The Great Rebel: Che Guevara in Bolivia

Luis J. González
Gustavo A. Sánchez Salazar

*Translated from the Spanish
by Helen R. Lane*

Grove Press, Inc.
New York

Contents

Preface

This book has no literary pretensions, nor does it intend to embroider doctrinal or ideological theories, or postulate or refute political conceptions and positions. It merely attempts to recapitulate, from the beginning, and in chronological order, the events surrounding the guerrilla center established in Bolivia in the course of the year 1967, its activities both as a political center, and as a center for combat. Its authors are two journalists with long professional experience in Bolivia. As such, they have preferred to embark upon the subject in the simple and comprehensible style that is theirs in their daily work, believing this to be the most adequate way of presenting an objective account of these events.

Much has been said and written about Che Guevara's guerrilla campaign in Bolivia and about the trial of French theoretician Régis Debray before a court-martial in the town of Camiri. But many of these accounts were obviously motivated by publicity-seeking, interested parties and, with their imaginary flights of fancy, they were often self-defeating. There has been no investigation of the facts in the light of the numerous documents and the original sources available. Consequently accounts of these have been marred by confused and nonsensical distortions in books and periodicals.

This book attempts to present to the public the strict truth of what happened, as it emerged after difficult and patient investigation. We thus believe we are contributing to the clarification of many blurred chapters in the story, enabling the reader to detect the undercurrents of the events shaping the world today, and setting more facts before those who want to judge, interpret, and give direction to the unrest shaking Latin America. This is the first attempt to tell the entire story of how Che Guevara, this most lonely of contemporary revolutionaries, intervened in Bolivia at this historical juncture, and of his theory, in which one may perhaps find some parallels to that of Herbert Marcuse, the master who has inspired and guided the action of many young rebels of our time.

The authors cannot—and do not—pretend to conceal their solidarity with the movements of national liberation for which marginal peoples in the most diverse areas of the world are fighting. Possibly, this has made this book not altogether impartial. Nonetheless, despite this commitment—or perhaps because of it—the authors have made every effort to be as objective as possible.

Apart from our personal investigations, a large part of the material here published is the fruit of the invaluable collaboration— in the form of criticisms, suggestions, information, etc.—received from journalists and Bolivian and foreign Catholic priests, from university professors and political leaders, from soldiers, noncommisioned officers, junior officers, senior officers and chiefs of the Bolivian armed forces, from peasants and residents of the zones in which the insurrection took place, and from surviving guerrillas. To each and every one of them, we express our profound gratitude.

We especially want to express our gratitude to journalist Luís González Quintanilla, who did the final editing of several chapters of the book.

Dedicated to the Memory

of Bolivian presidents Germán Busch and Gualberto Villarroel, early martyrs to the cause of the economic and social liberation of the Bolivian people;

of the pupils of military institutes, conscripts, soldiers, peasants, and guerrillas who fell in the fight, the direct or indirect victims of the injustices reigning in this part of the world;

of Bolivian writers Carlos Montenegro and Sergio Almaráz Paz, stubborn defenders of the potential resources and the active riches of the nation belonging to the inalienable patrimony of this crucified people beneath the Southern Cross.

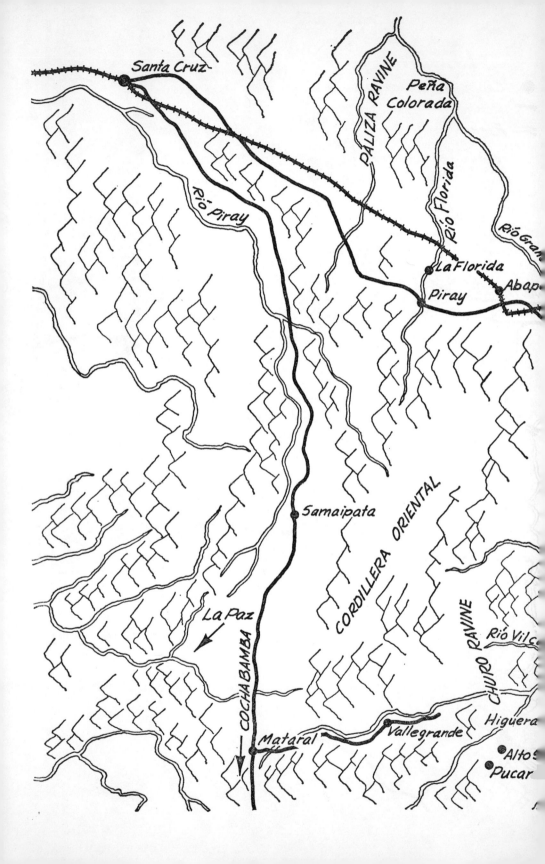

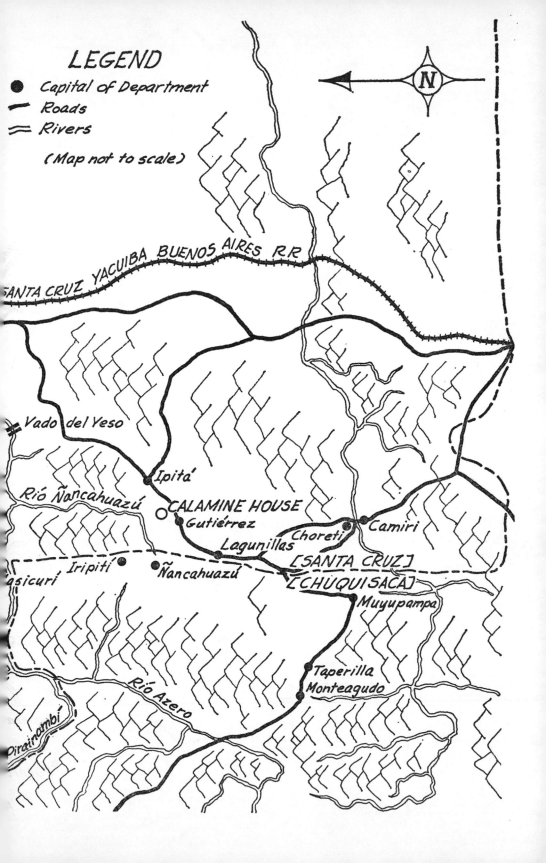

In the middle of the morning, a man in Pucara, a town some nine miles from Higuera, was using all his influence to get to the place where Che was being held prisoner. The authorities, however, stood in his way, and after using all his powers of persuasion he had to call on his ingenuity. He arranged for a horse to be taken out of town, and then he left the village on foot so as not to arouse suspicion. He was the Redemptorist Father Roger Schaller, a Swiss, the parish priest of Pucara.

He whipped his mount and arrived in Higuera around four-thirty in the afternoon. At that very moment, the bodies of the guerrillas were placed in a helicopter to be transferred to Valle Grande. The blanket-shrouded stretchers tied down at the edges were spattered with blood. There were also dark spots of blood on the ground. The priest kneeled near Guevara's body, blessed the lifeless corpse, and said a prayer.

Twenty minutes later the helicopter landed in Valle Grande, where the surprised, anxious, and nervous journalists and military officers changed the tone in the next scene of this tragedy.

In the modest church of Higuera at seven o'clock that night, Father Schaller said mass for those who had died during the day's battles. Officers, ordinary soldiers, and townspeople attended. In a corner of the little chapel, as if hiding themselves from the questioning stares of the curious, were the warrant officers who had killed the two guerrillas. On the altar next to the Gospels was a plastic bag

11

full of something unusual: dark wet earth. Father Schaller had gathered it up from the blood-soaked floor of the schoolroom, along with two of the bullets that had passed through Guevara's body.

As people left the church after the mass, two officers were seen casually smoking old pipes: they had belonged to Che. The commissioned and noncommissioned officers of the unit that had fought the guerrillas in Churo ravine kept everything the guerrilla leader and his men had had with them. It was explained that everything had been divided up among the victorious soldiers as spoils of war.

1

Introduction

Latin America is a volcano threatening eruption at any moment. For four centuries its native masses have lived in the shackles of a colonial system, victims of voracious foreign exploiters and their servile mestizo intermediaries. But this system is in its death throes. All classes and leaders must prepare themselves to confront this crucial stage in its history. Men must correct the remnants of systematized depredation, without violence if possible, with violence if necessary.

It is not the purpose of this book to repeat other studies of the objective reality of Latin America. We wish only to present data that will situate the events that interest us in their environment.

On the surface, the world at present is torn by the struggle of two antithetical concepts of life, two opposing ideologies: on the one side, the all-embracing organization of corporate capitalism, and on the other, the vertical structure of the dictatorship of the proletariat. Both systems, however, share a common objective: attracting into their sphere of influence the greatest territorial area possible, with all its exploitable human and natural resources. Thanks to this common denominator, the real division in the world, which is masked beneath this apparent division, becomes clear. In plain terms, the world is divided into superindustrialized nations and underdeveloped nations, that is to say between peoples who are scientifically, technically, and economically advanced and peoples who are backward or marginal. Any other so-called division would be totally artificial. Apart from the fact that it exaggerates geographical reality, to speak of East and

West, of communism versus Western Christian civilization—to take two instances—is a deliberate, prefabricated lie to escape or mask the obscure games being played throughout the world.

Since it has fallen within the hegemony of the United States, the condition of Latin America is automatically defined: it is a semi-colony. Today's technocrats like to use politer terms. They speak of "underdeveloped" countries, countries "in the process of development" or "relatively developed," and so on. Despite so much politeness, the problem remains the same: Indian America continues to be a semi-colony. It is an aggregate of dependent countries organized for the sole purpose of supplying raw materials at ridiculously low prices. In almost every case producers of a single product, the nations which constitute Latin America represent for the industrial powers the cheapest and most strategic regional market for the extraction of raw materials. As a result of this state of dependency, none of these countries has either a voice or a vote in the mechanism that regulates interchange. They cannot count on permanent markets nor fix stable prices for their raw materials, much less set up their own industries for transforming raw materials into final or intermediate products; nor can they diversify their economies. Thus, these impoverished nations fulfill the paradoxical task of keeping the American economy more than solvent by contributing more than three billion dollars yearly in exchange for a slogan: the Alliance for Progress.[1]

In the judgment of experts, the countries of Latin America, with a few specific exceptions, fulfill all the conditions which make for a subdeveloped region or nation. If any doubt that this is true remains, it can easily be dispelled by reading the numerous reports and conclusions of the intergovernmental and specialized private organizations in the hemisphere. It can also be corroborated by reading over the deliberations of American and world economic conferences in the sixties, whose most dramatic revelations have been produced in São Paulo, Alta Gracia, Geneva, Algiers, and New Delhi.

To keep the actual reality before our eyes, we shall cite some of these conditions, in no particular order: low income per capita, an

---

[1] We have the utmost respect for the enlightened President, John F. Kennedy, the generous initiator of this ambitious project. His untimely assassination at the hands of obscure reactionary forces caused this visionary enterprise to fail.

extremely low rate of internal savings and investments, the absence of viable infrastructures, population pressure on purely agricultural activities, low energy production rates, low industrial productivity, underemployment, lack of jobs, lack of special regulations for women and children who work, a high death and morbidity rate, a high birth rate, especially among the lower classes, hunger and restricted caloric intake, illiteracy, housing shortages, oligarchies which do not respond to pressures and the consequent marginal status of the masses, administrative disorder, disorders in the tax structure, the compromising of national sovereignty, ideological colonialism, etc.

This is the culture in which foreign intervention thrives. The people have not had an opportunity to play a role in the elucidation of national problems so as to forge their own destiny. There is bipolarity in Latin-American society. It is divided in two, one part consisting, in socio-economic terms, of the upper class, the oligarchy, as it is called in many places, and known in Bolivia particularly as the *rosca*; and the other part consisting of the great mass of marginal beings, something like a *lumpenproletariat*, with a disastrously infrahuman standard of living.

This first sector of Latin-American society is the active instrument for making the subhuman way of life of the other part of the community permanent. Imperialism—either subtly or openly—uses that part of the population working against the country's good so as to rule as lord and master. How this is done is well known: balkanizing the continent and causing artificial regional problems to arise; arming puppet governments and setting up compliant dictatorships; buying politicians and generals, writers and journalists; domesticating lawyers of foreign companies; and, finally, strengthening uniformed anti-civilian oligarchies.

The Bolivian writer, Sergio Almaráz Paz, says that the nineteenth century is not yet over in Latin America. This is painfully obvious. Because of pressure from extra-national forces and the dictates of their own self-interest, the minority castes have kept native communities in a perpetual state of submissiveness and total underdevelopment. But history, luckily, does not take place in a vacuum. Without fail, the future will be in the hands of the people. Politicians and statesmen, sociologists and liberal thinkers agree that it is necessary to destroy the established order, or "established disorder," as Emmanuel Mounier would say. The *real* nation sees revolution as the only way to replace the sclerotic social structure. The fictitious nation, on the other hand, is forced to construct a labyrinth of weak reforms of the superstructure as a concession. "It is not necessary to be a Marxist to see that a revolution is needed in Latin America; Catholics, Communists, and fearful liberals agree on this. But the debate has above all centered on the type of revolution and not on the means to make it succeed."[2]

The confrontation is between revolutionaries and small, alienated groups in the service of imperial power. Reformism is a sort of conformism, in disguised form, for the continuation of the *status quo*. Revolution is the only instrument of historical transformation. There is general agreement on this point. Opinions differ, however, when it comes to deciding what means shall be used. Are reparations of violent injustice to be looked for in revolutionary violence or in some sort of nonviolent revolution? Will institutional violence be destroyed with massive social uprisings or with the present emptily democratic juridical-political means at hand? Can systematized injustice be overthrown by "two, three, many Vietnams," or only with Lenten fasting? Will the solution come in the form of "just violence" or in the form of an evolving human solidarity? The answer is in the hands of the people, because it is the people who, in the last analysis, bring about decisions.

As we await the end of codified injustice, it would be well for those who wield power at the moment to recall these words of Pope Paul VI: "It is a matter of building a world where every man, regardless of race, religion, or nationality, may live a fully human life, freed of the servitude imposed on him by other men and by a nature not yet wholly tamed; a world where freedom is not a vain word and where poor Lazarus can sit down at the same table as the rich man."[3]

On October 9, 1967, at 1:40 P.M., Warrant Officer Mario Terán of the Bolivian army, entered a schoolroom in the small Bolivian village of Higuera, and with a volley of shots from his M-2 carbine

---

[2] Richard Gott, research professor in the Instituto de Estudios Internacionales of the University of Chile and director of the *Revista de Estudios Internacionales*. See "El Congo a partir de Mobuto," in No. 3 of this review.

[3] Paul VI, *Populorum Progressio:* p. 47. Cf. *Acta Leonis* XIII, t. XI (1892), p. 131.

killed the wounded man held captive there. The man was Major Ernesto Guevara. The order for his death had been received from President René Barrientos at 10 A.M. that morning.

The following chapter will attempt to give the reader a summary of the political and social climate in Bolivia—a climate that would lead, almost inexorably, to the intervention, and ultimately, the execution of the man who had said: "Many would call me an adventurer, and I am one; only one of a different sort, one of those that risks his skin to demonstrate what he believes to be true."

2

Bolivia:
Chaco War to Che

Bolivia, hemmed in on all sides, is the heart of South America. It has an area of 412,777 square miles, and approximately four million inhabitants, with a high proportion of Indo-mestizos. The Andes Range bifurcates as it majestically enters the territories once called Alto Peru, and divides the country into three geographical zones. The mountainous zone and the Andean *altiplano*, situated between the eastern and western Cordilleras, counterforts which come together again in the south, with a median altitude of 12,000 feet above sea level, have the densest native population. Four rocky peaks, wreathed in perpetual snows, stand out above it, their altitudes varying from 19,000 to 21,000 feet: Huayna Potosí, Illimani, Illampy and Sajama. The area has crops typical of every mountain region, and varieties of unusual animals such as the vicuña, the alpaca, the llama, and the chinchilla. But its greatest potential lies in its mineral resources: tin, tungsten, bismuth, silver, zinc, salt, sulphur, copper, and gold.

The valley region, centered in the *departamento* of Cochabamba, with an average altitude of 15,000 feet, has a relatively dense population dedicated almost exclusively to farming. Its mild and uniform climate is the pride of its inhabitants. Because of its geographical location it is destined to become an industrial center and a nucleus for the general development of the country.

The third region takes in the forests and plains of the east, joining the Amazon Basin on the north and northeast, and the Plata Basin on the south. This thinly populated region comprises almost two-thirds of the territory of Bolivia. Its climate is like that of the tropics, with occasional—intensely cold—rainy spells called *surazos,* which are due to air currents from the Antarctic. The north and northeast are known for their cattle raising, forestry, and farming. Toward the south lie the richest petroleum deposits being presently exploited, and great reserves of natural gas. In the east are enormous mineral resources that have not yet been exploited, especially the Mutún fields, one of the most coveted iron deposits in the world. Gas and iron, like petroleum in earlier days, are of great interest to international consortia and consequently play a large role in the political life of the country.

Bolivia is a nation of decided contrasts. The climate varies from 14° F. in the *altiplano* to 104° F. in the southeast and northeast. It is a mining country, but 70 per cent of its Quechua and Aymara population is engaged in farming. In the valleys and the *altiplano,* mechanization is still a myth and the wooden plow a reality; nevertheless, in some of the mining centers men use the most modern technical tools. It is the only country which is a part, by its ethnic, mineral, and geographical variety, of all three of the continent's most important basins, that is, the basins of the Atlantic and Pacific oceans and of the Amazon River. Yet Bolivia and Paraguay are the only countries that have been hemmed in on all sides, with no outlets to the sea, by the depredations of their neighbors.

About two-thirds of the population belong to the Aymara and Quechua groups, distributed in the *altiplano* and the valleys. In the east there are a multitude of very small forest-dwelling tribes (Guayaros, Mosetenes, Tobas, Movinas, Itenez, Clulupis, Matacos, Yanaiguas, etc.) with a mixture of traditions, beliefs, and dialects. An important number of mestizos, and a white minority making up the rest of the population, are distributed in all the areas of the country. The very small number of immigrants is represented by Yugoslavians, Italians, Arabs, Germans, Jews, and, in recent years, by settlements of Japanese and of Canadian Mennonites.

Approximately 83 per cent of the total population is concentrated in the *altiplano* and the valleys, while the eastern regions—the largest in area—just barely contain the remaining 17 per cent. Thus the great imbalance in the demographic index of density is a factor working against any attempt at socio-economic development.

The principal cities of Bolivia are: La Paz, the administrative seat and the center of the economic, cultural, and political life of the nation; Oruro, a mining center and the railway connection with the Chilean coast along the Pacific and the Plata Basin; Cochabamba, the second largest metropolis in the Republic, a city in which local interests run strong and which serves as a strange catalyst in national politics; Santa Cruz de la Sierra, the principal urban center in the east, noted for the elegance and great beauty of its women; Tarija, on the southern border, lusty and tinged with memories of Spain; Sucre, the constitutional capital and one of the cradles of South American emancipation; and Potosí, the mining center that has supplied the world ever since the Spanish Conquest.

Each one of these cities—the capitals of *departamentos*—has a prestigious university that carries on relations with the largest intellectual and cultural centers in the world. The Universidad Mayor Real y Pontífica de San Francisco Xavier de Chuquisaca, in Sucre, is one of the oldest in America. A similar institution for graduate studies has recently been created in the *departamento* of Beni.

Dependency and exploitation that give rise to poverty among the people also typify Bolivia, leaving what are perhaps deeper marks within the mosaic of countries south of the Río Bravo. Its unusual social, economic, and cultural characteristics serve to underline the peculiar schema of Latin American backwardness in Bolivia. Up until April, 1952, there was a proverbial dichotomy in the country, a division—according to Augusto Céspedes—of the country into the "formal" country and the "real" country. In the middle of the twentieth century, Quechuas and Aymaras, the heirs of the advanced pre-Colombian civilization of Tawantinsuyo, find themselves in the sad condition of downtrodden and humiliated peoples at the very limit of human servitude. The structure of production in Bolivia pointed to the continued existence of feudal lords when the era of nuclear energy was opening its wide gates to humanity. Illiterate, starving, and without hope of a decent life, this major portion of the population carried on its productive labor resignedly, without even satisfying the demand within the country. The benefits of this productive system fell to a privileged social class with limited aspirations: the legal profession, politics, various cultural activities, and tourism were its principal occupations.

The feudalism in the countryside generated an economy of the handcraft type in the cities: little factories, little laboratories, little infrastructures—enterprises, that is to say, that were the counterparts of the kind of spirit of their founders. Nevertheless, extraordinary installations embodying every technical innovation for efficient exploitation were installed in the Bolivian mines. This country with its long mining tradition—the silver mines of Cerro de Potosí alone financed the wars and the court life of the Spanish crown for three hundred years—poured out tribute for their owners even more diligently in the Republican era. But, following tradition here too, these riches were never used for the benefit of the people.

Patiño, Hoschild, and Aramayo, names representing three dazzling fortunes amassed in Bolivia, were specialists at grinding down men and mountains to extract minerals. And these minerals, transported in the beginning on the backs of llamas or mules, and later by railroads, were turned into capital, factories, industrial plants, and titles of nobility outside the country. As the mines poured out their riches, these men, better known as the "tin barons," internationalized their capital by playing the stock market with careful deliberation, and setting up residence in London, Paris, or New York. Bolivia thus came to occupy a doubly important strategic position in the vortex of imperialist consortia.

The great mine owners formed what has been called a "superstate," a power greater than that of the state itself, which latter they dominated and forced to do their bidding. Many battles were fought in Bolivia to free the country from this subjection, but until 1952 all these isolated efforts remained futile.

Nonetheless, the Chaco War against Paraguay (1932–1935) awakened a sense of national identity that roused Bolivia from its lethargy. It gave rise to new nationalist, anti-feudal, and anti-imperialist parties which began to replace the traditional groups, which in the eyes of the people were now responsible for all the mistakes of the past, as well as the existing state of collective injustice. From this time on, with the seesawing and bickering that were part of the process, the people organized to win their just rights.

The most aggressive forces in national life bent their efforts toward reaching two objectives that in their eyes would achieve the liberation of the nation: agrarian reform and nationalization of the mines. The first was to be a deathblow to feudalism and the second another to the "tin barons," who in this era were the genuine representatives of foreign interventionism.

The contradiction between a national state and imperialism was unusually disruptive where internal political relations were concerned. It was reflected just as strongly in the periodic massacres of miners, with military forces and police being used for this purpose. More than once, union fights ended with the physical annihilation of both workers and mine executives. This is why the capacity for resistance and the fighting spirit of the Bolivian worker, especially the miner, borders on the heroic. These situations, which were so carefully "cleaned up," are also the reason why Bolivian writers, intellectuals, and politicians fustigate and denigrate the national army, and characterize it as an instrument, though often an unconscious one, of the repression of the people.

Two years after the end of the Chaco War, in April, 1937, the government, basing itself on legitimate contractual rights and the rights of sovereignty, declared that all property rights of the Standard Oil Company within the Republic had lapsed because of fraud proved by tax authorities.

This decision on the part of the government was a milestone in the Bolivian people's new way of thinking. On June 7, 1939, the government, headed by Colonel German Busch, completed the work that had been begun by decreeing the expropriation of foreign currency and obliging the mine owners to hand all of it in to the Central Bank, rendering an accounting of their expenses abroad, and selling what remained to the bank. The decree was drawn up by the Minister of the Treasury, Fernando Pou-Mount.

This marked the beginning of an authentically nationalist awareness on the part of the Bolivian people, led by young intellectuals and veterans of the Chaco War, and the beginning of the long struggle for national sovereignty and economic independence in the face of foreign exploitation. The most representative sectors of the nation have joined this great crusade: workers, peasants, students, university professors, journalists, and independent writers and members of nationalist parties, among them the Movimiento Nacionalista Revolucionario (MNR), the Partido Revolucionario de Izquierda Nacionalista (PRIN), the Falange Socialista Boliviana (FSB), and the Partido Demócratica Cristiano (PDC), some of them obeying genuine convictions and others aiming at the enlistment of popular sympathies.[1] A majority of the governments and leaders that have succeeded each other since this time have set themselves up as convinced anti-imperialist apostles and fervent defenders of the internal frontiers of the nation, although there have been a few periods of regression or restoration of the oligarchy.

This is also the consistent attitude of the Catholic hierarchy, laymen, and priests who, either in groups or singly, have recently come out in defense of the human capital and the economic patrimony of the nation. At the beginning of April, 1968, the highest representative of the national church, Cardinal Clemente Maurer, Archbishop of Sucre, in an interview with the press in Santa Cruz, expressed the general feeling of the nation: "Evidently there are capitalists who come from abroad to further exploit us and make us poor," the prelate pointed out. He then added that "this is not acceptable either to the Church or to the State; but since the Church does not have the means for coercion at its disposal, it is governments who must take it upon themselves to end such injustices and such abuses. In this sense the Church can support any legitimate and justifiable movement to end them."

This determination to oppose any sort of paternalist or colonialist interference in Bolivia is thus not a concept that has come to it from outside the country; it stems from a deep collective impulse. It is the firm expression of its anxious hope of destroying this enormous subcontinental ghetto and joining a community of Latin American nations.

In the forties the struggle between the real Bolivian people and the mestizo oligarchy began to turn in favor of the former. In Santiago, Chile, in 1938, a brilliant nucleus of young Bolivian students founded the FSB, a party of "impassioned patriotic fervor," subject to a "strict hierarchical discipline, a hierarchy that is the result of the selection of the most competent." Later years saw the successive organization of the PRIN (1940), of Marxist-Leninist-Stalinist persuasion, and the MNR, a staunch nationalist party.

The MNR grew more vigorous as it stubbornly defended the national resources and the interests of the people. It became an outspoken accuser of the great mining interests and the anti-national

---

[1] A table of the English equivalents for the abbreviations can be found on p. 233.

rosca, taking upon itself the task of being the first to give voice to the anxieties of workers, peasants, and progressive members of the middle class. In conjunction with members of the military who had fought in the Chaco War, it brought Gualberto Villarroel, who at that time had the rank of Major, to power in December, 1943. He collaborated with the MNR during a large part of his administration, and made the country swallow his strong revolutionary tonic. But on the mad morning of July 21, 1946, President Villarroel was hanged from a lamppost in the Plaza Murillo, along with several of his collaborators—the handiwork of two strange bedfellows: Latin American Marxists and the *rosca*. The MNR then went into exile for almost six years. But the FSB did not have the chance to wield the full power of the state and the PRIN did not succeed in lining up its principles with national realities.

In the elections in May, 1951, the leader of the MNR and candidate for the Presidency, Victor Paz Estenssoro, was elected by a majority vote. But the *rosca* brought pressure to bear on the army to have it take over in a bloodless and cynical *coup d'état*. In a general order, the Commander in Chief of the armed forces, General Ovidio Quiroga, designated a government military junta with General Hugo Ballivián as presiding officer. The popular will having thus been flouted, the doors of insurrection were opened to restore democratic representation in the Republic. On April 9, 1952, after three epic days of battle, the people of La Paz (factory workers, railway workers, university students and professors, miners from Milluni, peasants who had united with the middle-class sectors of the MNR, nationalist military personnel, and the National Guard of Carabiniers) defeated the military forces. In Oruro, miners armed with dynamite forced well-equipped and well-trained regiments of the army to surrender.

The MNR revolutionary government thus began with its constitutional regime doubly ratified—by votes and by the blood of the people. The first revolutionary administration received massive support that was unparalleled in the life of the Republic. On October 31, 1952, the mines of the "tin barons" were nationalized in Oruro, and on August 2, 1953, the Agrarian Reform Law was promulgated in Ucureña. With the nationalization of the mines the people won the right to make use of the national resources that their efforts had developed as they saw fit, and they regained the political power to work for the good of the entire nation. With the agrarian reform the system of land appropriation or landholding was altered, the organization of production in rural areas was transformed, the great *latifundios* were broken up, small tracts were handed over for the benefit of those who worked the land, and, basically, human dignity was conferred on two million natives who had lived in virtual slavery: simple Indians now scrambled up the social ladder and attained the status of "peasants."

A new Educational Code, moreover, restructured the educational system within this new social reality so as to enable the masses to exercise their fundamental rights responsibly; provisions were made for urban reform; the economy was diversified; industrialization was stimulated for the first time; international financial agreements were concluded so as to immediately begin construction of the first hydroelectric plant in the country; various parts of the nation were linked by means of communication that opened vast regions far from the great centers of production and consumption; socio-economic development got under way, and, thanks to these measures, a relatively large internal market was created where once there had been no market at all. Universal suffrage was decreed, workers were given a voice in the administration of para-national enterprises, the rights of labor unions were protected by law, and the most advanced social laws were passed. The powerful Central Obrera Boliviana (COB) was set up and for several years was the principal power—excepting the MNR—in the political life of Bolivia.

Oddly enough, the feeble national oligarchy did not understand, or refused to understand, the importance of the transformations under way. It did not understand the extent to which the various classes had cooperated with each other in an alliance in which it should naturally have been included. It continued to be a very minor executor of orders as the delegated representative of neo-colonialist interests. The oligarchy itself made light of its function as a cog in the hierarchical machinery of the nation. "The large mining interests reduced the national plutocracy to such a small circle quantitatively, to such a tiny minority of persons rotating their functions, that they caused it to also lose its status as an oligarchy or a bourgeoisie, having reduced themselves to a depressed upper crust of a proletarian nation," the writer Augusto Céspedes has written.

This limited vision of the "depressed upper crust" hardly comes as a surprise in a country in which, according to certain experts fond of statistics, there have been something like 160 "revolutions" and coups in its 142 years of existence. The *rosca* perhaps believed that this was but one more chapter in the long history of coups and barracks revolts. From the first day of the revolution, therefore, this upper crust took it upon itself to combat its theories and sabotage its accomplishments. The fact is that men suffer from an almost universal failure to realize the magnitude of contemporary events. As Régis Debray says in *Revolution in the Revolution?*, we are never completely contemporary with our present.

Semicolonial peoples cannot wreak havoc on the account books of plutocratic powers with impunity. From the very moment it arrived in power, the national revolution was confronted with an unfair propaganda campaign and threats of blackmail on the part of the great monopolistic consortia. During the Second World War the MNR was accused of being Fascist, and when it took power it was called Communist. But once convinced of the uselessness of this endeavor to blacken it, the counterrevolution hastened to destroy the new state of affairs by other means, taking advantage of the economic weaknesses and the resulting galloping inflation that the revolution produced. ("Freedom is one of the most expensive things in the world," Gamal Abdel Nasser once said.) Orders were given to recover the ground lost by putting a brake on the masses' rise in the social scale; it was found necessary to set the popular government and the people at odds with one another, that is to say, to create conflicts between the revolutionary power and labor organizations. *Divide ut regnes.* On the one hand "American aid" was proclaimed, and on the other hand numerous powerful obstacles were put in the way of the revolutionary process. (In reality such aid is only a restoration of part of the wealth of the nation—tin, rubber, tungsten—extracted from the country through political blackmail during the Second World War for the "defense of democracy.") On October 26, 1955, the government of Paz Estenssoro approved, within a climate of economic coercion that was already well established, the much-debated and onerous Petroleum Code, one of the most negative accomplishments of the MNR, and a major attack on the economy and the national patrimony. This law is commonly referred to as the "Davenport Code," because the original draft was approved in an American office belonging to an American lawyer named Davenport, in cooperation with the legal adviser of the Yacimentos Petrolíferos Fiscales

Boliviana (YPFB), Dr. Jorge Fernández Santivañez. Sheltered by this legal body, a flood of United States oil companies inundated the country, among them the powerful Bolivian Gulf Oil Company, the company which benefited most from this state of affairs, and the one which continues to increase its generous dividends at the expense of the Bolivian people.

The second revolutionary government, headed by Hernán Siles Zuazo (1956–1960), suffered even more from outside pressures and found itself obliged to impose a program for stabilizing the Bolivian monetary system. Jackson Eder, a business expert who came to Bolivia as a technician to establish this program, became a virtual czar of the Bolivian economy. One of his first decrees was aimed against various projects for developing the country and diversifying the economy. He brought about a total paralysis of the nation, and a wave of unemployment with its explosive charge of potential poverty and resentment spread over the whole country, thus contributing to the sapping of the revolutionary vitality of the people.

The third revolutionary period (Paz Estenssoro: 1960–1964) reaped the consequences of this state of affairs, and internal repercussions led Estenssoro to even greater collusion with the U.S. State Department and the Pentagon. The government, whose security lay in the armed militias of workers and peasants, was obliged to restructure the armed forces along conventional lines. In April, 1963, the government received a bald request that it occupy the mining centers militarily, which Paz Estenssoro categorically refused to do; but on the other hand the authority of the military has been strengthened by certain politico-administrative offices and by the Acción Cívica Militar, a sort of rural national guard, operating with the covert or overt assistance of Colonel Fox of the American Embassy. In return for this, the bureaucracy of the Alliance for Progress constantly points to Bolivia as an example of its efforts. The cumulative effect of these things, here summed up very rapidly, was responsible for the fact that the masses aligned themselves against the government.

At this stage, furthermore, all the impediments that go along with revolution came into play. The lack of revolutionary awareness and the lack of preparation of the majority of political and labor leaders created factions. Labor leaders, especially those in rural areas and in the mines, created their own fiefs. Personal ambitions hastened the internal divisions of the MNR. In April, 1964, when the party had split into a thousand fragments, Paz Estenssoro accepted his third term as President and assumed office on August 6 of that year. This was all that was needed to set off the powder keg. On the morning of November 4, 1964, the armed forces, taking advantage of popular disturbances in the streets, staged a *coup d'état* and took over the government.

It would be a great error to state that all these revolutionary changes over the years were carried out perfectly. Even though foreign powers concurred in obstructing the development of the revolution, it must not be forgotten that it also bore within itself the seeds of its own destruction. Its principal defects were its taking on of the characteristics of the middle class and its slow submission to imperialist power. But despite all its errors and deviations it is necessary to emphasize, so as better to understand certain future events, especially those that involved guerrillas, that the MNR transformed the old economic, social, and political structures in accordance with the objective conditions and the possibilities that obtained at the moment that it was called upon to act. It opened the way and led the people through the first stages of a necessary revolution that had no other precedent in Latin America, except for the Mexican Revolution. It fulfilled its historical responsibility, and, as we can see, the structural transformations that it brought about are irreversible.

René Barrientos Ortuño, a general in the Bolivian air force and Vice-President during the last MNR government, and General Alfredo Ovando Candia, the Commander in Chief of the armed forces, were the leaders of the military insurrection. The event is interpreted by General Ovando as a "revolution within the revolution," but by public consensus it is commonly referred to as the "restoration revolution." A military junta was installed in power, headed first by Barrientos, then later by Barrientos and Ovando, and by the latter in a third stage. On August 6, 1966, Barrientos assumed the office of the Presidency, provided for in the constitution of Bolivia, and Ovando returned to his former function as head of the armed forces. A "restoration" took place as certain political, social, and economic sectors returned to their privileged pre-revolutionary positions. This meant a halt in the process begun in 1952, and as a result, problems of all sorts became still more crucial. The government of the new regime could not confront the disorders natural to every revolution-in-progress in any positive sort of way. Very soon the political parties of the left, who had joyfully saluted the coup of

November 4, saw themselves pushed aside and their leaders jailed, confined to their residences, or exiled. In May, 1965, Juan Lechín Oquendo, the former Vice-President of the Republic, the leader of the miners, the head of the PRIN, and the executive secretary of the COB, was arrested, as were former-President Siles Zuazo and other political leaders and labor leaders. The COB declared a general strike. Repression of the masses became the order of the day. Disregard for the legal rights of labor unions, attacks on and destruction of union headquarters, "red" and "white" massacres of factory workers and miners, massive cuts in the salaries and wages of the working population, armed violence against students, university professors, and teachers, and other anti-popular measures created hunger, terror, and resentment. In May and September, 1965, workers' blood ran in the cities and the mines as a foretaste of the tragic "red night" of San Juan (June 24, 1967), in which men, women, and children died in the mining centers of Catavi and Siglo Veinte. Even the Catholic Church began to worry; 108 prelates and priests petitioned the government, urging humane treatment for the workers and humane political relations within the country.

From the end of December, 1966, until March, 1967, the public's attention was monopolized by all sorts of rumors concerning the stability of the regime, and their preoccupation was echoed, more or less discreetly, by journalists and newscasters. The Frente de Revolución Boliviana (FRB)—a political grouping which had proposed Barrientos' candidacy, but which had never inspired much confidence—dissolved, and there were open conjectures about the apparent unity of the armed forces, the real basis on which the superstructure of the regime was built. Discussion of the possibility of a military coup at any moment came to be a daily pastime in clubs and political cabals. Around March, these rumors became even more insistent as the first revolutionary thunderheads gathered in the southeast.

3

A Don Quixote of
the Twentieth Century

Ernesto Guevara de la Serna was born June 14, 1928, into a family
with a long line of worthy ancestors and one related to members of
the "upper aristocracy" of the country. He was born in the city of
Rosario, Argentina, where his parents, Ernesto Guevara Lynch and
Celia de la Serna, were eventually to settle.

The life of the family was permanently influenced by Ernesto's
chronic illness—asthma—the first signs of which he had shown at the
age of two. They had moved to Buenos Aires when Guevara was
born, and by the time he was four, they were forced to move to
Córdova, on the advice of doctors, so as to have the best possible
climate for their son. They eventually settled in Alta Gracia where
Guevara went to grade school. The family moved back to Buenos
Aires in 1944 and Guevara graduated from the Colegio Nacional in
1946. He entered the University of Buenos Aires as a medical
student.

Guevara was timid, but was never the shy and lonely introvert
that many people say he was. "There is a difference between timidity
and introversion. He was an excellent student, and had the makings
of a leader ever since he was small," his father said.[1] During his youth
he directed all his activity, sometimes to the point of obsession, to
overcoming his asthma. He forced himself to take part in violent

---

[1] *Gente* (Buenos Aires, No. 18).

physical exercises—the hardest sports, such as rugby, were his favorites. A young sportsman using a vaporizer became a common sight on various playing fields. He also regularly went on hikes and marches.

At the university he was an outstanding student, but he did not spend all his time studying; he had girl friends and fell in love for the first time. "Ernesto didn't know how to dance, but women were very much attracted to him," a friend of those days says.

His political activities also began at this time. His parents actively opposed the ruling regime of General Juan Domingo Perón and passed their anti-peronista convictions on to their son: he joined, organized, and led opposition groups in the university, clashed with the police, and participated in anti-government demonstrations. Despite this, he carried a heavy program of studies: the last year before his graduation he took eighteen courses. He graduated from the university in 1953.

During his years at the university, his love of travel became increasingly evident. In 1950 he visited twelve Argentinian provinces on a bicycle he had equipped with a little motor. He later made his first trip through South America; he intended to go as far as Easter Island, a Chilean possession in the Pacific, 2376 miles off the coast, to work in the Rapa Nui leprosarium. Though the Easter Island portion of his trip never came off, his travels did give him the opportunity of getting acquainted with Chile and Peru, where for the first time he met people from the lower classes. In Iquitos, on the Marañón River, he worked for a time in the San Pablo leprosarium. From there he went to Colombia, to Venezuela, and then on his first trip to the United States, where he visited Miami for three weeks. At the end of this trip he returned to Buenos Aires and caught up on his studies, passing his examinations in the Faculty of Medicine and receiving his degree as a doctor of medicine.

He immediately began his second trip around South America, and at the end of 1953 he went to Bolivia. Nine months earlier— in April, 1952—a socio-political movement of enormous importance had shaken the Andes. The Bolivian national revolution was the most striking uprising of the masses thus far in this hemisphere in this century. On January 6, 1953, a rightist coup against the government of Paz Estenssoro was put down in a few hours. Guevara witnessed, and long remembered, the spontaneous mobilization of the people to defend their revolution; he saw miners' and peasants' militias arrive in La Paz to put down the counterrevolutionary coup, carrying old guns wrested from military regiments the April before. He would never forget these days spent among the people. In La Paz he found a job in the State Information Agency and later in the National Service for Agrarian Reform. But when he saw the worm of reformism impatiently gnawing the revolutionary body politic, he sought a purer form of revolution and visited the nationalized mines in the company of Ricardo Rojo, the student director of the Unión Cívica Radical Intransigente in Argentina and today a well-known lawyer in Buenos Aires, whom he had met in La Paz. He met men who were starving, exhausted, and suffering from silicosis but who nonetheless wanted to be masters of their own souls. Guevara's visit to the mines awakened his admiration for the revolution and for the Bolivian miners.

It is not known exactly where and when he picked up Marxist ideas. In secondary school and at the university he read a great deal about a great many things; the masters of scientific materialism also passed through his hands. His travels, which gave him the opportunity to see the subhuman world of the exploited, confirmed his revolutionary convictions and his hatred of the capitalist system.

After visiting the mines, his wanderlust next took him back to Peru, again with Ricardo Rojo. On September 11, 1953, they crossed the border in a truck, "with Indians, potatoes, and onions," as his traveling companion later put it. He was faced with a moral dilemma: should he choose the relative comfort of the cab of the truck or sit in the back with the peasants and the load? He chose the second.

He did not stay in Lima long, but took advantage of his stay to make contacts with Peruvian leftist and youth groups. He then went traveling in the north, crossing the Ecuadorian border on September 16. He stayed in Guayaquil for a time, living with five Argentinian leftists who had been exiled by Perón.

When an almost spontaneous revolution broke out in Guatemala, the young Argentinians were curious, and, using the influence of friends, managed to get onto separate United Fruit Company ships going to Panama. Thus, ironically, the American company unwittingly collaborated with the Latin American revolutionary who was later to fight against its economic interests. Guevara left the ship in Panama and from there went to Costa Rica, where he met his comrade Ricardo Rojo. Rojo introduced Guevara to the top leaders of Latin American social-democratic parties who were waiting their turn to govern: Juan Bosch, Raúl Leoni, and Rómulo Betancourt—though he found that he had little in common with the latter. In San José he heard for the first time of Fidel Castro—from exiled Cubans who were desperately hoping for an amnesty for the leader of the attack on the Moncada barracks. But Guevara's goal was Guatemala, and that was where he went.

In Guatemala, he had time to observe the revolutionary politics of Jacobo Árbenz's government. Árbenz adopted measures aimed principally at the United Fruit Company, whose policies were forcing Central American countries to remain nothing but immense banana warehouses, but he could not defend his country's interests without suffering himself, and the reaction came soon. Colonel Carlos Castillo Armas headed an expedition against the democratic government, with an army organized and equipped by the Pentagon, the CIA, and the United States State Department under John Foster Dulles, a declared enemy of progressive movements in Latin America. As a last desperate step, the people were armed and popular militias were organized. The young Argentinian doctor, who had tried fruitlessly to persuade revolutionary youth groups that a popular army was necessary, organized and taught, trying to stop the avalanche that the forces of the seditious colonel represented. But it was too late. Perón's ambassador to Guatemala saved Guevara from reprisals, giving him asylum in the embassy. He eventually left for Mexico, leaving behind Hilda Gadea, a young Peruvian militant with the Acción Popular para la Revolución Americana (APRA) in Guatemala, who had helped him over the roughest spots.[2]

Once on Mexican soil, Guevara did a little bit of everything in order to live decently until Hilda Gadea arrived and put him in touch with a nucleus of Cuban revolutionaries. They were the survivors from the handful of 150 men who had attacked the Moncada barracks in Santiago on July 26, 1953, in an attempt to overthrow Batista. Their central figure was a young lawyer, Fidel Castro Ruz. Guevara tells of his first meeting with the Cuban leader:

> I met him on one of those cold nights in Mexico, and I remember that our first discussion was about international politics. By the wee hours of that same night—dawn, really—I was one of the members of his future expedition. But I should like to clarify how and

[2] Later, Guevara married Hilda Gadea and they had a daughter named after her mother. Fidel and Raúl Castro served as witnesses at the wedding ceremony.

why I met the present head of the government of Cuba in Mexico. It was in the aftermath of the democratic movements of 1954, when the last American revolutionary democracy in this area—that of Jacobo Árbenz Guzmán—succumbed to United States aggression. One came back from there defeated, united in pain with all Guatemalans, hoping, seeking a way to make a future for that anguished country. And Fidel had come to Mexico in search of a neutral terrain on which to prepare his men for the big push. . . .[3]

Guevara, an Argentinian, was accepted by the Cubans; his profession made him a valuable asset to the movement. The future combatants' difficult preparations against Batista began. Colonel José Bayo, a Cuban who had done military service in Spain and a famous expert on guerrilla fighting, gave the group military instruction. A little farm served as a training center. A short time after their training had begun, the group was surprised and arrested by the Mexican police. After two months in jail, they continued training even more enthusiastically than before. Finally, on November 25, 1956, eighty-two men sailed from Tuxpan, Veracruz, on the frail and now historic yacht "Granma" to liberate Cuba.

The days after the disembarkation in Cuba, at Playa de las Coloradas on December 2, 1956, were ill-starred. The province of Oriente witnessed the destruction of the "Granma" and the butchering of many members of the expedition. Only twelve men were left after the first clash with Batista's army, and the chiefs of staff of the Cuban revolution were to come from this group: Fidel, Raúl, Ernesto, Camilo Cienfuegos. The revolutionaries went up into the Sierra Maestra, the base of the first rebel column, named after the Cuban patriot José Martí. In the mountains they gathered strength and began the process that would culminate in the flight of Batista and his acolytes on January 1, 1959. In the course of the struggle, Ernesto Guevara de la Serna turned into the Che Guevara of the history books, or simply "Che," a name given him because he frequently used this Argentinian form of getting someone's attention. He distinguished himself by his capacity for leadership, his courage, and his sense of responsibility, and soon became the trusted lieutenant of the Castro brothers. He took an active part in the creation of new guerrilla zones and in the preparation of the general offensive. New fronts were established in different provinces, based on columns

---

[3] *Sucesos* (La Paz, December, 1967).

that split off from the "mother cell" or "single central nucleus," to use guerrilla terms. On August 25, 1958, Fidel Castro assigned to Che the mission of leading Column Number 8, "Ciro Redondo," from the Sierra Maestra to the province of Las Villas and there organizing a new front, and gave him command of all the rebel units of the 26th of July Movement operating in that region. The column went through 350 miles of territory controlled by the enemy. The march was extremely difficult and painful—Guevara's campaign diary is an eloquent record of their sufferings—but now the guerrilla war entered another phase and the young revolutionary leader covered himself with glory. The rebel columns "Ciro Redondo" and "Antonio Maceo," the latter commanded by Camilo Cienfuegos, entered Havana together. There was a glorious and historic welcome awaiting Guevara. He took on Cuban citizenship and settled down in the fortress of La Cabaña to keep watch over the triumphant revolution.

Once the revolution had triumphed militarily, there were grave responsibilities awaiting Guevara as he undertook the task of organizing it economically and socially. He successively occupied the posts of President of the National Bank of Cuba and Minister of Industries.[4] He took over as Minister of Industries at a time when the revolution was attempting to become truly radical. Gradual reform no longer had a place in Cuba: drastic measures were taken against American capitalist interests, and the national economy was modeled on Socialist patterns. Guevara wanted to transform the economic structure totally and his first measures were directed at putting an end to the monoproduction of sugar and making Cuba self-sufficient in other respects. The first industries to be created were those which would not have to depend on products imported from the United States.[5]

The imperialist reaction came quickly, and an American economic blockade was set up. The makers of Cuban economic policy were forced to step up their programs for industrialization and let agriculture be second. There was criticism of this policy, and in

---

[4] In the first post he signed Cuban paper money with a simple "Che."

[5] At about this time Guevara divorced Hilda Gadea and married a Cuban schoolteacher, Aleida March, who had been his secretary and assistant. They had four children: Aleida, Camilo, Celia, and Ernesto.

public sessions of self-criticism Guevara recognized his errors and vowed to act more carefully thereafter.

In August, 1961, Guevara represented Cuba at the meeting at Punta del Este, Uruguay, that produced the declaration of the Alliance for Progress. He took the floor at the conference to denounce repeatedly imperialist exploitation in that part of the world. His distinguished addresses revealed him to be a consummate statesman and an eloquent and convincing speaker; in no other international conference has there ever been such severe criticism of the foreign policy of the United States from an official Latin American representative. Guevara urged that the United States fulfill its moral duty by giving back, through a suitable plan, the riches that had been extorted from the Latin American countries by American consortia. The meeting ended with the Declaration of Punta del Este, which Major Guevara did not sign, and Cuba was excluded from President Kennedy's plan for Latin America. We do not hesitate to affirm that if these two illustrious Americans had seen eye to eye, there would have been positive repercussions for the peoples of this hemisphere; we believe that the two men represented two forward-looking conceptions of what revolution should be in the contemporary world. Because of the spontaneous enthusiasm that Che's personality inspired, he stole the show in Punta del Este, to the dismay of those diplomats pickled in formaldehyde on government shelves.

After Punta del Este, Guevara went to Argentina for a lightning-quick, ultra-secret meeting with the President of Argentina, Arturo Frondisi, at the latter's request. In the capital of Brazil the next day —August 19, 1961—Guevara was decorated with the "National Order of the Southern Cross," the highest Brazilian decoration given to foreigners.

Guevara's strong personality caused mixed reactions; he was one of those people who cannot be ignored or pass unnoticed. Luís Simón, a member of the 26th of July Movement who was later to go into exile in Miami, illustrated these differing reactions when he said of Che: "He is presumptuous, cynical, a night owl, and highly emotional; but at the same time he is studious, stoic, courageous, and decisive." He grew more prickly in the camps of the Sierra Maestra, in Las Villas, in La Cabaña, and in the high public offices he held, and his men always found him a tough and demanding leader who was just as hard on himself as he was on them. Revolutionary battles proved that he was an extraordinary combatant and the construction of Cuban Socialism showed him to be a strict and austere government leader.

In 1964 and the first months of 1965, Cuba went through a political crisis. Because of the massive economic, technical, and cultural aid that the Soviet Union was lending Cuba, pressure was put on the Cuban Communist Party to toe the Moscow line—this was the time of the historic division of the world Socialist movement into two antithetical camps, the Russian and the Chinese. There were repercussions in Cuba; it was said that Che was the leader of the Maoist tendency and that this was evidenced by his clear and definite position on moral incentives for workers and by his energetic advocacy of continental revolution. In Guevara, Fidel Castro found the ideal man to execute his plan to turn the Cordillera of the Andes into an immense Sierra Maestra and to organize the principal revolutionary *focos* in Latin America.

In November, 1964, Guevara took a four-month trip. Moscow was the first step in his itinerary, but he stayed there only a short time. He returned to the Western hemisphere and gave a vigorous speech attacking peaceful coexistence in the General Assembly of the United Nations. December 17 found him in Africa, and he visited Algeria, Mali, the Congo, Dahomey, Guinea, Ghana, Tanzania, and Egypt. He had a concrete objective—to organize a grand internationale of marginal or underdeveloped countries—and during his trip he made contacts and put forth his ideas on the subject.

In February, 1965, he represented Cuba at the Second Afro-Asian Economic Seminar. He returned to Havana on March 14.

According to Ricardo Rojo, on his return to Havana Guevara wrote his mother of his decision to work for a month in the sugar cane fields, and then to work for five years in one of the factories that he himself had organized when he was Minister of Industries. Celia de la Serna de Guevara answered him in the following letter:

> My dear,
> My letters seem strange to you. I don't know if we have lost the naturalness that we used to have when we talked to each other, or whether we never had it and have always talked to each other in that slightly ironic tone that we who live on the shores of the Río de la Plata have, aggravated by our own family code, which is even more hermetic.
> The fact is that worrying has made me abandon this ironic tone

and be direct with you. It seems as though that is when my letters are not understood and become strange and enigmatic.

In this diplomatic tone we have adopted in our correspondence I also have to read between the lines for a hidden meaning and then interpret. I read your last letter as I read the news in *La Prensa* or *La Nación* of Buenos Aires, digging out the real meaning and import of each sentence, or at least trying to.

The result has been a sea of confusion, and even more worry and alarm.

I am not going to use diplomatic language. I am going to be direct. It seems to me to be real madness when there are so few heads with organizational talent in Cuba for all of them to go cut cane for a month as their principal occupation, when there are so many good "machete-wielders" among the people. To do so as a volunteer, during a time normally dedicated to resting or amusing oneself, for a Saturday or a Sunday, is something else again. It also makes sense to do so as one's principal labor when it is a question of demonstrating conclusively the advantage and the necessity of using machines to cut cane, when the harvest and the number of tons secured will earn foreign exchange that Cuba is counting on.

A month is a long time. There are probably reasons [for your decision] that I don't know about. Speaking now of your personal case, if after this month you are going to devote your efforts to running a factory, the sort of work done rather successfully by Castellanos and Villegas, it seems to me that this is mad to the point of absurdity —especially if this work is going to be carried out for five years so as to set a genuine example.

Since I knew your eagerness not to take a single day off from your Ministry, when I saw that your trip abroad was becoming too prolonged, my question was: Will Ernesto still be Minister of Industries when I arrive in Cuba? Who has been right, or who has come out on top, in the dispute about the motivations that cause people to work the hardest?

These questions are half answered. If you are going to manage a factory, it means that you are no longer Minister. Knowing whether the dispute has been settled wisely depends on who is named in your place. In any case, for you to stay five years managing a factory is too great a loss of your talents. And it isn't your Mama who's speaking. It's an old lady who would like to see the whole world converted to Socialism. I think that if you do as you say you're going to, you won't be a good servant of world Socialism.

If for some reason there are paths no longer open to you in Cuba, in Algeria there's a Mr. Ben Bella who would be grateful for your organizing the economy there and advising him, or a Mr. Nkrumah in Ghana who would feel the same way. Yes, you would still be a foreigner. This seems to me to be your permanent fate. . . .[6]

In the middle of April, Major Guevara disappeared from public view and extraordinary stories began to circulate about his possible whereabouts. Many political commentators—"specialists in Cuban affairs"—agreed with the conclusions of the CIA and said that Fidel Castro was responsible for his death. They said that they had learned from absolutely trustworthy and truthful sources that Che had died at the hands of the Castro regime when his differences with the leader of the Cuban revolution grew too great. "Many famous journalists, such as Lartéguy of *Paris Match*, stand behind the thesis that Guevara has been physically eliminated."[7]

These stories, which were made up out of whole cloth, obliged Castro to read in public on October 3, 1965, in the presence of Aleida March, a letter that Che had sent him when he left his government post. The text reads as follows:

> I remember many things at this time: the time I met you at María Antonia's, the moment when I decided to come [with you to Cuba], all the tension of the preparations. One day people came by asking who should be notified in case we died, and the real possibility of dying struck us all. Later we found out that this was how it was, that in a revolution one triumphs or dies (if it is a true revolution). Many comrades were left along the wayside on the road to victory.
>
> Today everything is less dramatic because we are more mature, but the same thing is happening all over again. I feel that I have fulfilled that part of my duty that tied me to the Cuban revolution in its territory and I say good-by to you, to our comrades, to your people, who are now my people.
>
> I formally resign from my responsibilities in the leadership of the Party, my post as Minister, my rank as Major, my Cuban citizenship. I have no legal ties to Cuba, only ties of another sort—ties which cannot be given up as appointments to office can. Reviewing my past life, I believe I have worked honestly enough and dedicatedly enough to consolidate the triumph of the revolution. My only serious

---

[6] Ricardo Rojo, *My Friend Ché* (New York: The Dial Press, Inc., 1968). The remainder of the letter is news of the family and friends.

[7] *Clarín Internacional* (La Paz, No. 50: November, 1967).

fault is not having trusted you more from the very first moments in the Sierra Maestra and not having understood your qualities as a leader and a revolutionary soon enough.

I have lived magnificent days and felt at your side the pride of belonging to our people both in the bright and in the sad days of the Caribbean crisis.

A statesman has seldom shone more brightly than you in those days; I am also proud of having followed you unhesitatingly, identifying with your way of thinking and seeing things and being aware of dangers and principles.

Other lands in the world call on my modest talents. I can do what is denied you because of your responsibility to Cuba; the hour has come for us to separate.

Please know that I am both happy and sad to do so: I leave behind here my purest hopes as a builder, the dearest among the persons I hold dear . . . and I leave a people who took me in like a son; this rends a part of my spirit. I will bear on new battlefields the faith that you inculcated in me, the revolutionary spirit of my people, the feeling that I am fulfilling the most sacred part of my duties—to fight against imperialism wherever it may be. This is ample comfort and heals any wound there may be.

I say once more that I free Cuba of any responsibility, except that which stems from her example. That if my final hour comes under other skies, my last thought will be for this people and especially for you. That I thank you for your teachings and your example, and that I shall try to be faithful down to the last consequences of my acts. That I have always been identified with the foreign policy of our revolution, and I still am. That wherever I stop, I will feel the responsibility of being a Cuban revolutionary and will act as such. That I leave my children and my wife no material possessions, and this does not sadden me; I am happy that this is so. That I ask nothing for them, since the State will give them what they need to live and get an education.

I would have many things to say to you and our people, but I feel that they are unnecessary; words cannot express what I should like them to, and it is no use to scribble page after page.

I embrace you with revolutionary fervor. Ever onward to victory. The fatherland or death.

Che

When he left Cuba, Guevara wrote his parents the following letter, which also does not skirt the subject of death, a subject which always played a role in his visionary dreams.

Dear Mother and Father,

I can feel Rocinante's[8] ribs beneath my heels again; I am beginning my travels again with my shield on my arm.

About ten years ago I wrote you another farewell letter; I regretted not being a better soldier and a better doctor. The latter no longer interests me, and as a soldier I'm not so bad.

In essence nothing has changed, except that I am much more aware. My Marxism is firmly rooted and purified. I believe in armed struggle as the only solution for the peoples who are struggling for their freedom and I act in accordance with my beliefs. Many would call me an adventurer, and I am one; only of a different sort, one of those that risks his skin to demonstrate what he believes to be true.

This may be the end. I do not seek it, but it is in my calculus of probabilities. If that's the way it turns out, here is a last embrace.

I have loved you very much, only I didn't know how to express my affection; I am extremely rigid in the way I act, and I believe that at times you did not understand me. Moreover, it was not easy to understand me; believe me today.

A will that I have polished with the delight of an artist will now sustain my weak legs and tired lungs. I shall do what must be done.

Remember this little *condottiere* of the twentieth century from time to time.

A kiss to Celia, to Roberto, Juan Martín and Pototín, Beatriz, to everyone.

A big hug from your prodigal and recalcitrant son,

Ernesto

Nonetheless, the stories about Guevara's death continued and he was well on his way to becoming a mythical figure. Major Guevara, the impenitent world-wanderer, traveled about the globe astride the fevered imagination of many journalists and amid the dehumanized rattle of the teletypes. Wherever a people tried to cut the noose that tied them to imperialism, there was Guevara's ghost. He was reported to be fighting with Francisco Camaño's troops in the Dominican Republic; there were rumors of his death in Santo Domingo; he was said to be in Vietnam or fighting with Mulele's troops in the Congo; an Italian newspaperman "interviewed" him in the forests of Peru; his presence was announced on the border between Paraguay and Brazil, and on that between Bolivia and Brazil; he was reported to have been seen with the Guatemalan guerrillas—the

---

[8] Rocinante was Don Quixote's horse.—*Trans.*

stories were limitless. He died a number of deaths in the sensationalist press.

But the real story was different. In July, Guevara left Cuba and went to Cairo, where he immediately contacted Somaliot, the leader of the rebellion in the Congo. He then went to the Congo and participated actively in the struggle against Tshombe's mercenaries, where his guerrilla experience was put to use. His base was Brazzaville, and he sent a birthday letter to his daughter Hilda from there in February, 1966:

> I'm writing you today, although the letter will arrive quite a while later; but I want you to know that I am remembering you and hoping that you're having a very happy birthday. You are almost a woman now, and it's not possible to write to you as you do to children, telling them silly stories or little lies.
>
> You should know that I am still far away and that I will be away from you for a long time, doing what I can to fight against our enemies. It's not very much, but I am doing something; and I believe that you can always be proud of your father, as I am of you.
>
> Remember that it will take many years of struggle, and even when you're grown up you will have to do your part in the struggle. Meanwhile, you must prepare yourself to be a revolutionary, which at your age means to learn a great deal, as much as possible, and to always be ready to support just causes. Obey your mother, too, and don't always think you're the one who's right: you're too young. That will come later.
>
> You must make a big effort to be among the best in school. Best in every sense—you know what I mean: studying and a revolutionary attitude mean good conduct, seriousness, love for the revolution, being a good comrade, etc. I wasn't like that when I was your age, but I was in a different society, where man was the enemy of man. You now have the privilege of living in another era and you must be worthy of it.
>
> Don't forget to watch over the other children around the house and tell them to study and to behave nicely. Especially Adeilita, who looks up to you because you're her big sister.
>
> Well, old girl, once again, have a happy birthday. Give a hug to your mama and Gina, and here is a great big bear hug for all the time we won't see each other, from your
>
> *Papa*

He was soon called back to Havana—his presence in the heart of the African continent seemed to have added fuel to the fire in the undeclared war between the Russians and the Chinese. When he reached Cuba in March, 1966, his arrival was an absolute secret, for he had decided to take up the revolutionary cause in an unexpected place: Bolivia.

The organization of Bolivian guerrilla groups, which had been discussed in detail with the Bolivian revolutionaries, was planned. The nucleus around Che was made up of Cubans, veterans of the Sierra Maestra and of Escambray. As we have seen, Che arrived in Bolivia for good in October, 1966.

Che was slowly entering the mist of legend. His words were heard only once again, in a document read for him to the Tricontinental entitled "Message to the Peoples of the World."

It was principally the war in Vietnam that occupied Guevara in this speech. To the guerrilla, a Vietnam left entirely to its own devices was illogical, unjust, and cruel. He blamed the great Socialist powers for having permitted this situation. He believed that imperialism could be defeated by the creation of other Vietnams in America. His resentment of the United States, which had begun during his first visit there, grew as his anti-imperialist political conception of that power deepened. The revolutionary war, he told the Tricontinental, must be directed fundamentally against imperialism—the cause of the backwardness and misery of the people of Latin America. Although the fight would be long, cruel, and bloody, and the best soldiers of the revolution would die in battle, he hoped that the insurrectional *focos* would constitute the death blow to those who were sacking the natural riches and trampling on the national sovereignty of the peoples who had been made the vassals of neo-colonialism.

In many circles, Major Guevara's message was held to be a fake. The fertile imagination of professional information officers and politicians well-established in the hierarchy of their countries stirred up the flames of the calumny that had it that Guevara's death was a corollary of a cruel purge within the Cuban regime. The old saying, "The revolution devours its children," was used to strengthen the hypothesis that Che had died a violent death.

During the events which followed, the stories about Guevara took on their original form and he again became the revolutionary fighter fulfilling his duty "making revolution," the Don Quixote charging down the world's roads to "right wrongs."

4

Preliminary Stages of the Guerrilla Effort

This was the political and social background out of which the guerrillas suddenly emerged in the southwest corner of Bolivia in the first months of 1967. The *foco*[1] was located in the last counterforts of the Central Cordillera of the Andes, whose average height is from 3000 to 3600 feet above sea level. The principal command post and the area of operations were located in a rugged region called Ñancahuazú, in Cordillera province in the *departamento* of Santa Cruz. The zone is part of the Río Grande Basin, a river into which small streams and secondary rivers flow. In this part of the country there are no population centers to speak of. The natives speak Quechua and Guaraní. Place names in the zone come from the Guaraní language.

With the exception of the fact that water from the ravines can be counted upon, the region is hostile; the landscape with its grayish trees is typical of the dark and miserable Chaco plain. Prickly branches, plants that tear the clothes and skin with their spines, a multitude of bloodsucking insects, clouds of exasperating mosquitoes, all exist in this wild region. Scratching out a living is difficult, and hunting and gathering wild fruits are not very reliable ways of supplementing the diet in emergencies. It is a place lost in the mountain fastnesses, with scant vegetation; a place where the climate and the

---

[1] A *foco* is the center of the guerrillas' operating zone.—*Trans.*

44

topography exhaust anybody hacking his painful way through the underbrush with a machete and climbing up and down the rugged rock faces of the mountains. Everything here is adverse, discouraging, insurmountable, with the torrid climate contributing to a rapid dehydration of the body.

No doubt the isolation of the spot, closed off as it is by very narrow defiles and almost perpendicular rock walls, was the reason that it was chosen for a refuge that would arouse few suspicions, while the farmhouse bought by the guerrillas would serve as a supply center for moves to other places.

It is hard to know exactly when and where preparations began, but it is quite likely that such a purpose—the creation of many Vietnams in Latin America—was in Guevara's mind when in April, 1965, he decided to disappear from public view in Cuba. It is likewise obvious that its antecedents were bound up with guerrilla *focos* in Peru and Argentina that had been made ready with the effective help of known leaders of the Partida Comunista Boliviano (PCB). It must be remembered in this regard that the abortive Peruvian revolt of 1963 that took place in Puerto Maldonado, an unhealthy tropical zone close to the Bolivian *departamento* of Pando, had the collaboration of Bolivian Communists in its preliminary phases and that the uprising in Tartagal, Argentina, in September, 1963, was carried out by young Argentinian guerrillas who had been trained by Cuban veterans in the zone of Emborozú, near Bermejo, in the Bolivian *departamento* of Tarija.

Bolivia, the heart of the continent of South America, seems to have been an *idée fixe* in Guevara's revolutionary plans following his brief visit to the country in 1953. When the realities of that time are analyzed, furthermore, the Argentinian leader's plan had a certain logic to it. Between 1958 and 1962 Bolivia had resisted all American pressures to break diplomatic relations with Cuba. In the cadres of the MNR, the governing party, and within the Central Obrera Boliviana, that at that time was an important focus of power—it was the last stage in the co-government of the MNR and the COB—there was strong sympathy for the Cuban revolutionary experiment. The first group of anti-Castro exiles which arrived in Bolivia at this time was received with hostile demonstrations of workers led by militants of the MNR and directives from the COB. Some deputies even came around to proposing the expulsion of the anti-Castroites as *personae non gratae*. The later deterioration of the MNR regime, which reached its low point in the middle of 1962, and the subsequent socio-economic unrest that the country has suffered from up to the present, gave greater impetus to the choice of Bolivia as a new preparatory center for revolutionary war.

The abortive attempts at revolt in Argentina and Peru began to have repercussions within the internal machinery of the PCB, which was at this period still monolithically controlled by its Central Committee. The leaders of the Party were rudely accused of having betrayed the Peruvian revolutionaries. Many of these revolutionaries sought refuge in Bolivian territory, bringing with them a great amount of armaments that, according to rumor, are still secretly buried somewhere. Almost all of them were arrested by the Bolivian police, but the police were not very hard on them and within a short time they were set free. Some of them stayed in Bolivia and took up residence in the mining zones, where they could count on the solidarity and aid of the miners.

The faction of the PCB that later was to become the pro-Peking wing constantly pointed a finger at the directors of the Party as having acted irregularly when called on to cooperate with the Peruvian rebels, though the Chinese wing never produced any proof of this.

Events in Puerto Maldonado hastened the division of the PCB into two wings, one pro-Soviet and the other pro-Chinese. Several Peruvian guerrillas who had settled in Bolivia also contributed to this split. José Negrón, also known as Chino,[2] a university professor who later married a woman from Beni, was one of those who most insistently pointed to the top level of the pro-Soviet leadership as having been partly responsible for the fiasco at Puerto Maldonado.

The Communist leaders were also blamed for the abortive uprising in Tartagal, although only a few isolated militants had taken part in it. The sum of all these antecedents made for further recriminations within the Party and hastened its final breakup. In April, 1965, in the mining district of Siglo Veinte, an extraordinary congress of the PCB took place, and out of it was born the organization that was to follow the ideological orientation of Peking. Since then the PCB has had two wings, two antagonistic sets of leaders.

---

[2] In certain leftist circles in the first months of 1968 this same Negrón was repeatedly said to be an agent of the CIA.

Mario Monje Molina, Jorge Kolle Cueto, and Ramiro Otero remained at the head of the pro-Soviet wing, and the leadership of the pro-Peking wing fell to mining leader Federico Escobar—now dead —and Oscar Zamora Medinacelli.

For reasons of political strategy, Bolivia, up to this point, had been a sort of neutralized zone as far as any guerrilla activity was concerned. It was merely a center of subversive movements radiating outward to neighboring countries, and the directors of the subversive movements had even put the damper on several strike attempts so as to make the country appear tranquil. All these previous failures and the division of the PCB led the leaders of the guerrilla movement to create a real guerrilla *foco* in Bolivia.

To this end Che Guevara took advantage of the presence in Cuba of a resolute group of militants from the Bolivian Communist youth group, which arrived in October, 1965, to complete its politico-military training. In the group were the most outstanding members of the military commission of the PCB: Coco and Inti Peredo, Aniceto Reinaga, Orlando Jiménez Bazán, Jorge Vásquez Viaña, etc.; and even the top leader of the Party, Mario Monje, who had several times visited Cuba, the USSR, and other of the Socialist countries. Guevara reached an understanding with them directly, leaving the Central Committee of the PCB somewhat out in the cold. Che's strong, authoritarian personality tended to be rough when it came to dealing with people who claimed to have as much authority as he had, except in the very particular case of Fidel Castro. The young Communist group trained in Cuba and controlled by Monje—a man whom the Cuban Communist Party trusted—became Che's general staff when they assured him of their total support and respect.

In January, 1966, the Tricontinental Congress took place in Havana, and was attended by two Bolivian delegations, one headed by Mario Miranda Pacheco, the leader of the Frente de Liberación Nacional (FLIN), known as the electoral arm of the pro-Moscow PCB, and the other headed by Lydia Gueiller de Möller, representing the Consejo Democrático del Pueblo (CODEP), made up of larger and stronger popular parties. This latter delegation, in which the Trotskyite Partido Obrero Revolucionario (POR) and the pro-Chinese wing of the PCB were also represented, arrived in Havana, thanks to personal efforts in its behalf by Senator Sálvador Allende at the

Cuban Embassy in Mexico City, but the delegation was not received or seated at the Tricontinental Congress.

It is not possible to clarify every aspect of the cooperation given Guevara by the pro-Moscow PCB. Jorge Kolle Cueto, the Secretary-General of the Party, referred to these interweavings in a political seminar in La Paz in December, 1967, and said among other things: "This does not presuppose, as might be thought, that the leadership of the Communist Party rejects or denies, or simply is not preparing for, the eventuality of armed struggle. Nothing could be falser. The Bolivian Communist Party has never rejected the possibility of taking this route. Indeed, it considers it criminal not to prepare the Party and the masses for the predominance of this form of struggle in all its various guises. And this is being done, avoiding the lack of preparation that, given the limitations that obtained, prevented the Party in other periods from playing the role that circumstances demanded." Later on in his speech he cited part of the report on his interview with Ernesto Guevara in Ñancahuazú, which was presented to those leaders by the First Secretary of the pro-Moscow wing, Mario Monje Molina, and which reads as follows: "1. No organism of the Bolivian Communist Party, no leader or militant of ours knew of the plans of comrade Guevara concerning Bolivia until January of this year [1967]. 2. No leader or militant knew of the arrival of comrade Guevara in the country on November 6, 1966. He later contacted a few comrades who succeeded in keeping the news of his presence absolutely confidential, as he had requested. As First Secretary, I went abroad on November 3, 1966, and returned on December 24, 1966. 3. At the end of December, I was invited to meet comrade Guevara at a place that was not specified . . . "

Nothing need be said about Kolle Cueto's thoughts on the matter. The report attributed to Monje Molina, on the other hand, does not appear to be entirely true, since various known leaders and members of his party actively participated in the preparations the guerrillas were making, as is evidenced by many accounts that are public knowledge.

On this particular, Dr. Ricardo Rojo says:

> A hard alternative faced the Bolivian Communist Party. It could not reject outright its analysis of the situation, beginning with the need for armed struggle. But if it chose the latter, it was clearly running counter to Soviet strategy, and if it didn't, Guevara would depend

exclusively on the hated pro-Chinese and the more abysmal Trotsky-ites. The Central Committee wavered, not knowing which way to turn. Many of the orthodox Communists feared that in such a confusion of different tendencies split by old conflicts the Party would end up having worked against Moscow's instructions and having lost the guerrilla movement as well.

In the beginning of December 1966 Mario Monje, the Secretary-General of the Bolivian Communist Party, traveled to Havana to discuss the matter with Castro. The Cuban leader found himself in an awkward position. He could not ignore the pacts between the Latin American Communist Parties and Moscow, and at the same time he had to obtain the support of the Bolivian Communists for his friend Guevara. What Castro was practically asking Monje was to let the political leadership on the continent be transferred from Moscow to Havana.

Monje returned with a clearer picture, and on New Year's Day, 1967, he asked to be taken to the camp at Ñancahuazú, where he had a long but not very friendly talk with Ché. Guevara had already noticed various signs of disaffection on the part of the Bolivian Communists. His agitators in the mines had been ignored, and in other cases men who had seemed ready to join the camp had changed their minds at the last minute.[3]

Moreover, an episode illustrative of the dissension within this branch is said to have occurred in Cochabamba. A select group of Communists (doctors, professors, workers, etc.) decided to lend their full support to the insurgents in the southeast, and therefore consulted with the region's First Secretary. This leader could not come to any concrete decision because of his limited power, and therefore asked the heads of the Central Committee of the Party to come. Jorge Kolle Cueto arrived from La Paz; he did not officially authorize the collaboration that they had planned, but left each Party member personally responsible for his position in the face of the events taking shape.

As for the role of the pro-Peking wing of the PCB, it was excluded from participating in the struggle from the very beginning. Thus, in a separate number of its clandestine official periodical,

[3] Ricardo Rojo, *op. cit.*

Liberación (No. 50), we read: "Participation in the guerrilla move-ment was neither sought from nor proposed to our party. Had this been suggested, we would have considered such positions in the light of the Marxist-Leninist conception of armed struggle, which is what guides the footsteps and the life of our party." This assertion is con-firmed to a certain degree by the pro-Soviet wing, which in its clandes-tine official publication, *Unidad* (No. 327–XI–67), says: "The Boliv-ian Communist Party did not go back on any promise in the tragic experience in the southeast, an experience which, for once, the chief, Zamora, had no part in. We can affirm this too, even though he puts on a holier-than-thou act." (The reference is to Oscar Zamora Medinacelli, the First Secretary of the pro-Peking wing.)

The conclusion that the pro-Peking group played no role what-soever in the guerrilla movement (aside from a few of its militants who acted on their own) is acceptable, since we know of several events that took place before this: the breaking of relations with the Cuban Communist Party; the contacts and close ties of the Monje-Peredo group (who were anti-Maoists) with the Cuban directors of the guerrillas; and the role of Moisés Guevara as a recruiter of guer-rillas—despite the fact that he had been a member of the pro-Peking wing, he had been expelled as a disruptive element.

When the movement ended with the death of Che, the relations between the two wings worsened, and the accusations became public. The part of the press partial to the pro-Peking sector openly accused the pro-Soviet PCB of having betrayed the uprising in the southeast. The official organ of the pro-Soviet wing, in turn, taxed the pro-Peking sector with having turned its back on the revolutionary under-taking from the very beginning.

The Trotskyite POR, divided into two or three different fac-tions, lent no aid—at least officially—in the preparations for guerrilla warfare. It did not go beyond lyrical expressions of solidarity, despite its known theoretical dissent concerning revolutionary means and in spite of the fact that it was neither consulted nor invited by the top leaders who were organizing the movement.

To sum up: The leaders of the pro-Soviet, pro-Peking, and Trotskyite factions undoubtedly looked upon the guerrilla uprising with a certain romantic sentimentality, with the exception of certain elements that lent it their personal support. But only the first two played a direct role in the rather disorderly preparatory stages, if only to clarify their position for or against the creation of a *foco* in the

Andes. At all events, the orthodox Marxists never came to agree with the new guerrilla scheme of action, and less still with its central theory of the *foco*, as these were outlined by the Cuban veterans and South American and European theorists.

The only elements which remained totally loyal to Che Guevara, right or wrong, were those ideologically defined as Castristas, who are still not definitely organized as a separate faction. These elements did support the revolutionary war in all its manifestations. Apparently there is no opportunity at present for a reconciliation of bureaucratic dogmatism and the urgencies born of the new socio-political context in Latin America. This dialectical struggle is still going on, at times becoming violently destructive. The truth and the responsibilities devolving on each of the parties will come to light only when the surviving protagonists of Ñancahuazú can make their voices heard. Meanwhile there can as yet be no reply to the caustic anathema that Che noted down in his campaign diary: "Bolivian Communists are pigs."

But in what is an incomprehensible paradox, Communists of all persuasions are vying with each other to glorify the memory of the great rebel now that the guerrilla struggle is over, while they train their big guns on the young French philosopher Régis Debray, whom they have stubbornly and repeatedly accused of disloyalty.

Yet Debray, in a tape recording in the authors' possession, expresses the following opinion of the relations between the Communists and the guerrillas:

QUESTION: What role did the Communist Party play in the guerrilla uprising?

ANSWER: Look, this is a very delicate problem. I am not a Bolivian. It is very difficult for me to speak. Do you know what I mean? I don't belong to a Communist Party either. I am not a French Communist; I am an independent Marxist. I don't think we should inject any more poison into all this. The press does everything it can to poison things. Señor Monje will be able to talk some day and explain what happened. And I want to say something else: those who died there, those who gave their lives for the revolutionary cause, came from the Party. They came from Communist Party bases and some of them were Party leaders. I believe that it is public knowledge that they had had disagreements with the Party. But it must be recognized that they were Party militants. I really admire them a great deal . . .

5

The Guerrillas Organize

The reasons for the much-discussed choice of Ñancahuazú as the guerrilla center of operations are still not known. The motivations for such a controversial decision could be set in the proper light only by Che and those closest to him. Nevertheless, persistent investigation has turned up a few facts.

Before Guevara arrived in Bolivia, Alto Beni, in the *departamento* of La Paz, had been chosen for the establishment of the "mother cell," as the central guerrilla nucleus is called in revolutionary terminology. The preparations were so close to being finished by the middle of 1966 that Orlando Jiménez Bazán, called Camba, had already bought a plot of land in that region for that purpose. As soon as he arrived in the country, Guevara learned of the reluctance of the Central Committee of the PCB to give their complete support to the movement and of the dissension that existed within its cadres. These circumstances and his natural mistrust of what he called the *camarilla,* or inner circle, led him to modify his plans immediately, abandoning all the work that had been done. As a consequence, after consulting with his intimate friends on the Military Commission of the Party, he chose the zone of Ñancahuazú, not as a principal center of operations, but simply as a reserve area for preparation and training. His main idea was to make the asphalt highway between Cochabamba and Santa Cruz (three hundred miles) the principal axis for mounting attacks, carrying out command operations, etc., with the mobility and flexibility that must characterize all guerrilla warfare. He carefully chose for his operations the stretch between Comarapa and La Angostura (168 and 284 miles southeast of Cochabamba respectively), along which there are various important towns, such as Mataral, Mairana, Samaipata, Valle Grande, and others less important, which offered the possibility of crossing the highway toward the north where he could have at his disposal a classic "guerrilla sanctuary," represented by the wooded cordillera of Amboró.

This project was acceptable as a rational plan for guerrilla action in view of the various political interferences. Yet in spite of this decision, it appears that Guevara did not definitely abandon his original project in Alto Beni, since, when the campaign was going through its worst crises, he alluded several times in his diary to the necessity of establishing a new front in this zone and in the province of Chapare, in the *departamento* of Cochabamba.

It is interesting to note at this juncture that Guevara never intended to head a social revolution in Bolivia, but rather merely to create and fortify a guerrilla *foco* until it could subsist on its own under the command of Bolivian leaders. Pertinent to this is the following declaration of the Bolivian guerrilla Camba, taped by the authors.

"Well, I think that he [Guevara] had no intention of abandoning the guerrilla group, especially the Bolivians. He wanted us to have complete confidence in him as the leader of the guerrillas. He didn't have the heart—he told us—to abandon his group that way. He would leave if things went right with the group, when the guerrilla army was able to fight and when there were competent new leaders to lead the struggle. 'Then I'll be able to leave with the cadres I came with, to organize somewhere else,' he used to tell us. He intended to spread guerrilla *focos* to other countries."

According to nonofficial sources, guerrilla experts and foreign cadres arrived in Bolivia in March, 1966. The first one to arrive was an important member of the Cuban intelligence service, presumably sent by Guevara, who is known only by his nickname of Papi.[1] This

---

[1] As this book was going to press, it was learned that Major Papi and

man was extremely active for a month, establishing various contacts with parties and political groups with leftist and revolutionary tendencies. Later Ricardo arrived for the same purpose—he was later to be one of the most outstanding guerrilla leaders. Other emissaries serving as couriers, and collaborators who had been in Bolivia before, arrived later. All of them received the invaluable and permanent cooperation of an agent named Tania, who had been there for several years.

Papi and Ricardo were to be responsible for analyzing the general situation in the country, which could potentially be thrown into chaos, and to evaluate the objective conditions so as to plan the armed struggle.

General Alfredo Ovando Candia said in reference to the beginning stage of the guerrilla movement: "Ever since the fourth quarter of 1966 we have had more and more reports on the preparation of the guerrillas in our territory, without our having thus far been able to obtain definite proof. On November 24, 1966, it became known that Ernesto Che Guevara was in the country between the fifteenth and the twenty-second of September, 1966, and left immediately thereafter." He then added: "Roberto Peredo Leigue came to Camiri between the months of October and December, 1966, in order to set up a guerrilla base in Ñancahuazú. Born on March 23, 1938, in the *departamento* of Beni, with identity card Number 229195, he had twice visited Mexico City; he was a militant of the Bolivian Communist Party, and a professional chauffeur. This man contacted various persons in Camiri, Choreti, Lagunillas, Pincal, and Ñancahuazú, and expressed his desire to acquire land for a ranch. The opportunity presented itself when Señor Roberto Villa sold him part of his property in Ñancahuazú for the sum of 15,000 Bolivian pesos. Once the ranch house was built, farming and cattle-raising seemed to be going on, and two men were hired as ranch hands for these purposes."[2]

This declaration of the Commander in Chief should be rounded

Ricardo were one and the same person, and that this person also used the nickname Chinchu. This guerrilla was with Cuban Majors Hermes Peña Torrez and Raúl Dávila in Emborozú, directing the guerrilla organization of Tartagal, Argentina, which ended with the death of Dávila in the one battle that was fought, and the disappearance of the Argentine journalist Jorge Massetti, who headed this guerrilla group under the name of Major Segundo.

[2] *El Diario* (La Paz, September 9, 1967).

out with the testimony of neighbors in Camiri and Lagunillas. According to them, Roberto (Coco) Peredo first appeared in the zone in August, 1966, just a few days after his return from Cuba, frequently accompanied by another person, presumably Jorge Vásquez Viaña (Loro), one of the most valuable members of the Bolivian Communist Party because of his personal bravery, his ideological background, and his education.

As for the acquisition of the farm, the Bolivian magazine *Suplemento de Primera Plana* printed the following: "The ideal site was finally found, an abandoned ranch in Ñancahuazú, whose owner, Victoria de Padilla, sold it for a relatively small sum, since the place was not suitable for the preparation of *chacos* [arable plots of land] or for the raising of cattle because of the thickness of the vegetation. Roberto 'Coco' Peredo Leigue is said to have been the one entrusted with making the purchase, but as a matter of fact there is no written record of such a transaction because the dealings were completely informal, since the buyers did not want there to be any proof of this operation." In reality, the transaction took place between Coco and Roberto Villa Mariscal on August 26, 1966, involving the sum of 15,000 Bolivian pesos. (One United States dollar is worth twelve Bolivian pesos.)

According to further statements made by General Ovando Candia, Guevara came into Bolivia for the last time with two Uruguayan passports issued in Montevideo: Number 130220, dated December 2, 1965, in the name of Ramón Benítez Fernández, and Number 130748, dated December 22, 1965, and made out to Adolfo Mena Gonzáles. The strange thing is that the visas of both passports establish that their holders entered and left the Madrid airport on the same day: on the ninth and the nineteenth of October, 1966, respectively. The same thing occurs on passport Number 129918, also issued in Montevideo, on October 29, 1965, and made out to Raúl Borges Mederos.

Ovando Candia also stated that Guevara and Antonio Garrido García (passport Number 12394, issued in Montevideo on December 16, 1964) arrived in São Paulo, Brazil, on November 1, 1966; and that after obtaining legal vaccination certificates with consecutive numbers, they continued on to La Paz on November 3, without any of their documents showing an entry stamp to prove they entered the country legally. There are thus no precise official data on the exact date that Guevara entered Bolivia for the last time.

Some of the Communist Party leaders Guevara contacted affirm that Guevara arrived in Bolivia in July, 1966; others say September; and some say it was in October. What appears certain is that he came into the country at the end of July, remained only a few days, and returned for good in the last week of October. Upon arriving in the country he took charge of the organization of the guerrillas and had interviews with high Communist leaders and labor leaders, especially the leaders of miners' unions. Unconfirmed reports have it that he spent a short time giving himself medical treatment in a farm in Muñecas province, in the *departamento* of La Paz.

Versions that seem reliable have it that Che visited the city of Cochabamba toward the end of October, where he conversed with leaders and supporters of one of the wings of the PCB. The lawyer, Ricardo Rojo, also supports this thesis; according to him Guevara arrived the second week of September, via San Pablo–Corumba, after having entered at Puerto Suárez, then moved from Santa Cruz to Cochabamba, where he stayed for quite some time. According to Roper, he had an interview with Jorge Kolle Cueto of the Party secretariat, but despite Che's insistence, Kolle could not give Che assurances of his collaboration, since only the Central Committee of the Party could decide this.[3]

The truth is that Guevara, as we said before, entered Bolivia with two passports, preferring to use the one made out in the name of Adolfo Mena Gonzáles. He used this passport to get credentials from the National Board of Information of the Presidency of the Republic on November 3, 1966, which described him as "a special envoy of the Organization of American States making a study and gathering information on economic and social relations in rural areas of Bolivia." By using disguises, special accessories, and cosmetics, he went about incognito, circulating freely without any special danger to himself.

To sum up, Che Guevara was in La Paz at the beginning of November, 1966, and appeared in Ñancahuazú on the seventh of that month to assume command of the new guerrilla *foco*.

Coco Peredo and Vásquez Viaña settled down on the 548-acre

---

[3] Ricardo Rojo, *op. cit.*

farm located a few miles to the north of Lagunillas, the capital of Cordillera province. They erected the first and only building on the place, a primitive structure with a calamine or corrugated-zinc roof, which gave it its name of "Calamine House." It was a roomy shack with walls of tree trunks plastered together with mud, and served as a dormitory, storehouse, and meeting place. It also had a kitchen that was even more primitive, corrals, garden plots, and a few country conveniences.

The sites for various camps were prepared about five miles to the west of the ranch, in a spot sheltered by thick woods. The buildings on them were slowly improved up until the middle of February.

While this was going on in the mountain fastnesses, the cities were being transformed into secret, but very active, laboratories for subversion. The various mechanisms were now adjusted. Communist factions of the most diverse persuasions bustled back and forth, and there was much movement among La Paz, Cochabamba, Oruro, Sucre, Santa Cruz, and the mining districts by politicians of the extreme left. Leaders and militants of the pro-Soviet and pro-Chinese wings of the Communist Party held secret meetings, and there was an unusual amount of movement from one city to another. They bought underwear, clothes for tropical climates, padded jackets, medicines of all sorts, and so forth. "In Camiri, a busy commercial town, foodstuffs, especially flour and canned goods from Argentina, were bought, while ranchers of the region provided, at a low price, the first two head of cattle, which were put in cattle pens to be fattened up for the guerrillas who were already known to be on the way," the magazine *Primera Plana* states.

Recruiting was entrusted to Communist militants of the pro-Soviet wing under Coco Peredo and Jorge Vásquez Viaña. Moisés Guevara, José Negrón, and Tania also helped with recruiting.

There seemed to be ample opportunity for the gathering of human materiel. The country at this time was living through one of the most painful crises of the last three decades. Within this panorama of near-despair, it did not appear to be difficult, at first sight, to recruit guerrilla cadres. Workers who had been laid off, and unemployed miners with uncertain futures, were hired or specially invited to join. Nonetheless there were few who hastened to join out of real conviction. Most joined as a way out of the precarious economic condition of the moment and as a means to keep the wolf from their families' doors. Those who enlisted out of ideological conviction were for the most part people from the middle classes who had more awareness because of their education; and miners, because of the firmness of their class consciousness and their vigorous tradition of armed resistance. Among the Bolivian guerrillas, these showed the strongest moral fortitude and revolutionary faith, fighting to the last breath.

According to the magazine *Primera Plana*, José Negrón first recruited among the miners and then tried to secure the cooperation of the Maoist wing of the party in La Paz, but the head of this section of the party, Oscar Zamora, forbade his subordinates to attend meetings called by Negrón, or to help the guerrillas. According to this magazine, this occurred in November, but it did not interrupt the recruiting, especially in Siglo Veinte, where the number of unemployed was greater.

This report in *Primera Plana* should be clarified. It has been established that it was not El Chino Negrón, but the ex-leader of a miners' union, Moisés Guevara, who took on the job of recruiting. Negrón merely assisted Moisés Guevara, planning his strategy from behind the scenes. There was no direct understanding between the pro-Peking leadership and Negrón or Moisés Guevara, because the latter had already been expelled from that group in May, 1966, "for having entered into contradiction with the Party line."

It has also been learned from reliable sources that Oscar Zamora's activities in Oruro were aimed at destroying a presumed splinter group in the bosom of the Party, which was supposedly inspired and organized by Moisés Guevara.

The attitude of Zamora naturally prejudiced the task of recruitment that the guerrilla organization had entrusted to Moisés Guevara. Once his attempts to enlist the aid of the militants of the pro-Peking wing had failed, Moisés Guevara enrolled unemployed miners and personal friends, without first having submitted them to a scrupulous examination of their moral solvency and their positions on fundamental points. Because of this, men hired for pay or deceived by false promises of much more money than they deserved were accepted by the guerrillas, instead of people with strong ideological commitments. And this also explains the large number of informers and the deserters in the guerrillas' midst; it is calculated that approximately nineteen men, almost all of them supposedly unemployed miners, suddenly disappeared from the rebel camp.

Nonetheless, many convinced Communist militants of the pro-Peking sector of the Party who had ties with Moisés Guevara entered the guerrilla group, occupying a place apart from the leadership of the group; among them were Simón Cuba (Willy), Raúl Quispaya, Francisco Huanca (Pablo), José Castillo (Paco), and Apolinar Aguirre Quispe (Polo).

One other event that will serve to confirm the lack of harmony between the pro-Soviet PCB and the guerrilla command took place at the beginning of 1967. On January 7 of that year a plenary session of the Moscow-leaning Central Committee was held to analyze its future relations with the directors of the guerrilla movement. It was decided that a personal courier should be sent to Castro in Havana with the official list of conclusions that had been drawn up, explaining the position of the Party and its conditions for effective and total cooperation with the revolutionary insurgent movement.[4]

Castro replied that he could not intervene in the matter, in view of the fact that Che Guevara had the power to resolve any problem concerning the guerrilla uprising. Some days later, an account of these events was sent to Guevara in Ñancahuazú by Castro himself, who suggested that Che resolve any ambiguity or disagreement that there might be with the PCB.

From November, 1966, the guerrillas who had been recruited slowly formed in groups and made their way one by one toward the camp. The Cubans made the move using two routes that they usually used: Mexico-Madrid-Prague-São Paulo and Mexico-Moscow-Zurich-

---

[4] In general terms the document was a repetition, in more detail, of the plans that had already been set forth on various occasions by the top leaders of the PCB, Monje and Kolle. It cited the nonexistence of the proper objective conditions: "Previous preparation of the Party and other revolutionary forces for the armed struggle; the grouping and the militarization of the popular armed forces on a national scale; the coordination of simultaneous actions in the cities, mines, rural regions, and mountain areas; the initiation of the fight at a moment of extreme political crisis, not as a continuation of a simple strike or in response to repressive measures of the government; subordination of the military command of the guerrillas to the political authority of the Party," etc. The bearer of the message was Jorge Kolle Cueto, the Secretary-General of the Party.

Santiago, Chile. Once on Bolivian territory, the last stage of the trip to the guerrilla camp usually took them through Camiri, a last "escape hatch," to use the apt expression of the Argentinian journalist García Lupo.

The end of November saw the arrival of Braulio, in whose diary we read: "On October 25 I left home, leaving my wife behind with tears in her eyes. On the twenty-ninth I left Havana. The second adventure was beginning; I was going to Bolivia with the name of Braulio, with a Panamanian passport and $26,000: a thousand for my expenses and $25,000 for Ramón.[5] The itinerary was Moscow-Prague-Chile-Bolivia. On November 25 we arrived in Bolivia. It was just a month since I had left home. On the twenty-sixth we left for the mountains."

On December 12, Guevara received a select group of veterans of the Cuban revolution and organized the command structure and the combat orders using these veterans as a cadre.

On the last day of 1966 there was an important political meeting in Ñancahuazú. On December 28, the First Secretary of the Bolivian Communist Party, Mario Monje Molina, had arrived in Camiri for this meeting, having been driven by Coco Peredo from La Paz in a jeep. On the thirty-first he had a long interview with Major Guevara.

The details of this much-discussed meeting of the leaders come from the following five sources:

ONE: Mogambo, a doctor and a Cuban guerrilla, writes openly in his campaign diary: "December 31. Today Mario Monje, the Secretary of the Bolivian Communist Party, arrived. He talked with Ramón. He informed him of three conditions for his staying in the guerrilla group. First: that he give up his post, because his party is not supporting the guerrilla movement, and separate himself [from the Party] but not from its political line; second: that he be recognized as political and military leader of the guerrillas while they are operating in Bolivian territory; third: that he be free to talk with all the parties in order to secure their aid. Of the second condition Ramón said to Monje: 'I'm the leader.' Then Monje left the camp,

---

[5] Ramón was one of Che Guevara's code names.

without any agreement having been reached." (Testimony of the Military Prosecutor, Colonel Remberto Iriarte Paz, in the trial at Camiri, October 18, 1967.)

TWO: Jorge Vásquez Viaña, who went to say good-by to the head of his Party at the Camiri airport on January 3, 1967, along with Coco Peredo, told a militant of the Bolivian Communist Party who was there the details of the interview between Guevara and Monje. His version goes as follows: "Ramón had a long conversation with Monje. Monje came back utterly defeated, after having asked for political and military command. Ramón offered him only the political leadership, which would be subordinate to the military command, since the struggle was already well under way. Monje was quite indecisive when he came in, since he did not have the support of his party. His proposals were made knowing that Ramón would not accept them. He did not want to be taxed with the responsibility of having promised not only his own personal participation but also that of his best people (Coco, Inti, Jorge Vásquez, Saldaña [Gabriel], etc.) and even that of the Party. He was sure that on his return to La Paz the Central Committee would get rid of him and he was resigned to renouncing the Party, withdrawing from politics, and going home. 'I am from Alto Perú; I can't help it,' he commented, referring to his indecision about coming in and above all about facing his group. On leaving the camp he gathered his comrades together. He told them that if they wanted to stay they could, but that the Party absolutely would not come in; he insisted that they leave with him. Orlando Jiménez (Camba), Aniceto Reinaga, Wálter Arancibia, Jorge, Coco, Inti, and others answered by looking at him impassively. In the face of this silence he asked sharply whether they were staying. 'Yes, we're staying,' they replied. Jorge Kolle is less guilty because he is consistent. He always opposed this line, unlike Monje, who backed out at the last moment.

"If Ramón had seen more decisiveness on the part of Monje, he might have given him absolute command. He noticeably demonstrated little ideological and personal fortitude. The experience in Venezuela is enough for us and we can't risk having our way of carrying on the struggle betrayed." [There exists a handwritten declaration by this militant, who served as a contact with the cities and visited the guerrilla camp several times.]

THREE: In reference to this episode Jorge Kolle Cueto, the Secretary-General of the pro-Soviet PCB, transcribed the following report that Monje Molina presented to his party in this regard. This is part of it:

"4. At the beginning of the talk, Major Guevara said that his presence in Bolivia and his intention of realizing his ideas here was his responsibility alone: that he was making this declaration so as not to damage the relations between the Bolivian and Cuban Communists.

"5. That it was his intention to begin the fight with all those who were now with him. That his destiny was none other than to fight for socialism against Yankee imperialism, to victory or death. That he would fight anywhere because all of America was his country. He therefore asked for the support of the Bolivian Communist Party and the incorporation of its First Secretary in the guerrilla movement as political head, subordinate to the military head.

"6. I replied that the Bolivian Communist Party and I were in a position to begin a serious discussion of the problem of the Bolivian revolution. That the experience that we had showed errors in confronting such a task, which by now should be well under way, but without subjecting ourselves to schemes that were specific and approved in each case, and without our experience being copied; that the Bolivian revolution should be carried out along a path that the experience and the awareness of our people could render viable. The whole leadership of the revolution should therefore be in the hands of Bolivians and not just the office of political chief subordinate to the military.

"7. As he argued in each case, Major Guevara asked whether my stand was open to argument and subject to bargaining. I told him it wasn't. I asked the same thing in turn about him, and he also answered no.

"8. Since it was impossible to reach an agreement, I asked permission to inform my party and the Bolivian comrades who were with him. He indicated that I was free to do so, that he wouldn't stand in my way, that I could abandon the camp whenever I pleased in the company of those Bolivian comrades who shared my point of view.

"9. I reported to the Bolivian comrades who were present and then comrade Guevara gave a complete summary of the matter, without there being any contradiction whatsoever in the two reports.

"On leaving the camp I assured him that although I did not know the opinion of the leadership of the Bolivian Communist Party, nothing would weaken our solidarity with the Cuban revolution, that we would keep the matter secret and if the fight began, the Bolivian Communist Party would express its solidarity, but it would do so while defending its conception and its own line."[6]

FOUR: From the diary of the Cuban guerrilla Braulio: "Monje did not want to have a guerrilla war in Bolivia unless he were the only leader; but he left dissatisfied. Later, out of rancor, he did not name the young leaders whom he saw in the camp to responsible positions within the Communist Party."

FIVE: An interview with Pombo, one of the three surviving Cuban guerrillas, by Edgardo Damommio, a correspondent from the Inter-Press Service:

"Wasn't there support from the peasants?"

Pombo hesitates.

"Yes, there was, but they were afraid. Afraid of the army, because they were the ones that were powerful."

"Wasn't there any support from the PCB?"

"We had its moral support."

"Of what use was this support to you?"

"It was of no use at all."

"So there wasn't any support?"

"Some sectors of the Party didn't want to support the guerrillas. Others did want to, but they wanted to wait."

"Did you know of the conversation between Mario Monje, the secretary of the Bolivian Communist Party, and Che Guevara?"

"Che told us: 'Monje insisted on three things. First: that the Bolivian pro-Chinese wing was not to be allowed to participate in the guerrilla effort. Second: that the military and political leadership was to be from the Party. Third: that there should be a waiting period, and that aid of all the Latin American Communist parties should be sought.' Che disagreed on these three points. And in one of them he wouldn't give an inch: retaining the leadership of the movement until a Bolivian force was ready. Monje did not accept this. As a

---

[6] Jorge Kolle Cueto; La Paz, December 19, 1967: in a political forum organized by the Law Students' Center of the Universidad Mayor de San Andrés.

leader of the Party, he gave a speech to all of us on December 31, before he left. And he said that he, personally, not as a member of the Party, wanted to take part in the guerrilla effort. That he would explain his position to the Party and would come back and join us. It's a known fact that he never returned." (Santiago, February 24, 1968.)

On this same night of December 31, 1966, three militants of the PCB, indignant and disillusioned by Monje's attitude, suggested that he be killed. Major Guevara was absolutely opposed and allowed no discussion of the proposal.

On January 1, 1967, Chingolo and Eusebio, who had been recruited by Coco Peredo in the middle of December, 1966, in La Paz, arrived at the camp.

The last men to join the guerrillas made up another section, led by Moisés Guevara and consisting of Vicente Rocabado Terrazas, Pastor Barrera Quintana, Salustio Choque Choque, Francisco Huanca, Casildo Condori (Víctor), José Castillo, and Simón Cuba, all Bolivians. The first six had left Oruro on the night of February 10. Cuba joined them in Cochabamba the next day; like many others he had already been in the camp. From there they all took the road that leads from Sucre to Camiri. On the night of the eighteenth Coco picked them up at the Oriente and Londres hotels to drive them in his jeep by way of the Calamine House to their final destination, which they reached at about noon on the nineteenth.

Moisés Guevara, the robust leader of the miners, made his report. The guerrilla leaders had objections since the latest recruits had been selected from among unemployed miners. With the exception of Simón Cuba, an ex-leader of a mining union, the political background of these recruits was not known. In the meeting it was again emphasized that one of the most powerful arms of the revolutionary fighter is the firmness of his ideological conviction. There was reason for doubt in this regard, and later events were to prove that the skeptical leaders had been right.

On March 6, a select group of visitors, who had apparently been awaited for a long time, suddenly appeared in Ñancahuazú. The group was made up of Régis Debray, Carlos Alberto Fructuoso, and Tania.

The exact number of guerrillas has never been known. Military sources progressively raised the figure from eighty to five hundred, without the total number of insurgents ever having been precisely determined. To judge from such factors as the casualties that were identified, the many desertions, the almost permanent visitors, and the survival of six guerrillas, it would seem that the total never reached seventy.

As soon as Major Guevara had arrived the previous November, the work of organizing the movement began. When he had welcomed his staff of experienced Cubans, almost all of whom had won fame in the revolution against Batista, Che got on with dividing his forces into three basic groups: the vanguard, under Marcos; the center, under his direct command; and the rear guard, under Joaquín. Each group was composed of at least ten to fifteen men. He appointed Inti and Coco Peredo as political commissars. He also entrusted the former with the funds he had at his disposal for the support of the guerrilla movement and made him responsible for giving the men instruction in Bolivian politics. There were other appointments: Alejandro was named chief of operations of the guerrilla command, and Ricardo was appointed communications officer and radio operator.

Following a practice observed in guerrilla movements all over the world, each man was baptized with a *nom de guerre*. It was at this juncture that Che Guevara became known as Ramón.

The land was now divided into a central camp and three secondary camps. Paths were hacked out leading to the Calamine House on the east and to the different observation posts and lookouts to the east and northeast, places that they named The Post, The Cliff (with a telephone connection to the central command), the Bear Camp, and the Fox Trail. Ditches and trenches were made with the materials at hand; a henyard was also built, and a patch of land laid out as a vegetable garden. The future guerrillas spent their time hunting wild animals for food, receiving instruction on guerrilla theory and practice, improving their marksmanship, making short marches to get acquainted with the zone, and so on.

The theoretical preparation and the classes in general education took place just as day was ending, under the direction of El Chino, a Peruvian. These sessions were held in a specially prepared site: a sort of semicircular amphitheater with rows of steps and a lectern for the speaker in front. The works that were most popular were those of Che and Mao Tse-Tung on guerrilla warfare; works on Marxist theory; the *History of Small Republics,* by Bartolomé Mitre; the *History of Bolivia,* by Enrique Finot; *Reports,* by the Venezuelan, Mario Menéndez; and, toward the end, a copy of the book *Revolution in the Revolution?* by Régis Debray, sent in by Fidel Castro with a guerrilla who had been taken into the group later than the others. The rebels read a great deal. In the caves (subterranean storehouses) of the Ñancahuazú camp, a surprising number of books, leaflets, and literature of all sorts was found immediately after they had been abandoned, along with war materiel and other effects. Apart from his campaign diaries, Guevara himself, when he fell prisoner in the Churo ravine, had in his knapsack—according to his captors—political works, several general notebooks, books of verse, poems of his own, and a notebook with evaluations and observations on his subordinates.

A correspondent of *Prensa Libre* sent the following dispatch from Camiri describing guerrilla life:

> Life among the guerrillas is not only oriented toward the overthrow of a regime. In the case of the Bolivians, they continue to demonstrate that they are also trying to wipe out ignorance through intensive preparation.
>
> The rebel "bearded ones," as some people like to call them, were obviously disturbed this morning when the commandant of the Fourth Division displayed, for the sixth time, in Monte Dorado, the belongings captured from the rebels.
>
> The lot includes drugs of various sorts, two light machine guns, four automatic pistols, a mortar, six old rifles and ammunition, and maps. But the most outstanding discovery was that of books of recognized authors, both Bolivian and foreign, who are part of the intellectual heritage of the whole world.
>
> The guerrillas, as far as we could see, share their tasks in an orderly fashion. They know that it is just as important for them to win battles against ignorance as it is to win victories over what they consider to be the enemy. Among the authors who "kept the guerrillas company" are Leon Trotsky, Nicolás Guillén, Roberto Alexander, Guillermo Lora, Albert Camus, Bertrand Russell, and others. It can be seen that the guerrillas are students of socio-economic phenomena in

"the world and its environs," as a childhood friend of mine would say.[7]

Commenting on this, the columnist Fredo Fredin[8] of the same newspaper said, in part:

> This means that the guerrillas, apart from their rigorous work of bearing arms, which is fraught with danger, also desire to enter into the full light of culture. If Russell, Camus, Trotsky, and others are in their hands, it is because their eyes and their spirits are anxious to know, thirsty to know, either because of the exigencies of their cause or because of sheer restlessness; but when all is said and done, [it is an] impulse to drink from the fountain of culture. And in such circumstances, in the tangle of the forest, with a horde of bulldogs after them, Camus, Guillén are nothing so much as a redoubt where freedom begins to be redeemed.

Each day around 8 P.M., orders were given for the tasks of the following day. While Guevara was in camp the orders were written, but in his absence, because of the relaxing of the rigid discipline that he had imposed, the orders were given verbally. Up until the first engagement—on March 23—the Calamine House was the general supply center. Coco took on the responsibility of making the necessary purchases in the stores in Camiri, bringing them out immediately to his "ranch," and from there guerrillas expressly responsible for this work transported them, an operation which they called "the *góndola* service."

On Christmas and on the last day of 1966 there were celebrations in the camp. Pigs were barbecued, Cuban-style, and sweets, rum, wine, beer, grapes, and other fruits were served. Life went on without any startling surprises; it was a sort of camping trip, a peaceful country outing rather than preparations for armed combat.

---

[7] *Prensa Libre* (Cochabamba, August 27, 1967).
[8] Pseudonym of the journalist Alfredo Medrano.

6

Che's March

On January 31, Guevara decided to leave Ñancahuazú and go north and northeast. He intended this trip to be a training march, so as to get his men in good shape physically, explore the terrain, and above all, get in contact with and study the attitudes of the peasants in the small hamlets. On February 1, the three groups already organized, each one composed of between twelve and fifteen men, began the march. Each man was armed and had field equipment and food supplies weighing between fifty and sixty pounds. Guevara was planning to go as far as the outskirts of the relatively important center of Valle Grande and return to Ñancahuazú on March 1 at the latest. Nevertheless, unforeseen factors forced him to put off his return for nineteen more days.

About twelve men remained in the camp under the command of Antonio, as the column marched off. Possibly neither Guevara nor his companions properly appreciated the difficulties that lay ahead of them. Though the march went on without harassment from the enemy, the desolation and the rough terrain wore them down relentlessly. Sickness and the avalanche of tropical insects, the unaccustomed physical effort, and the general absence of support from the inhabitants of the region demoralized the men, and the first desertions by Bolivian recruits took place. The hard trip over inhospitable mountains doubtless reminded the Cubans of the 350-mile march that Column Eight ("Ciro Redondo") made from the Sierra Maestra to Las Villas to establish a new rebel front against Batista in Cuba.

The three units (the vanguard, the center, and the rear guard) marched separately. Che was in direct command of the center, but he moved from unit to unit. On February 9, they made their way along the right bank of the Río Grande until they came to the houses of some peasants who welcomed them cordially, gave them food to eat, and informed them that there were military forces in the area— some three hundred soldiers busy building a road from Valle Grande to Lagunillas. Che stayed there two days, and on the eleventh they began to march north again. On the thirteenth and fifteenth they met other peasants who treated them cordially, and sold them food and supplies. For the next two weeks they marched along the Río Rositas, in whose waters Benjamín drowned on February 25. During this time the insurgents had a very discouraging time of it, tired and weak as they were from the effort that they had made. Their food supply ran very low.

On this same day the rearguard committed one of its numerous indiscretions. General Ovando Candia states in this regard: "Information was also received that between the twenty-sixth and the twenty-seventh of February, 1967, five foreign-looking individuals had contacted residents of the zone and asked questions about different things, the roads, etc., to get to the Río Grande. These five persons were again sighted swimming across the Río Grande. In order to rest, one of them took off a belt, the kind that has many pockets, in which there were great quantities of dollars and Bolivian pesos which he dried in the sun, in the presence of the peasants who lived around there, who saw this."

On the twenty-seventh they encountered new difficulties as they crossed the Río Rositas again, and the main body lost contact with the vanguard led by Marcos. On March 2, they retraced their steps and again crossed the river, trying to locate the group that had been separated from the rest. Braulio had severe cramps, some were weak from hunger, and others had serious tropical diseases. Inti managed to get some food and shoot some animals, but it was not enough to appease the hunger that gnawed at their vitals. "Two Bolivian recruits deserted and things weren't going well," we read in Braulio's diary.

On March 10, there were more desertions by Bolivian insurgents. Che's sections—the center and the rear guard—still had no news of the vanguard, but the men continued their march back to the camp.

On the fourteenth they arrived at the flooded mouth of the Ñancahauzú, where Carlos was drowned as he tried to cross the river on an emergency raft that they built there. On the twentieth Che writes in his diary: "We left at ten o'clock at a good pace. Benigno and El Negro preceded us with a message for Marcos in which he is ordered to take charge of the defense and leave administrative work to Antonio. Joaquín left after having erased the footprints going into the arroyo, but with no anxiety." A little later he notes: "At 15:00 hours, as we were making a long halt, Pacho appeared with a message from Marcos. The report gave more detail about Benigno's first report but it was more complicated now since the guards, numbering sixty, had stationed themselves along the road to Vallegrandino, and captured a messenger of ours from [Moisés] Guevara's group, Salustio. They took a mule from us and the jeep was lost. There was no news from Loro, who had stayed behind in the post at the little house. We decided nonetheless to go as far as the Bear Camp . . ." A few minutes later the men led by Guevara entered the camp mentioned, three miles north of the other one, "just in time to take the defensive because the army is close by, following Marcos almost into the camp."

Marcos, for his part, on seeing himself separated from the other two groups, and remembering that Guevara had said that he wanted to return to Ñancahauzú during the first few days of March, decided to march back to the camp. He pretended not to have heard Guevara's precise instructions and made several errors. He did not follow the route that had been decided on; he made distinctions between Cubans and Bolivians when assigning work, causing the justified resentment of the latter; he handled his men with a strictness that was almost brutal; and on certain occasions showed up in various towns with all his men, instead of making discreet personal contact with the peasants. In Tararenda he was again imprudent, and in the province of Valle Grande he was discovered by a hunter from the zone, and a supposed petroleum worker called Epifanio Vargas. When Vargas got suspicious, Marcos made up a story: "We're a group of geologists and we're exploring for an oil company," he told Vargas. But not all of Vargas' misgivings were put to rest, and he decided to follow the armed group surreptitiously, and then go to Camiri and announce their presence.

On March 17, as Marcos was heading for the Calamine House so as to enter the central camp immediately afterward, in spite of orders to the contrary from Che, his forces, to their surprise, suddenly met the peons of Ciro Algarañáz Leigue, a semi-official informer for the authorities, and the owner of the next ranch in Ñancahuazú. Hours later, they clashed at the Calamine House with a small platoon, and one soldier died in the encounter. That same morning this army unit captured the guerrilla sentinel Salustio Choque Choque in the insurgent observation post, located less than half a mile from the house. Marcos' unit then returned to the central camp.

The balance sheet of this march gave those who were on it a glimpse of the drama that they were beginning to live. The rough march through rugged territory among phlegmatic people was a bitter experience. Most of the peasants showed little willingness to cooperate. If at times they did so, it was out of fear, or else they were attracted by the generous sums that the guerrillas were in the habit of paying for supplies and services. A few peasants received them with cold courtesy, gave them the hospitality of their houses, and sold them the fruits of their meager harvests; others occasionally served them as guides, and some were willing to supply the guerrillas with information on the same terms that they supplied it to the army. As inexpressive and inhospitable as the land itself, the dour Bolivian mountaineer concealed himself behind a disconcerting impassivity. This moved Guevara on many occasions to note his disillusionment in his diary in phrases such as: "The inhabitants are as impenetrable as stones. When you speak to them it seems as if they are making fun of you deep down in their eyes." It must not be forgotten that these people had benefited from the 1952 revolution. Also, a large percentage of them had Guaraní blood in their veins: this is a race accustomed to facing the world with a calm resignation that resembles Oriental fatalism.

The terrain did not make the guerrillas feel optimistic either. This rural zone has no farm settlements, cattle ranches, or ranges of any importance. People are few and far between. The little hamlets and villages are dozens of miles apart. Production is on a very primitive level, hardly enough for survival. The people turn their backs on civilization. The system of communication could not be worse; it was for exactly this reason that the army was busy building a trunk route between Valle Grande and Lagunillas, so as to link two important regions separated by huge mountains. There are only footpaths and paths for beasts of burden here.

Hunting is very difficult in this area. To the west of the Río Grande and the Ñancahuazú the streams coming down from the mountain tops lack the rich variety of fish of other regions of the country. The insects are voracious and readily attack human beings.

After wandering about in this hostile milieu for fifty days, the men came back worn out, ragged, and disillusioned. Their clothing was in tatters, and some of them had their feet barely covered with pieces of leather, jungle vines, and scraps of their extra clothing. Wasted away, weakened, sick, their return to the central camp was a disheartening sight. In a statement to the newspapers, Régis Debray described the scene in these words: ". . . When I saw Che for the first time in my life, there on March 19,[1] I found him wasting away; they said that he had lost some forty-four pounds because he had gone hungry for a period of forty terrible days. There were guerrillas who also had swollen hands and feet; they could no longer walk. Joaquín, Alejandro, and Che were the worst off. I still think they could never satisfy the hunger that they had endured, because their hunger persisted."

This march, which was only intended to be a training exercise, with no enemies to face, demoralized some of the guerrillas and brought on one desertion after the other.

Debray, Fructuoso, and Tania had arrived in Ñancahuazú in the absence of Che, who was at the time marching in the north. Therefore Debray could not do the reporting that had brought him to Bolivia, and Fructuoso could not attend the political conference he was invited for. Both of them decided to await Guevara's return so as to complete their respective assignments and leave immediately afterward for their own countries. Like Monje Molina and others, both of them were to remain in Ñancahuazú only for the time strictly necessary to complete their missions, and then immediately leave for the outside with Tania, but the change in plans was to lead them into a web of events that brought unexpected disaster. The three visitors were thus

---

[1] In reality, Guevara returned on March 20. The error is Debray's.

hemmed within the camp by sheer accident. There was nothing for them to do but adapt themselves, as other visitors had had to do, to the rhythm of life in the camp. Therefore, they joined in the routine activities of their accidental companions. They were each given a hammock to sleep in, a blanket, a nylon tent, a haversack for personal effects, and supplies for individual use. Tania helped with the cooking, served as secretary, and hunted. Bustos and Debray also helped on secondary missions: hunting, target practice, keeping the sentinels company in their lonely observation posts, standing guard within the camp, attending the sessions on theory and the cultural lessons. All this was done out of respect for a rigid principle that ruled the life of the guerrillas: "A man who doesn't work doesn't eat," as Bustos and others testified. They each received a *nom de guerre*: Debray was called The Grandfather, Danton, the Frenchman, or Ebré, and Bustos was called the Argentinian, Fructuoso, Carlos, or El Pelado. All these activities— unconnected with their missions—were to later serve as the basis for accusations at their trial, in the absence of more or less certain proof, that they had performed missions as belligerents before, during, or after the first engagements.

When the day set for Che's return went by and the wait for him was prolonged, the camp's occupants became increasingly worried. As the days passed and their leader still did not arrive, the guerrilla rank and file became edgy.

On March 11, the order of the day stipulated that Vicente Rocabado Terrazas and Pastor Barrera Quintana were to go hunting for a supply of meat. Instead of carrying out the order, the two men decided to defect, disappear in the dense woods, and escape to Camiri, via Lagunillas. On the fourteenth they surrendered to the authorities, and agents of the Department of Criminal Investigation took down their initial statements, which were immediately passed on to the headquarters of the Fourth Division of the army in Camiri. One of the fugitives had had previous connections with the DIC and the Control Político; in his statement, appended to the proceedings of the trial in Camiri, he declared that he entered the revolutionary zone to carry out "an information-gathering mission," intending to receive some benefit from his denunciation. These two men offered important data on the rebel organization: the approximate number of combatants in the camp and the number of those who were off on the march, the names and nationalities of a large part of the guerrillas, defensive emplacements, means of access and communications, means of transmitting information, etc. They also talked of the presence of Che, disclosing his *nom de guerre*, the date and route of his entrance into the country, and other details relating to him. In a tape in the authors' possession, Rocabado confesses that he heard on January 12, 1967, in La Paz, that Che was in Ñancahuazú; this was told to him in confidence by Moisés Guevara.

Moreover, the guerrillas had not been at all reserved toward these two deserters; they had told them, in confidence, everything that they needed to know about the situation, as if they were full-fledged members of the group, even going to the extreme of showing them numerous photos of the insurgents and their leader. It appears that Antonio told them more than he should have.

The military patrols arrived at Calamine House on the seventeenth, and Salustio Choque, in the guerrilla observation post, surrendered to them without putting up any resistance at all. According to his confession, the guerrillas had given him this pretended mission because they had serious doubts as to his loyalty to the revolution. Choque confirmed all the facts revealed to the authorities by the other two deserters.

On this same day, the seventeenth, Marcos and his men committed the indiscretions that we have already mentioned. The rancher, Algarañáz, then left to inform the military authorities of the guerrillas' presence. Some hours later the supposed petroleum worker Epifanio Vargas showed up in Camiri, informing the authorities of the guerrillas' activities and offering to serve the army as a guide, as had the two deserters. On this date, also, Rocabado and Barrera were transferred from Camiri to the General Headquarters of the Military High Command in La Paz.

With this information and the other intelligence it had previously garnered, the military command was fully acquainted, by March 18, with the general situation of their adversaries. The subsequent action of the military forces in this zone was therefore to be of the nature of a military operation against an openly declared enemy. The magazine *Primera Plana* confirms this statement in these terms: "This [the death of a soldier at Calamine House] happened on March 17, and the event acquires extraordinary importance, not only because this humble conscript was the first victim of the guerrillas, but also because it thus established that the armed forces were already fully acquainted with the existence of guerrillas, and the patrols that later penetrated deep inside the so-called 'red zone' were not on a peace mission—laying out roads or opening trails—but rather on a one hundred per cent war mission."

There was increased activity in the zone controlled by the insurgents. When Marcos arrived at the command post and failed to find Guevara, he assumed the leadership of the forces grouped there. He decided to abandon the main camp in order to set up a line of resistance farther back in the mountains, north of the Río Grande. Preparations were made and couriers were sent to tell Che of the unexpected change in the war plans and warn him of a possible offensive by the Fourth Division.

Major Guevara got back to his operations post at Ñancahuazú on March 20, and did not hide his displeasure at the steps that had been taken. He immediately restored rigid discipline, which had virtually ceased to exist in the camp during his absence. With the concurrence of Coco and Inti he ordered the expulsion of four Bolivian guerrillas for "lack of morale, robbing the food supply, and great unwillingness to do chores around the camp." These men did not leave the zone immediately but instead stayed in the camp waiting for the right moment to leave.

7

The Visitors

Jules Régis Debray, born in Paris, on September 2, 1940, belonged to the well-to-do French middle class. His mother, Madame Jannine Alexandre Debray, says in her short biographical account of her son: "His family is composed entirely of men and women belonging to the liberal professions; the family does not have a fortune, but it does have the great social awareness proper to a healthy middle class that has an honorable name in Paris and in France. Since all the family are practicing Catholics, they are prompted by a vigorous Christian spirit."[1] His father, Georges Debray, is a civil attorney recognized by the Paris bar, a member of the Lawyers' Council, a chevalier of the Legion of Honor and of the Equestrian Order of the Holy Sepulchre; he is not a political militant. Madame Debray is also an attorney recognized by the Paris bar, a councilor of the *département* of the Seine, Vice-President of the Paris Municipal Council, and ex-Vice-President of the General Council of the Municipal Treasury of Paris; she has belonged to the Independent National Center political party, and at present belongs to the Democratic Center, a rightist party headed by Jean Lecanuet. The Debrays were members of the resistance during the Nazi occupation; neither of them shares the political convictions of their son.

This account is given only to show that Régis Debray was not a resentful social rebel. He was educated according to the strictest

[1] *Prensa Libre* (Cochabamba, August 26, 1967).

family traditions, and as befitted the family's social and economic position. He followed the normal educational pattern in primary and secondary schools. At seventeen he received, from the hands of his own mother, the philosophy prize in the annual General Competition among the brightest pupils from all the secondary schools. In the Lycée Louis-le-Grand he received the highest grades in the school and prepared for the École Normale, the advanced normal school that has given France some of its most enlightened figures. In 1959, his parents rewarded him with a trip to the United States; he unexpectedly took off from Miami for a trip to Havana, and from Havana he returned to Paris to prepare for his master's degree in philosophy.

In 1961, he once again left for South America, stayed several months, and then returned to continue his studies, already greatly impressed by the worrisome social problems of the continent. In 1963, he traveled to Venezuela, having been sent there by the French television network and a movie director to make a documentary film. He returned to Paris at the end of 1964, after a year and a half on the continent, during which time he visited every nation in Latin America with the exception of Paraguay. During this period he wrote a well-known and extensive essay, "Castroism, or The Long March of Latin America," which appeared in the monthly *Les Temps Modernes*, edited by Jean-Paul Sartre.

During this last trip, he visited Bolivia for the first time as a correspondent of *Les Temps Modernes*, entering the country from Chile with all his documents in order. On this trip he was accompanied by Elizabeth Burgos, a young Venezuelan girl who had studied philosophy in Germany and whom he had met in Caracas. (On Debray's return to France, she stayed behind in Bolivia, dedicating herself to intellectual activities and eventually occupying a top post in the Secretariat of the Ministry of Mines and Petroleum.) Debray remained in the country about three months, giving lectures in universities, and forming ties in the academic milieu, especially with the universities of La Paz, Cochabamba, and Oruro. He maintained permanent contact with the embassy of his country and through its cultural attaché, M. Molombou, he met high public officials, including ministers of state, journalists, political personalities, intellectuals, labor leaders, etc. He gave speeches on sociology and other related subjects in the mining districts which, at the time, were agitating against the government of Paz Estenssoro. Back in

France once again, he received his diploma as an *agrégé* in philosophy and elected to teach in Nancy.

In the middle of January, 1966, by virtue of a cultural agreement between France and Cuba, the Minister of Foreign Relations of his country chose him as Professor of the History of Philosophy at the University of Havana, and several times during his professorship he had the occasion to meet and interview Fidel Castro and other high officials of the Cuban revolution.

Since he was preparing a doctoral thesis under the direction of Professor Godelier, a specialist in Latin American affairs at the Institute of Social Anthropology of the University of Paris, he was commissioned by this body to do work on this specialty in Chile and Bolivia. On arriving in Bolivia, he made several studies in social and economic anthropology in the region of Alto Beni and in the province of Chapare, of the *departamentos* of La Paz and Cochabamba respectively, a long distance away from what was to be the *foco* of the guerrillas later on. In order to round out his knowledge of the country, he bought books and maps on these zones in the Military Institute of Geography and in other public offices and shops. All this was for the purpose of making comparative studies on spontaneous colonization and the transplanting and acculturation of human groups in a strange milieu, as he had done in Chile and as researchers and scholars from all over the world habitually do nowadays, moving about Latin America in great numbers. He traveled through the country as a journalist, visiting several mining districts once again to obtain various interviews that were to be published outside the country.

At this time he was already known to his friends in private and official circles as a Marxist intellectual of Castrista persuasion. His entry into Bolivia, his movements, and his departure from the country are matters of public knowledge, legally proved by his personal documents and authenticated by credentials from the National Information Service of the Presidency of the Republic. In some cases, furthermore, he traveled in the company of national officials and in other cases with personnel from the Banco Interamericano de Desarrollo (BID).

He never joined the French Communist Party, even though for two years—until 1963—he belonged to the Union of Communist Students, whose members generally go on to formally join the Communist Party. He stuck to his position as an independent Marxist, and did not take part in the ideological conflict between the leaders of traditional Communism.

Upon his return to France in 1966, new missions awaited him, this time purely as a journalist. The well-known French publisher François Maspero—as Debray says in his declaration to the authorities—sent him to Latin America to get an interview and write a report of unusual importance for the international press. In another version, Debray is said to have received, while he was still in Havana, a letter from Ernesto Guevara in which Guevara asked Debray to interview him, and suggests Maspero as an intermediary. Whatever the truth of the matter, Maspero gave Debray two thousand dollars for tickets, travel expenses, and various other expenditures; he gave him precise confidential information about where he was to go and how he was to acquire the proper credentials, and even fixed the place and the subject for the interview; he provided him with documents that included a passport in his name, credentials from Maspero's publishing house, the University of Paris, and the Mexican magazine *Sucesos*, directed by Mario Menéndez Rodríguez. These documents were all later seized by the Bolivian military authorities. The French journalist came to Bolivia with all the legal documents needed to exercise his profession, and he also had the credentials that any publisher or newspaper usually provides to its correspondents or special representatives when they are chosen to carry out confidential missions, either openly or off the record.

A few days before Debray left, Maspero informed him that the mission was to be carried out in Bolivia and that the person to be interviewed was Ernesto Guevara. He also entrusted him with a brief personal message for Guevara from his wife: That she was fine, that she was taking care of the children, that she had good grades at the University, and that's all. Debray then left for Bolivia, entering the country at the end of February, 1967, by rail via Antofagasta, Chile. He got off the train in El Alto, the last station before the railroad center of La Paz, going by car down the steep short cut to the city; this is the usual procedure passengers who know the line use so as to gain time, since the train takes almost an hour to come down from El Alto, which is on the ridge of the *altiplano*. He then went to the Hotel Avenida, registering in his own name and presenting his personal papers.

According to Guevara's campaign diary, the journalist was supposed to arrive in La Paz on February 25, and meet a contact in the Mexico movie theater on the twenty-eighth at 9 P.M.: if this failed, the diary adds, he was to come back to the theater on odd days of the month at the same time to meet his contact. Nonetheless, Debray, in his statement, says that his first contact was a man named Andrés, who had instructions to meet him every Tuesday at 6 P.M. in front of the Sucre Palace Hotel located on the principal square of the city, with a copy of *Life* magazine in his left hand. He identified himself to Andrés by asking him questions about his watch, as had been agreed. After a hurried talk, Andrés immediately put him in touch with a woman whose name—Tania—he learned later. She carried out the preparations for getting them to the place where the interview was to be held, and told him that they would be accompanied by another person, an Argentinian. Two days later they started the trip on one of the buses of the Flota Galgo company. In a restaurant along the route from La Paz to Oruro, where the bus stopped to let the passengers have lunch, Tania introduced him to his traveling companion, Carlos Alberto Fructuoso. They arrived in Sucre and stayed at the Gran Hotel for two days. Debray showed his personal documents, Tania hers, and the Argentinian a passport in the name of Carlos Alberto Fructuoso. The next night they went on to Camiri in a rented car. The car broke down in a place called Padilla and on the recommendation of people who lived there, they went on in a jeep, a vehicle more suited to the rough road they had to take. At midday on March 5, having reached Camiri, Tania settled her companions in rooms she had rented in the Hotel Oriente, half a block from the main square, and went out in search of her contacts. Since he did not have clothes suitable for wear in the country, Debray bought a shirt and slacks. Tania came back around 7 P.M., telling them that she had found the people she was looking for and advising them to take only a few personal effects with them, leaving the rest in the hotel since they would be back in two days at the very latest. They went out to eat and at 10 P.M. they left in a jeep for "a ranch" in the company of another person who was driving, and who turned out to be Coco Peredo. During the trip Coco had an animated conversation with Tania. Through her Debray and Fructuoso realized that the "ranch" was the now-famous Calamine House and that it had been broken into several days before, following a denunciation by the guerrillas' neighbor, Ciro Algarañáz Leigue; they also learned that it was feared the authorities would come back because they suspected that the movements of its occupants involved the operation of a clandestine cocaine factory.

They arrived at the house early on the morning of March 6, and were received by four or five supposed ranch hands. These men told them that the person they were to interview had thought the authorities might break in again and had therefore decided to hold the meeting farther up in the mountains, in a site that had been prepared for that purpose.

They left the Calamine House on foot at approximately seven o'clock, taking turns carrying haversacks and packages of provisions that Peredo had bought in Camiri. After walking half an hour they stopped to rest in a shady spot and wait for guides who were to take them to their destination. When the guides arrived, Tania introduced her companions by saying: "This one is the Frenchman, and this one is the Argentinian." Among those who came down from the mountains was Antonio, who was at that time the leader of the guerrilla camp in Guevara's absence. All of them went on together, arriving about 2 p.m. at the central guerrilla post at Ñancahuazú. The recent arrivals were welcomed with the satisfaction and enthusiasm that were to be expected from men who had long been cut off from any contact with the outside world.

Carlos Alberto Fructuoso was a pseudonym. His real name was Ciro Roberto Bustos Marco, a native of Córdova, Argentina, age thirty-five, married to Ana Maria Castro, and father of two daughters, aged three and two. He had studied the plastic arts in Buenos Aires and taught courses in that subject in his native city and in Mendoza; his specialty was portraits. He had held jobs as a newspaperman and as a commercial artist, and had ties with important artistic centers in Montevideo and Buenos Aires. Politically, he had participated in university, intellectual, and artistic forums under leftist auspices. As a man concerned with social progress, he had had contact with the guerrillas who appeared in the north of Argentina in 1963.

In his statement before the military judge he said that he was not militant in terms of any of the tendencies of Argentinian Communism; that he did not share Ernesto Guevara's political ideas concerning armed struggle; that he had never been in Cuba, the USSR, or Red China; that he had not participated in the guerrilla movements in Vietnam and Algeria, as persistent rumors had it. According to his first statements, at the beginning of 1967 he was in Córdova to ask for economic aid for the young people who had joined the Argentinian guerrilla *foco*. At about that time a certain woman named Emma came to invite him to participate in an important meeting of a new political front organized in Bolivia, without telling him any more about it. Bustos said that his visitor at no time spoke to him of any guerrilla plan for Bolivia and that he knew nothing about one. He added: "I don't know Emma's real name or nationality. She spoke to me in the name of a new political front organized in Bolivia. She never told me the name of this front, but it was a leftist organization; nor did she tell me the name of the person at the head of it. I also do not know who financed her activities, but Juan Lechín gave her $150 to underwrite the cost of my trip." Bustos supposes that "a passport counterfeiter" named Rutman, who lived in Buenos Aires, gave Emma his address in Córdova, knowing of his activities in behalf of his guerrilla compatriots.

Once he had accepted Emma's invitation and arrived in Buenos Aires, Rutman provided him with false documents in the name of Carlos Alberto Fructuoso. These were the circumstances—still according to his statement—under which he went to Bolivia, led there by the interest he had in the agenda of the meeting, which focused on the socio-political and economic problems of Latin America. He arrived in La Paz on February 28, and, following information he had received in Argentina, immediately sought contact with Andrés, who told him that a young woman named Tania was waiting for him in "a café near the Universo movie theater," to which he took him in a taxi. The young woman who appeared for the meeting turned out to be that same Emma he had previously met in Córdova. Tania-Emma told him that the political meeting would not take place in La Paz, but in the interior of the country. From that point on Bustos, Debray, and Tania took the same route that was to lead them to the central camp in Ñancahuazú.

As for Isaac Rutman, it is noteworthy that neither the Bolivian authorities nor the Argentinian Military Intelligence Service—who know all the above details—have ever referred to Rutman's activities.

But among the pertinent documents in the possession of the Bolivian intelligence service there are two that are very revealing: 1. A portrait of Rutman sketched by Bustos along with those of nineteen other foreign and Bolivian guerrillas whom he had seen in Ñancahuazú, and: 2. A physical description of Rutman, along with that of twenty-seven others, also attributed to Bustos.[2]

The authors have enough information to assert that the intermediary called Andrés does not exist, being only an imaginary person created to put the authorities off the track. We have similar doubts about the existence of Rutman, but we are not certain enough to make a categorical statement that he is a fictitious person. As for Tania's trip to Argentina to invite Bustos, there are strong doubts about this as well.

Tania arrived in Bolivia from Peru, in March, 1965. She was then probably about twenty-seven years old. Tall, blonde, blue-eyed, with a slight German accent, pretty without being strikingly beautiful, she looked typically German. Attractive, vivacious, and well educated, she soon made her way into journalistic, intellectual, and official circles in La Paz and made friends with many people. She was tireless, and did many things. She worked for the fortnightly magazine *Esto Es*. She then got a job in the national information service of the Presidency of the Republic and on the state radio. She worked as a language teacher, particularly of German. She did research on antique ceramics and ethnology. She took up the study of folklore, and armed with a tape recorder made many records of native music. In 1966 she registered at the Faculty of Biochemistry and Pharmacy of the Universidad Mayor de San Andrés in La Paz. She married an engineer named Martínez, who soon abandoned her for a scholarship in Yugoslavia. The owners of the house where she stayed say that she was a charming young woman, soft-spoken, cordial, and discreet in every sense of the word, and report that she was never heard to mention political subjects. No one bothered to check on her background, since her conduct was always irreproachable. All she ever said was that she was a citizen of Argentina and had visited Mexico, Venezuela, and Cuba.

[2] See Appendix III.

Around the middle of 1966 she told her friends that she had received an inheritance of three thousand dollars, with which she bought a jeep and began to travel about within the Republic, usually in the east and southeast, visiting Oruro, Cochabamba, Sucre, Camiri, and Santa Cruz on several occasions. At the end of the year she disappeared for some time from La Paz, and her friends said that she had gone to Argentina.

At the end of the year she moved into the Hotel Oriente in Camiri, leading an uneventful life, although she made frequent trips in her jeep to La Paz, most of the time by way of Muyupampa-Monteagudo-Padilla-Sucre-Cochabamba. She was often seen in shops in Camiri in the company of the two new owners of the Calamine House ranch. On the Zararenda radio station in Camiri she started a program called "Advice to Women," a service of advice to the love-lorn that interested a large audience. But more than once, there was something odd that called attention to her program: she frequently employed a certain terminology that seemed strange and even incomprehensible to her listeners. Much later it was determined that her radio program served to transmit coded messages to the guerrillas, and that the two companions she was seen with were Coco Peredo and Jorge Vásquez Viaña, known as El Loro. When she suddenly terminated her radio program, her usual listeners experienced something like dismay, since her programs were a pleasant distraction in the monotonous lives of the population of this little oil town.

Around March 27, 1967, the first official bulletin was put out on Tania, stating that she had fled to Argentina. She was described as a contact and an emissary for the rebels and in charge of the conscription of contacts in the cities. All kinds of speculations were made about her, especially about her real identity.

It is certain that Tania was the principal axis of the contacts between the rebels and sympathetic forces in the cities. She had planned to leave immediately after her last entry into the guerrilla zone, but she was trapped there. Guevara writes in his diary: "Tania has been identified; years of good and patient work have thereby been lost." And in another passage he writes: "Tania is isolated here, since she came contrary to instructions and was surprised by events."

Official sources and Bolivian and foreign papers believed that they had identified Tania; the first reports, subsequently repeated by the Bolivian press, stated that she was Laura Gutiérrez Bauer, the name that was given on her personal documents. Some foreign papers maintained that her name was Laura Martínez, and stated that she was sometimes called Emma Gutiérrez in Bolivia. In September, 1966, she stayed in the Asunta Residence Hall in Santa Cruz under the name of Mary Aguilera. All of these papers stated that she was an Argentinian who was educated in Germany until the age of twelve, and that her father was a citizen of Argentina and her mother of German extraction.

Who was this restless young woman who died for her ideals and who doubtless lent a bit of tenderness to the bitter Calvary of the rough-and-ready combatants?

Tania's mother and father, Erich and Nadja Bunke, were violent anti-fascists who lived in Germany. Her parents had to emigrate to escape Nazi repression, arriving in Argentina at the end of the thirties, and their daughter was born in that country. After the end of World War II the family asked to return to the German Democratic Republic, but the matter dragged on because they had trouble getting papers and exit permits, and other such difficulties. Tania was still an adolescent when taken to Germany but she remained strongly attached to her native land and to all of Latin America because of the great politico-social experiment that was taking place in Argentina in this period. She entered an East German university, where she studied for several years, returning to Latin America in the early sixties. She went to Cuba to continue her studies at the University of Havana, and from that time on her parents had no news at all as to what had happened to her.

Ciro Roberto Bustos and Régis Debray, who had been awaiting Guevara's return since March 6, had their first interview with him on March 21.

Almost nothing is known about what was discussed between Bustos and Che. Nothing, or next to nothing, has leaked out about the results of the political conference for which Bustos had been invited, and official sources and documents do not shed very much light on this matter. Nor is there anything important about it in Bustos' statement of August 25, in which the interrogator does not emphasize this point. What is known from his confession is that Guevara gave him 2000 Bolivian pesos for his personal expenses and

$2000 to pay the fees of the attorneys defending the Argentinian guerrillas who had been sent to jail, "as a gesture of solidarity, but which obviously had a political purpose: it was a [baited] hook."[3]

In Che's diary there are many clear references to the role that Bustos played. For example, on March 21, Guevara writes: "I spent the day in talks and discussions with Chino—making certain points clear—the Frenchman, Pelado, and Tania." There is another reference to Bustos (one of whose code names, it will be remembered, was Pelado) in the diary entry for this day: "Pelado is quite willing, of course, to put himself at my service and I suggested to him that he be a sort of coordinator, contacting only Jozemi's, Belman's, and Stamponi's groups and sending me men so that they can begin training."

Guevara was in the habit of making a monthly summary of the activities of the guerrillas, and in the one for April we read: "Danton and Carlos fell victims of their almost desperate anxiety to leave and my lack of energy to prevent them, so that communications were also cut off with Cuba (Danton) and the scheme for action in Argentina (Carlos) is going by the board." In a message to Leche[4] there is another reference to Bustos: "I made contact with El Pelado [with the] object [of] organizing bases in the south and gathering Argentinians together; he too is bottled up here." Although no facts are known about the formal political interview for which Debray was invited, it may be concluded nonetheless that it actually did take place, since at this moment there were two other important visitors in the camp: Bustos and the Peruvian Chino, and also less important visitors, since at this time the guerrilla contacts and political contacts implicated in this subversive movement still moved freely in and out of the guerrilla camp.

From Debray's statement to the authorities and a few that he managed to make to journalists, it is known that he had three conversations with Guevara. During the first of these, on March 21, Debray told Che of the assignment that Maspero had given him. There was general discussion of the material that he would be pub-

---

[3] Bustos' statement.
[4] The code name for Fidel Castro.

lishing abroad; his first reports were to be published in *Le Monde* in Paris because of its good reputation throughout the world. In these reports Debray was not to make any reference to Ñancahuazú; he was merely to say that there was an important subversive *foco* somewhere in the Andes. Only after the guerrillas had publicly revealed themselves and it became known that Guevara was personally in charge was Debray to make a more complete report in the Mexican magazine *Sucesos.*

Among other things, Che told the French writer that the first objective in view was not precisely an immediate change in the government in Bolivia, but rather his fundamental idea was to bring about the installation of a popular, anti-imperialist government that would take the rich resources of Bolivia out of the hands of their present exploiters. The basic objective was to install a revolutionary anti-imperialist base that might serve as an example for all the peoples of Latin America. He was thinking above all of a catalyzing effect of the guerrillas, first in Bolivia and then later in all of South America.

The second interview took place on March 24, in a tense and preoccupied atmosphere, since the first serious engagement with the Bolivian military had taken place the day before. Debray questioned Guevara about various events in his previous life: from his departure from Argentina at the end of 1952, his travels in Bolivia, Venezuela, Guatemala, Mexico, and the Sierra Maestra, and his functions as a high official in revolutionary Cuba, to his later disappearance from public view in March, 1965. Debray's questions also covered Guevara's ideological position in the Socialist camp in the face of the Sino-Soviet dispute.

Impelled by his ideological affinity and sympathy for the guerrillas and seeing the straits they were in, Debray asked to become a combatant and suggested that his work as a journalist be turned over to someone else. He asked that he be assigned a number, such as all the combatants customarily received on being taken into the guerrilla group. Guevara refused to do this, explaining to Debray that the function of informing world opinion about his aims and his presence in Bolivia was as important as actually fighting. From that moment on, after the two of them had agreed on this, Debray repeatedly insisted on leaving the "Red Zone" immediately.

The third interview was the shortest. It was decided that Debray should leave the camp without taking the photos he had taken along with him because of the danger that they might fall into the hands of the government forces; Guevara promised to send all the material Debray had accumulated for his report on Ñancahuazú on to him in Paris. The initial reports in *Le Monde* could be published without photographs, as had been agreed, but this was not true for the articles to be published in *Sucesos*, which had to comprise a complete report. It was at this point that Guevara told Debray for the first time of his plans to stay only a short time in Bolivia, just long enough to shape a perfectly trained, homogeneous group thoroughly indoctrinated with his beliefs.

There are no concrete references in Che's diary to his conversations with Debray. There are, however, repeated allusions to him, from before his arrival in Bolivia late in February until after his imprisonment in Muyupampa. From these references it is possible to deduce that Debray brought confidential messages from Fidel Castro and that he left the camp with memorized instructions for him. At one point there is mention of the fact that he was carrying money to the guerrillas, but this does not seem to be borne out by events. Guevara also notes that apart from his mission as a journalist, Debray would also be carrying messages to certain personalities known throughout the world, among them Bertrand Russell and Jean-Paul Sartre.

From everything that is revealed in Guevara's diary it must be inferred that Debray, as an intellectual committed to an ideological position, could not help but play a role in the activities of the guerrillas, and that this role apparently was that of a top-secret liaison man.

8

The First
Engagement

On the morning of March 23, a well-equipped detachment of the army started out in the neighborhood of the Calamine House and made a sweeping exploration of the region, following the Ñancahuazú River westward. The small patrol was headed by Major Hernán Plata, accompanied by his immediate subordinates, Captain Augusto Silva Bogado and Second Lieutenant Rubén Amézaga.[1] As this patrol began operations against the guerrillas, it sustained severe casualties —dead and wounded—humble citizens who suffered in the performance of their duty. Let us follow the account of this action given by Captain Silva in Camiri to the special correspondent of *Presencia*:

> At 7:15 in the morning on Thursday, March 23, we began a patrol in search of some guerrillas that we had been pursuing for several days.
>
> We knew that they were located in the Ñancahuazú Ravine. We went on walking for a few minutes and arrived at the river of the same name. We kept going upstream. It was rough going. The soil was sandy and slippery. In some places we walked in water up to our waists.

[1] This operation was carried out in the sector assigned to the Fourth Division, commanded by Colonel Humberto Rocha.

89

At about 7:30 those of us at the head of the patrol managed to get out of the river. On the river bank we found fresh footprints left by the guerrillas. We rested a few minutes and waited for Major Plata who was following behind us. We had to get organized.

So we organized. It was decided that Major Plata would advance with the second squadron keeping a distance of twenty yards and that Second Lieutenant Amézaga would head the other one. It was decided that Señor Epifanio Vargas and I would be on point. Before beginning the march I told my men to be very careful and look right and left. Once the instructions had been given, we decided to advance, and did so.

"We may lose our skins"

"We may lose our skins up ahead," was the pessimistic phrase from the guide. "So we have to be very careful." "Don't worry; the others are going to back us up," was Captain Silva's reply as they walked up the river.

We came to a curve, took a right, and went on ahead. We had walked some thirty yards when we and the two patrols following us were surprised by heavy fire.

It was crossfire; the shots came from the left and from the right. We took action to protect ourselves and took up positions, crawling along the ground and firing in all directions.

I heard a cry and saw that Epifanio Vargas had fallen three feet from where I was. Then I saw soldiers fall.

When the battle began, Second Lieutenant Amézaga was in the middle of the river, and that was where he was wounded. Amézaga nonetheless kept on shooting at the mountain where the shots were coming from and I saw him hit a guerrilla. The Lieutenant managed to get to the river bank but he could not protect himself from a hail of bullets . . . that was where he died . . .

"Prisoners"

I was shooting to the right of where I was . . . I raised my head for a couple of seconds and a hail of bullets shot my cap off without hurting me.

After a few minutes more of shooting the Captain was taken prisoner. The guerrillas, who had beards and were wearing uniforms, took away his personal effects—his rings, his watch, his money, his documents. They did the same thing with Major Plata and the soldiers taken prisoner later.

Silva also had this to say about his experience as a prisoner: "The guerrillas were all right, they gave us coffee with milk and plain rolls, but they kept a close watch on us all the time and tried to get information out of us. They did not succeed in doing so."

" 'If you behave you'll be allowed to go free; if not . . . you'll be shot,' the guerrillas announced to the soldiers. They were allowed to go free after forty-eight hours."[2]

Captain Silva's declaration obviously contradicts the version which the army and the President of the Republic gave of the battle in Ñancahuazú. As a result the Minister of National Defense was later to announce that Major Plata and Captain Silva would be court-martialed, "for the purpose of investigating the result of the guerrilla action in which they took part on Holy Thursday . . ."[3]

In the brief account of this engagement the valiant way in which young Lieutenant Amézaga met death should be emphasized; wounded and bleeding in the middle of the stream, he continued to fight bravely until he was shot down in a hail of bullets on the bank of the river.

The inexperienced and inexpert platoon was overtaken by a panic that is understandable. Members of the platoon tried to repel the attack, firing as they crawled along the ground, without a single target in sight. The enemy hidden in the brush fought a hard battle, alternately firing and shouting repeatedly: "Long live the Army of National Liberation," "Long live free Bolivia," "Surrender, soldiers, we don't want to kill you." The three groups into which the detachment was divided all entered the fight. When they saw their comrades fall, some of the soldiers in the rear guard dropped their arms and fled. This compromising situation led the rest of the detachment to surrender. Vargas, the guide and the first to fall, was the same person who had told the authorities of the presence of guerrillas in the zone after Guevara's march; the guerrillas recognized him in spite of the camouflaged army uniform that he was wearing, according to what some of them said later.

The balance sheet of the action thus was: Lieutenant Amézaga, five soldiers, and Vargas the guide dead; Major Plata, Captain Silva, and eleven soldiers taken prisoner, with five of them wounded. After

---

[2] *Presencia* (La Paz, April 3, 1967).
[3] *El Diario* (La Paz, April 7, 1967).

disarming the men they had captured, the rebels treated them with unexpected cordiality. About three hours after the battle had ended, they gave them food, and guerrilla doctors attended to the wounded, sparing no effort to cure them, to the point of almost exhausting their available supply of drugs.[4] The officers were interrogated; they were told of the aims of the subversive movement and invited to join its ranks, a proposal that was not accepted. Speaking of these prisoners, Che Guevara writes in his diary: "They talked like parrots."

Forty-eight hours later, the prisoners received permission to return to their bases. Before the soldiers left, the rebels exchanged their own civilian clothes for the camouflaged army uniforms. The rebels were willing to allow the soldiers to recover their dead around noon the next day, recommending that the soldiers come naked to the waist so as to prove that they were not armed. It was fourteen days before the dead were finally picked up in a state of total decomposition.

The officers and their men were bade a cordial farewell by their conquerors, who kept them company along the way for a time. There then began another odyssey for the military personnel. Army units had surrounded the zone and were preparing to attack the guerrilla positions. Stripped of their uniforms, the former prisoners could easily be taken for a guerrilla detachment; to avoid this, the officers ordered their men to sing barracks songs, and thus this patrol managed to arrive at the government zone with no further mishaps.

Even though the guerrillas had set up a system of guard duty and had taken security measures, they were not expecting military action so soon. Debray and Bustos both say in their statements to the authorities that Che Guevara was in the camp at the time of the battle, and that at about ten in the morning, Coco arrived at the command post at a run, dripping with sweat, to announce the battle, explaining that it had taken place about two hours before near the Calamine House. He told Che that there had been several casualties and that a large quantity of arms and military equipment had been captured, and he requested reinforcements and doctors. Guevara immediately ordered Inti to go with a contingent to the spot where the encounter had taken place and get all the details, help gather together the equipment captured from the enemy, and interrogate the

---

[4] Debray's statement.

prisoners. He also ordered the doctors to attend to the wounded.

A few minutes later, he told Debray to go with the doctors to gather data for his articles, urging him not to approach any of the prisoners or converse with them so as to avoid being recognized later, since he would soon have to leave the camp; he ordered Bustos to accompany the other men so as to help collect the captured booty. Guevara did not leave the camp.

The engagement marked the beginning of the guerrilla war. Apparently the guerrillas' general plan was not yet in operation, and organizing and training was still in a preliminary stage. According to reliable opinions, among them those of the Commander in Chief of the armed forces of Bolivia himself, the guerrillas ought not to have revealed themselves until months later. Unforeseen factors precipitated things. The rebels found themselves entangled in events which proved to be beyond their capabilities. The apparent cause, according to several rebels who survived, was Marcos' repeated failure to obey Che's orders and the consequent revelation of where they were and what they were up to. Although this explanation may be oversimplified, it is true that from this point on, events were beyond the control of the guerrilla command.

On March 25, a meeting of combatants of all levels was held in the main guerrilla command post. Guevara made a series of critical observations on the events that had developed in the past and a formal evaluation of the situation at the moment. He announced new orders for the defense of Ñancahuazú, imposing more rigid discipline and recommending that they be as economical with food and drugs as possible. He demoted Marcos, relieving him of command of the vanguard, and that post was given to Miguel. "He says he was demoted for having given the guerrilla movement away last March. He also demoted him for having shot at an unarmed man."[5] In a tape-recorded statement, Camba says: "There were two reasons why he was demoted: first, because he had had fights with the Bolivians and was about to divide the guerrillas up into Cubans and Bolivians, which displeased Che; and second, for lack of discipline."

---

[5] *Presencia* (October 11, 1967). Extract from the diary of a guerrilla.

In the entry in Che's diary for this date, there is the following account:

> The day went by with nothing new. León, Urbano, and Arturo were sent to a lookout spot that dominates the entrance to the river on both sides. At 12:00, Marcos withdrew from his position in the ambush and all the men were concentrated in the principal ambush. At 18:30 hours, with almost all personnel present, I made an analysis of the march and its significance and exposed the errors of Marcos, demoting him and naming Miguel leader of the vanguard. At the same time the expulsion of Paco, Pepe, Chingalo, and Eusebio was announced, and they were told that they will not eat if they don't work. Their ——— is being suspended, and their personal things are being redistributed among the other comrades who need them more. I referred to Kolle's report that he will come for discussions which will take place at the same time as the expulsion of the members of the youth group present here. What is of interest is deeds; words that do not match deeds are not important. I announced the search for the ——— and the renewal of the study program.
>
> I talked with Pedro and El Médico, to whom I announced that I had raised the rank of almost all the guerrillas and with Apolinar, to whom I gave orders. I criticized Wálter for having gone soft during the trip, for his attitude in combat, and for the fear he showed of planes; he did not react well.
>
> We are clearing up details with Chino and Pelado, and I gave the Frenchman a long oral report on the situation.
>
> In the course of the meeting this group was given the name of Army of National Liberation of Bolivia and an announcement will be made of the skirmish.[6]

A manifesto to the Bolivian people was issued by the Army of National Liberation of Bolivia in April.[7]

On March 27, Guevara notes in his diary, concerning the battle: "Today the news broke, monopolizing every radio station, producing a multitude of communiqués, including a press conference by Barrientos." A military reconnaissance plane scattered leaflets "in the hunting grounds." In another part of his diary he writes: "Getting

---

[6] The dashes indicate illegible words in the text.
[7] See Appendix V.

people out is difficult now; I had the impression that Danton didn't find it at all funny when I told him so. We shall see later."

On this same day he ordered Benigno, Loro, and Julio to try to get to Pirirenda without being seen, so as to see how to get the visitors out. Then he writes: "Communiqué No. 1 is being drawn up, which we will try to get to the journalists in Camiri." Later he organized a "*góndola* service" to the "little house to pick up corn," and another to buy supplies in Gutiérrez, and finally, "a little diversionary attack that could be made in the mountains, between Pincal and Lagunillas, on the vehicles that go through there."

The communiqué referred to reads as follows:

TO THE BOLIVIAN PEOPLE:

COMMUNIQUÉ NO. I
REVOLUTIONARY TRUTH IN THE FACE OF
THE REACTIONARY LIE

The group of usurping gorillas, after murdering workers and preparing the ground for the total surrender of our resources to American imperialism, showed its scorn for the people in a farce worthy of a country fair. When the hour of truth arrives and the people rise up in arms to respond to armed usurpation with armed struggle, they attempt to continue their round of lies.

On the morning of March 23, forces of the Fourth Division, bivouacked in Camiri, numbering approximately twenty-five men, under the command of Major Hernán Plata Ríos, entered guerrilla territory along the riverbed of the Ñancahuazú River. The whole group fell into an ambush that our forces had set up. As a result of the encounter, twenty-five arms of all types fell into our hands, among them three 60 mm. mortars and the shells for them, and a large quantity of ammunition and equipment.

The enemy casualties were: seven dead, among them a lieutenant, and fourteen prisoners, five of whom were wounded in the encounter. These men were cared for by our medical unit as best our means permitted.

All the prisoners were set free after having received an explanation of the ideals of our movement.

[A list of enemy casualties follows.]

On making public this first act of war, we establish what will be the norm in our army: the revolutionary truth.

Our deeds will demonstrate the truth of our words. Let us regret the innocent blood shed by the fallen soldiers, but peaceful viaducts are not installed with mortars and machine guns as the puppets in uniforms with stripes on the sleeve claim, seeking to create the legend that we are vulgar murderers.

There was not a single peasant, nor will there be one, who can complain of the treatment he receives from us and of the way in which we obtain supplies, except for those who, betraying their class, lend their services as guides or informers.

Hostilities have begun. In future communiqués we will clearly indicate our revolutionary position; today we call upon workers, peasants, intellectuals, upon all those who feel that the hour has come to answer violence with violence, to rescue a country that has been sold slice by slice to Yankee monopolies, and to raise the standard of living of our people, who grow hungrier and hungrier each day.

THE ARMY OF NATIONAL LIBERATION OF BOLIVIA

On Tuesday, March 28, a commission of the Bolivian Red Cross decided to go to where the first Ñancahuazú encounter had taken place. Its principal object was to pick up the dead bodies of the company commanded by Major Hernán Plata Ríos, among which were the remains of Lieutenant Amézaga and several soldiers. The army had an interest in this operation, since the bodies would be evidence of the existence of the insurgent groups.

The commission was made up of Dr. Gilbert Flores Barrón, a doctor of the Bolivian Fiscal Petroleum Deposits; Dr. Manuel Sauna, a doctor from Lagunillas; a retired colonel named Torrico; three soldiers dressed as peasants; and a youth, Hugo Flores, the bearer of the Red Cross flag. They started out from Lagunillas in an ambulance, went through Pincal, and continued on toward Ñancahuazú.

At Kilometer 37 they made their first contact with the guerrillas: an armed man in civilian clothes stopped them, but allowed them to go after he had identified them. Farther on they made contact with an insurgent patrol. "One of the people in it," Dr. Flores said, "was a young Bolivian doctor, who, after indicating that we could go ahead, accompanied us a short distance. Farther on another guerrilla stopped us, warning us that we could not go on. The guerrilla doctor then told us that a truck had come along behind us, and several soldiers had climbed out. He said to us with a certain bitterness: 'We are receiving you peacefully, so that you can pick up your dead; but with troops behind you that will be impossible.' " In the face of this recrimination Flores retraced his steps so as to detain the soldiers. Dr. Sauna remained as a hostage until the impasse was resolved. The chief of the commission ordered that the troops be detained, while Mustang planes of the Bolivian air force flew overhead in the clear sky of Ñancahuazú. Despite this, the guerrillas led them to where the corpses were.

These could not be removed because they were in an advanced state of decomposition and the dampness had swollen the bodies and made them too heavy to be carried. In the face of this, the guerrillas told Dr. Flores that for humanitarian reasons they would grant a truce of forty-eight hours in order that the army might recover its dead. The commission returned to Lagunillas and told the military authorities what had to be done. Colonel Juan Fernández Calazana, the Chief of Staff of the Fourth Division stationed in that locality, answered: "The guerrillas may accord themselves the power to grant truces, but these mean nothing to the army, because they are a band of mercenaries and thieves. So even though there was talk of a truce, the army won't respect it, for there really is no such thing." For this reason, though the guerrillas supposed that the truce was in effect, the following day government planes flew over, dropping bombs and strafing the zone.

On March 31, Guevara went about preparing for a march south so as to evacuate the four visitors. On April 3, Guevara wrote: "I spoke with Danton and Carlos, laying out three alternatives for them: following us, going out alone, or going by way of Gutiérrez and from there trying their luck as best they could. They chose the third. Tomorrow we'll try our luck." The decision was to go out by way of Gutiérrez, about thirty-seven miles south of Ñancahuazú.

A more careful plan was drawn up to get Chino and Tania out, since the two of them were more important to the revolutionary cause. On April 3, at 3:30 A.M., the three principal groups, under the direct command of Guevara, set off, leaving a small platoon to guard the camp sites. Making their way along slowly, they passed the site of the March 23 ambush and then passed to one side of the Calamine House at about 8:30. They came across the remains of the seven corpses left from the first encounter, and Guevara says of them in his diary: "Only perfectly clean skeletons remained of the bodies of the seven corpses, on which birds of prey had responsibly exercised their function." The trip turned out to be fruitless since they could not achieve their objective. The attempt to get the visitors out was ended on April 4, when the guerrillas saw that a close watch was being kept on Gutiérrez by the authorities and that it was occupied by military personnel, making escape impossible. The information on the watch being kept on Gutiérrez was supplied by village contacts and residents, friendly peasants, and the guerrillas' own infiltration of the village. Confronted by this situation, Guevara decided to retrace his steps and reoccupy the positions he had had in Ñancahuazú. During halts along the way, they built little camps along the Las Piedras arroyo, with an eventual return to these spots in mind.

During the return trip, in view of his failure to get out, Debray again proposed to Che that he be taken in as a guerrilla, suggesting that someone else be given the mission of journalist that he had been entrusted with. But Che, reminding him of his limited physical endurance and his lack of experience in the field, gave him a characteristically cutting reply: "Ten city intellectuals are worth less to me as guerrillas than a single peasant from the region."

9

The First News
of the Guerrillas

The first movements of the guerrillas in the country came to light in an atmosphere of general confusion and incredulousness. At first neither the authorities nor the public seemed to believe the news. There were vaguenesses and contradictions of all sorts, and repercussions were felt outside the country. There were those who asserted that it was a question of a "simple intervention of General Barrientos' government for purposes having to do with domestic policy"; others referred to clashes between the army and the many clandestine manufacturers of cocaine, who were discovered almost every day in the country. The imagination of journalists, especially abroad, gave free rein to the most absurd speculations. An interesting report datelined Ñancahuazú, April 10, 1967, was made by Murray Sayle, a correspondent for the London *Times*, and a reporter with ample experience in Vietnam, who wrote: "Outside observers suspect that the Bolivian government invented the guerrillas or attributed more importance to them than that which they actually had, in order to obtain American support on the eve of the Presidents' Conference in Punta del Este, Uruguay." He then added: "In reality, an American diplomat said that in his opinion 'the Bolivians are trying to put pressure on us to extend more armaments aid'; and he asked me for an unofficial report for Americans on whether the guerrillas really existed. My information is that the facts are almost as fantastic as the rumors."[1]

The first official news came to light on March 2, 1967. The Minister of Internal Affairs stated that there existed armed bands organized by extremists with the object of physically eliminating high state officials, and added that " 'Poristas' [adherents of the Trotskyite wing of the Bolivian Communist Party] have bought a piece of property near Santa Cruz, where its militants are receiving instruction on guerrilla tactics."

Two days later, Colonel Félix Moreno, the prefect of Santa Cruz, spoke of the presence of guerrilla groups in the region of Río Grande, basing his opinion on information gathered from various sources; he stated that he had arranged for a rigorous investigation since this might constitute a danger to public order.

On March 7, however, the government denied the existence of guerrillas, affirming that the whole affair was nothing but a manifestation of subversive activities on the part of extremist parties, and reporting the adoption of preventive measures.

On March 9, General Robert Porter, the head of the Southern Command of the United States, with headquarters in the Panama Canal Zone, held a conference with the Bolivian Military High Command in Miraflores—a district in La Paz and the headquarters of the Armed Forces Command. It was then reported that the American armed forces had offered technical assistance to the Bolivian army whenever the situation should require it. General Porter was in Bolivia again later, visiting various military garrisons; on one of his trips, as he was making a swing around other countries bordering Bolivia, he entered the country accompanied by a general named Johnson, whose real identity and activities were kept a strict secret. At the same time the presence of guerrillas in Brazil, supposedly headed by Che Guevara, was announced. The following day, General Jorge Belmonte Ardiles, the Commander in Chief of the Bolivian air force, denied that guerrilla groups had appeared in the east. He maintained that information to that effect "is nothing but speculation—originated by extremist groups—that was not denied when it should have been by the government authorities; as for the Commander in Chief [Ovando Candia], I can state that he is visiting

---

[1] *Granma* (Havana, April 23, 1967).

no part of any garrison in connection with any presumed guerrilla activity."

On March 12, rumors circulated about the possible existence of armed groups in San José de Chiquitos, in the *departamento* of Santa Cruz. The head of these groups was said to be the lawyer Luís Sándoval Morón, a top leader in the MNR.

On March 14, Pastor Barrera Quintana and Vicente Rocabado Terrazas turned up, or were arrested by the authorities, in Camiri, having deserted the rebel camp on the eleventh. Ever since their arrival at the guerrilla center they had been suspected by their comrades, to the point that the latter resolved to let them go and were only waiting for the right moment to get them out. Unconfirmed reports have it that Rocabado was an agent of the Control Político, the political police of the MNR regime. In their confessions both these men agreed on the motives for their descrtion: failure to pay them what was promised them, discriminatory treatment because they were Bolivians, which took the form of assigning them to menial tasks—they were made to be cooks, bakers, and *"góndolas"*[2]— and indoctrination with "ideas contrary to the interests of the country." There was no official report of their detention. The two later served as guides during various army operations.

Some days later, in the zone of Monteagudo, in the *departamento* of Chuquisaca, there were suspicions that guerrillas had been organized and acts of sabotage carried out by extremist groups, according to a report by the local sub-prefect, Armando Betancourt. Orders were given for military groups to stand watch on the pipelines and the petroleum zones of the southeast. Political and military authorities in Sucre instructed radio stations to consult them before broadcasting information on the existence of subversive *focos* in the *departamento* of Chuquisaca. Journalistic censorship was thus imposed by subordinates, to be later countermanded by the President of the Republic. Radio La Plata was the first to be affected.

On March 17, Salustio Choque Choque, on duty as a sentinel in a tree near the Calamine House on the road to the central camp at

---

[2] *Góndola* is a Bolivian word for bus. The guerrillas used the word to designate those who transported supplies—in this case from Calamine House to the central camp.—*Trans.*

Ñancahuazú, fell prisoner, or surrendered, to an army unit headed by Colonel Alberto Libera. Like Pastor Barrera and Vicente Roca-bado, his comrades were suspicious of him and had sent him on this last mission as a test, according to what he reported when interrogated.

The capture of Barrera, Rocabado, and Choque permitted the Military Command to have information as early as March 17—six days before the first encounter in Ñancahuazú—about the guerrillas: their number, nationality, the participation of Che Guevara, their location, roads leading in to them, etc.

On the eighteenth there was talk of a possible meeting of military chiefs of the continent in the city of Cochabamba. On the nineteenth a cave or subterranean cache was discovered in a ravine in Ñancahuazú. Six suitcases and several satchels full of personal effects, in particular civilian clothes made in Cuba, with a label "Casa Alvion—Havana," were found in it. Documents and various papers of less importance were also found, according to General Ovando.

President Barrientos made a trip to Monteagudo on March 20. On the same day a state of alert was ordered in the garrisons serving in frontier zones. There was unofficial talk of "Castro Communist guerrillas operating in national territory." There were references to a dead soldier in the vicinity of Monteagudo, and it was reported that the army had ordered preventive measures and the recruiting of soldiers for the Fourth Division.

On March 21, the President stated that his trip to Monteagudo was simply a routine visit, having nothing to do with presumed subversive activities. He declared that the news reports about guerrilla movements were mere rumors. The Minister of Defense, for his part, had no important information to give out either; he merely stated that rumors had come to his attention since orders had been given for the recruitment for the Fourth Division of young men of age for military service and he made it clear that these conscripts would receive instructions in guerrilla warfare, apart from their normal military training. The newspaper *Presencia* stated that it had confirmed the existence of guerrilla groups in the *departamento* of Chuquisaca, directed by a Cuban and two men from Oruro, who were said to have been arrested, or at least identified, and it added that the army had suffered a casualty.

General Barrientos categorically denied the existence of guerrillas on March 22. In the face of newspaper articles to the effect that they did exist, he stated: "I deplore the fact that a few responsible organs have let themselves be taken in by informants who bring them news that is completely false; for instance, that a soldier has been killed by guerrillas, and similar reports, which are untrue." He repeated: "The guerrillas exist only in people's imaginations." Nonetheless, that same day the newspaper *Presencia* confirmed the movement of troops to the region of Monteagudo for the purpose of controlling the guerrillas. It specifically said that military units had been moved to the vicinity of Tarabuquillo, Lambayo, and Rossl. Despite all this, the government and the armed forces insisted that they had no knowledge of such facts.

On March 23, there was a report from Cochabamba that army units had been moved from the Centro de Instrucción de Tropas Especiales (CITE), with headquarters in that city, to the *departamento* of Chuquisaca. The military leaders consulted denied all reports of this.

This same day saw the first important encounter between the military forces and the insurgents in the sector of Ñancahuazú. The army had serious casualties: men dead, wounded, and taken prisoner.

In the course of the day the President of the Republic had one meeting after another with the heads of the political parties that supported his government and with the Military High Command. During the last of these meetings, the interim commander of the armed forces, General Jorge Belmonte Ardiles, reported that investigations of supposed guerrilla movements in the zone of Monteagudo had been carried out, and he categorically denied that the troops of CITE were being mobilized.

On the twenty-fifth President Barrientos was in Cochabamba. The evening before he had flown over the insurgent zone and in Camiri had received personal reports from the commander of the Fourth Division on the action in Ñancahuazú. At 8 A.M. he summoned the heads of the Military High Command and officers of the local garrison to his private residence, El Rosal, informing them of events and of the gravity of the situation.

A military leader who had held a high position in the administration since the coup of November 4, 1964, suggested that prompt and effective military aid in the form of armaments and personnel specially trained in anti-guerrilla warfare be requested from the American government. Those present were tense at the prospect of such intervention.

Colonel Joaquín Zenteno Anaya, the ex-Chancellor of the Republic during the military junta and at this juncture the head of the Marshal Andrés de Santa Cruz Command School and Military Staff in Cochabamba, took the floor. He was opposed to the plan, and made a long historical summary of the background of the Bolivian army. He spoke of its traditions, its academic training, its unity, and its capability. According to highly reliable authorities, Zenteno outlined the danger involved in an "intervention of foreign forces" in the country. Those who participated in this historic meeting affirm that Zenteno's intervention ended with loud and prolonged applause. It is said that the President then assured his comrades that, in any case, the problem would be considered calmly and responsibly by the government.

This attitude of the chiefs and officers of the Cochabamba garrison, most of whom played prominent roles in the fight against the guerrillas, prevented foreign soldiers from entering Bolivia and converting the country into another Santo Domingo.

On the following day the first news of the skirmish on the twenty-third leaked out. According to General Belmonte, a patrol of seven soldiers under the command of one officer disappeared, in the guerrilla zone, as it was surveying for a roadway between Masicurí and Lagunillas. It was announced that paratrooper units, Mustang airplanes, and a helicopter were sent to this region to fight against the rebels. General David Lafuente, commander of the army, telegraphed the sub-prefect of Muyupampa, Justino Corcuy, to organize groups of townspeople to repel the insurgents.

General Alfredo Ovando Candia, Commander in Chief of the armed forces, later declared that on March 25, "five foreign-looking individuals made contact with townspeople and asked about roads to get to the Río Grande. They swam across the Río Grande. They had with them a great quantity of dollars and Bolivian pesos."[3]

On the twenty-sixth the existence of guerrillas was officially admitted. A communiqué from the Commander in Chief of the armed forces stated: "As units of the armed forces were laying out the road

---

[3] *El Diario* (September 23, 1967).

from Valle Grande to Lagunillas, a group of soldiers which was surveying the road under the command of Second Lieutenant Raúl Amézaga, was treacherously attacked by unknown groups with automatic arms. We regret to report the death of Amézaga, six soldiers, and the civilian guide Octavio Vargas, a worker for the Bolivian Fiscal Petroleum Deposits, who were brought down by a cowardly fusillade."

In Santa Cruz, Barrientos announced the death of Major Plata in Ñancahuazú, and the death of ten soldiers whose bodies were to be taken to Cochabamba. The guerrillas, according to the President, had suffered fifteen deaths and four men taken prisoner. According to another source, the head of the nation reported that the army had attacked the guerrillas from the southeast, from the air and on the ground. And from Santa Cruz came reports of the arrival by air of American military advisers and armaments.

On March 28 it was announced that the guerrillas had retreated to the zone of Inaú. The newspapers reported that the President of the Republic had stated that "the guerrillas are a reality and we must fight." The presence of Ernesto Guevara in Bolivia was announced for the first time. It was stated that he had been in the country twice before and that "the hand of Che Guevara" was in the organization of the guerrillas in the southeast. He was said to have been seen in the city of Sucre. The following statement was attributed to General Belmonte: "Two of the guerrillas who have been arrested declared that Guevara was in La Paz twice, and participated in the organization of the guerrillas. Of the five guerrillas captured the day before yesterday by the armed forces, three are foreigners who are now in Camiri, and two are Bolivians, deserters from the guerrillas who are now in La Paz."[4]

General Barrientos and the Minister of Defense explained the current situation to the Cabinet of Ministers. It was realized that the country was being invaded by foreign, armed groups supporting Castro Communism, plus extremist agitators who were Bolivian nationals. The subversives were said to have committed acts of vandalism and terrorized peasants of the region. There were also said to have been encounters with the armed forces, who put the rebels

---

[4] The two Bolivians referred to are the deserters Vicente Rocabado and Pastor Barrera.

to flight. The extremist parties were accused of collaborating with "foreign mercenaries, among whom a Peruvian guerrilla nicknamed Chino Negrón has been recognized." Military units numbering two thousand were reported to be surrounding the guerrillas. A state of emergency was declared in the zone where the guerrillas were operating and forty-one political figures of the opposition were taken into custody.

On returning from the area of operations against the guerrillas, General Lafuente declared that the rebels were practically surrounded and under the army's control. There was also a report that the guerrillas had several airfields and that special instructors from the Liberation Forces of Venezuela and Peru were training the rebels. A series of encounters supposedly took place in the zone of the disturbances, which culminated in the capture of nine prisoners and the occupation of an airfield in the zone of Río Grande that gave signs of having been used recently; it was reported that among the prisoners was the Chilean Javier Ernesto Bilde Bonilla, who had been hired by a Cuban and was arrested as he entered Bolivian territory on foot along with other foreigners. One newspaper announced that an aide of Che Guevara's was in command of the guerrillas.

The existence of guerrilla urban contacts was now reported for the first time. General Lafuente announced that a woman named Tania, the principal contact, had fled to Argentina.

On the same date General Alfredo Ovando Candia, the titular Commander in Chief of the armed forces, returned to the country and declared that "the guerrillas deserve nothing but the total repudiation of the nation." On his way to Lima, Peru, he told the press that the Communist parties might be "proscribed," or declared outside the law. When President Barrientos was asked his opinion of General Ovando's statements, he said that "five poor wretches don't deserve any attention from us. The Communist Party in our country is not important enough for us to adopt this sort of measure. They aren't worth bothering about. The Communists will lose ground little by little."

On April 2, Colonel León Kolle Cueto,[5] the Chief of Staff of the

---

[5] Colonel Kolle Cueto is the brother of the Secretary-General of the pro-Soviet wing of the Communist Party, Jorge Kolle Cueto.

Bolivian armed forces and the President's special envoy to Argentina, Brazil, and Paraguay, declared in Buenos Aires that the situation in Bolivia was a delicate one. The same day Barrientos said that it was not true that Bolivia had been asking for economic aid to fight the guerrillas. According to the Argentinian journalist Rogelio García Lupo, Colonel Kolle officially confirmed to Argentinian authorities the presence of Ernesto Guevara in the zone that borders both countries, adding that "the Argentinian army worked on the theory that Guevara was intending to create a training camp for guerrillas in Bolivia so as to infiltrate them later into the north of Argentina." In a press conference Barrientos said: "The purpose of Kolle Cueto's trip is to ask the governments not to allow suspicious elements entry from their borders. They should likewise prevent the escape of guerrillas, which is very logical." The President reaffirmed his previous opinion on the supposed activity of Ernesto Guevara among the guerrillas: "I don't believe in ghosts; I still maintain that Señor Guevara is keeping Señor Cienfuegos and hundreds of others shot in Cuba company."[6]

The President stated that in his opinion the crisis in Bolivia was the work of international Communism, which wished to sow anarchy and chaos in the Republic and that the executors of this policy were international adventurers, with no ideology, recruited for the sole purpose of robbing and plundering.

Several days after his return, General Ovando Candia declared to the press in Santa Cruz that the guerrilla groups were larger than those that had acted in Peru, and that even though they did not constitute a real threat or danger to the country, the fight might last for months. He severely criticized the conduct of the anti-guerrilla operations, stating that if he had been in the country several days before, he would not have had recourse to bombing the insurgent zone, which led to nothing of consequence. In his opinion, it would have been better to intimidate the enemy with machine guns only, without trying to cause a great many casualties. He also emphasized that there had been contradictions in the information coming from military sources. He announced the adoption of more rational measures for the conduct of the operations, and expressed the opinion that the

---

[6] The reference is to Major Camilo Cienfuegos, who was lost in an airplane accident in Cuba.

guerrilla force probably made its appearance too early, due to some tactical error on the part of its organizers.

At about the same time the press in Santa Cruz announced the arrival in that city of an Argentinian military delegation made up of Colonel Raúl García Piñón, Colonel Pedro Lareigue, and other high-ranking officers.

On April 6, a communiqué from the armed forces announced the occupation of the Ñancahuazú pass by units of the Fourth Division after a short action in which planes of the Bolivian armed forces took part, provoking the disbandment of the guerrillas and their flight toward the mountains; he added that the armed forces were in control of the situation.

Colonel Joaquín Zenteno Anaya was appointed Commander of the Eighth Division with headquarters in Santa Cruz, replacing Colonel Roberto Vargas Claros.

This was the period when the authorities saw guerrillas everywhere. In Cochabamba a mentally deranged beggar, called Bulich, was arrested as a "suspected guerrilla." His relatives testified that he had recently escaped from the Pacheco Asylum in Sucre. Later, in October, he was again arrested on the same charge as he wandered through Oruro.

A journalist from *Presencia* reported "an anecdotal happening" in Camiri during the military operations: the chief of the Departamento de Investigación Criminal (DIC)—the new name for the political police—of this city was arrested by the Army Intelligence Service as a suspicious character. The authorities in Camiri later freed the man, who had had an extremely hard time convincing the military of his identity.

Some time later in Cochabamba, in—of all places—the Palace of Culture, during the awarding of prizes in the Annual Literary and Scientific Competition, with the President of the Republic and several legislators present, the Chuquisaca poet Mario Auza Catalano was arrested after his rooms at the Hotel Sucre had been searched. The authorities' suspicions had been aroused because he wore a beard.

The neurosis led to the arrest of a number of people as supposed "contacts" or potential guerrillas. Things were so sensitive that even the parish priest of Muyupampa, the Reverend Father Leo Schwart, was at one time accused of being a Communist by some soldiers because he had given food to some supposed guerrillas prowling around Ayango. The priest on this occasion had the backing of the inhabitants of the entire region, to whom he explained his case by saying: "Just because I take care of humble people, I am branded a guerrilla."

According to information from military circles, in a few days there was to be a trial of the five guerrillas who had been taken prisoner. The Military Prosecutor said that he would ask for thirty-year sentences for them as traitors to the country. Nothing was ever heard of these prisoners again.

On April 10, there were two bloody clashes in Iripití, north of Ñancahuazú. The military forces again had soldiers dead, wounded, or taken prisoner.

The newspapers attributed to Colonel Humberto Rocha, the Commander of the Fourth Division, the exaggerated statement that "the Castro Communist guerrilla groups, sheltered by the Ñancahuazú ravine, are using artillery to harass the advanced positions of the armed forces." In this way, the Commander was trying to emphasize the strong combat potential of the rebels.

On the eleventh, the Council of Ministers ordered the proscription of the Communist parties and the POR.[7]

On the next day, Tomás Rosales Vargas, a citizen of Camiri, hanged himself; he had been locked up for two weeks in a DIC cell, suspected of complicity with the guerrillas. There was no inquest.

The following day an army communiqué announced the action in Iripití and reported the deaths of Lieutenants Luís Saavedra and Jorge Ayala, noncommissioned officer Cornejo, and four guerrillas.

On April 14, the body of Lieutenant Saavedra arrived in Camiri. At the same time seven peasants captured by the military forces in the guerrilla region were brought to the town. In various cities in the nation, politicians belonging to the opposing MNR, PRIN, and militant Communist parties were arrested. On the fifteenth, units of the Eighth Division were transferred from Santa Cruz to the north of Ñancahuazú, along the banks of the Río Grande.

A special correspondent of *Presencia* reported that forty-three miles from Camiri, between Muyupampa and Ñacunday, "the bearded ones showed up." This zone is 160 miles from Iripití, where the last encounter had taken place. On the same date journalists

---

[7] The text of this order is given in Appendix IV.

Régis Debray (a Frenchman), George Andrew Roth (an Anglo-Chilean), and Carlos Alberto Fructuoso (an Argentinian) were arrested in Muyupampa.

It was announced that on the twentieth a patrol under the command of Lieutenant Néstor Ruíz dealt the insurgents a daring blow in the Ñacunday sector. The five guerrillas captured in the action were taken to Camiri. According to information given the press by Colonel José Carrasco, the commander of the military air base at Santa Cruz, there were an Argentinian and an Italian among the prisoners, passing themselves off as journalists. In La Paz, President Barrientos nonetheless announced to peasant leaders from Cochabamba that it was an Englishman, a Frenchman, and an Argentinian who had been arrested.

News programs on the radio announced the death of "three mercenaries: one Frenchman, one Englishman, and one Argentinian." Other news sources said that the Frenchman was a famous Communist, "an important member of the Castro hierarchy in Cuba."

On April 23, the command of the Fourth Division imposed a total censorship on the press in the guerrilla zone. This measure gave rise to vehement protest on the part of Bolivian journalists and accredited foreign correspondents. In spite of the fact that this measure was publicly rescinded by the President of Bolivia, there continued to be rigorous censorship until after the guerrilla uprising had ended and the trial in Camiri was concluded.

The governments of Argentina, Brazil, and Paraguay followed the development of events in Bolivia with justified apprehension. Apart from reinforcing their military garrisons on the borders they shared with Bolivia, they kept strict watch on these frontiers, offered all possible cooperation with Barrientos' government, and established a thoroughgoing exchange of information among all their security organizations. Argentina and Brazil, moreover, lent valuable aid in the form of food supplies and war materiel.

Foreign information agencies noted that the President of Paraguay, General Alfredo Stroessner, had declared his intention of participating with military forces in the destruction of the rebels, as he had done during the Santo Domingo crisis. This attitude of the Paraguayan government gave rise to protest on the part of the nationalist opposition parties (MNR, FSB, PRIN, PDC) and the various Communist parties. The MNR and the FSB, which have parliamentary representation, brought their anxieties to the attention of the national legislative bodies.

American intelligence organizations, in particular the FBI and the CIA, in close coordination with the Pentagon, also were no strangers to the drama being played out in the mountains. Experienced agents of the CIA in many cases cooperated—visibly, semi-secretly, and secretly—with the Bolivian investigation services and directly intervened in several important instances.

Advisers and military technicians, for their part, gave lessons in "Counter-Insurgency," or "Internal Defense and Development," as the specific activities of the famous "Green Berets" are now called. As for equipment and armaments, the government of Bolivia has repeatedly denied having received extraordinary aid from the United States, and has stated that the helicopters and planes sent by the United States government were already provided for in previously concluded agreements for the cooperation of the two nations.

Christopher Roper, the diligent Reuters correspondent in Lima, who visited Bolivia at various times during and after the insurgent uprising and the trial in Camiri, made an interesting analysis, on October 12, 1967, of the cooperation given Bolivia by the United States government, and the world scope of the American military and intelligence network and its relations with Bolivia.

As for the coordination of information, Roper said: "An American soldier told us in Santa Cruz that the intelligence service of his country aided Bolivians in documenting the presence of Che and the hunting down of his city contacts. 'You can say'—this official told us, pointing with his hand to the prosperity of Santa Cruz, where the Alliance for Progress has spent 115 million dollars and Gulf Oil another 100 million—'that we are fighting to defend all these treasures for the Bolivian people.'"

As regards military aid, Roper stated that the center of military cooperation was the former sugar mill, La Esperanza—built with funds from the Alliance for Progress—under the direction of Major Ralph (Pappy) Shelton, of Nashville, Tennessee, who had headed similar schools in the Dominican Republic and Laos before coming to Bolivia. In La Esperanza, Shelton had as an aide Captain Leroy

Mitchell, "an American Negro who had recently arrived from Vietnam."

Roper noted that "the Americans are taking the Bolivian situation very seriously." After the death of Che, Shelton said to him: "I'm a pessimist, and I don't think the guerrilla war has come to an end here; far from it."

The team led by Major Shelton which trained the Bolivian Rangers Battalion included as advisers specialists of the five branches of the Special Forces—arms, communications, medicine, demolition, and intelligence. They also concerned themselves with the "moral strengthening" of the human materiel and its "political education."

According to Roper, "It is very difficult to estimate the strength of the Americans in Bolivia, because of the discretion of their components and because the Bolivian authorities roundly deny that they have received any outside aid. Nonetheless, Colonel Joseph Rice, who is based in Cochabamba, declared that there are fifty officers and noncommissioned officers in this mission." Roper says in his dispatch: "The international imperialist network is really international."

10

Skirmishes in Iripití

As the month of March drew to a close, official reports on the guerrilla movement were contradictory and confused. A large part of the press didn't believe that it existed, and important sectors of public opinion were skeptical. Even though several days had gone by since the ambush of Ñancahuazú, the armed forces did not issue a report on the casualties. There were different versions of the encounter, some which were exaggerated and alarmist and others which underestimated the scope of the movement that had begun in the southeast. The President of the Republic announced to the country that it should be prepared to fight against a foreign invasion, and the Minister of National Defense, General Hugo Suárez Guzmán, stated that civil defense groups must be organized in the capitals of *departamentos*, provinces, and cantons. The first communiqué from the armed forces command also stated that the military units which had fought in Ñancahuazú were part of a company of sappers who had been building a road from Valle Grande to Lagunillas, and that given this circumstance, the members of the unit were the victims of a "cowardly ambush on March 23, set up by Castro Communists, with a great part of them being shot."

At this same time, the troops of the army were fulfilling their delicate mission in places known later as the "Red Zone." The company of Major Rubén Sánchez, composed of 120 men, whose platoons

113

were under the command of Lieutenants Ayala, Gutiérrez, and Ruíz, arrived at noon on April 3, at a place called Yuqui. At five o'clock the next morning, guided by the deserter Salustio Choque Choque, the company advanced to the west mouth of the Ñancahuazú Ravine so as to cut off the possible retreat of the guerrillas camped in its middle section. At the far east end of the ravine, at the Calamine House, another company was posted, with Captain Alfredo Calvi in command. After proceeding about three miles, Major Sánchez's unit was stopped by bombing and strafing from government airplanes: the detachment had been taken for rebel forces since at this date the guerrillas had camouflaged army uniforms at their disposal. After fifteen minutes the pilots identified the troops and switched from machine-gun fire to the conventional salute from airmen. The confusion had not resulted in any casualties. This error on the part of the air force is explicable not only for the reason noted, but also because no military force had ventured into the ravine for the last twenty days. Later a government plane flew over the area with Colonel Marcos Vásquez Sempértegui, the Chief of Staff of the army, and other top military officers as observers, all of whom saw the daring position the infantry unit had taken up. All day the air force continued to protect Major Sánchez's company as it went farther east in the ravine.

At midday, Choque Choque managed to locate some sentinel posts and guerrilla positions, and in order to neutralize them Major Sánchez directed on them all his available firepower for more than an hour.

From the heights there came some barely audible shots. Firing to soften the enemy up, the company continued to advance. Shortly after entering the ravine they began to see the first signs of the guerrillas' defensive organization. The location of the individual and collective positions, laid out in a circle on the heights, was evidence of how carefully the terrain had been prepared. The first camp had a field kitchen and camp cots. Farther on, a second camp, larger than the first, could be seen. The path linking the two camps was defended by trenches. This second camp, which was laid out much like the first, had, among other things, a baking oven and defensive fortifications built of earth and pointed stakes. Close by, there were vegetable gardens and a henhouse. Soon after, they discovered the path that led to the third camp, the largest of the three. In it were a sort of amphitheater with benches seating approximately forty men and a lectern from which the theoretical discussions among the guerrillas were directed. The army units spent their first hours in the camp looking for papers, documents, and anything else that would serve to augment their knowledge of the guerrilla movement. The photographer from the Palace of Government, Fanor Ugalde, found a photograph of Che Guevara. Studying it and comparing it with the flora of the place, the army was later able to prove that the photograph had been taken in this zone. It was one more piece of evidence to prove that the legendary revolutionary had been with the Bolivian guerrillas.

The journalist Murray Sayle said that he saw showers made of mule skin, crude operating tables, chairs, latrines, and receipts for medical equipment bought in La Paz between the eighth and the twentieth of November, 1966.

"Among refuse carefully removed from the dormitory," Sayle continued, "I found a photograph of Dr. Che Guevara, the ex-lieutenant of Dr. Castro, taken in the forest, and a copy of a speech by General Vo Nguyen Giap of North Vietnam, translated into Spanish, in which he advocated 'armed struggle of long duration for national liberation, and prolonged resistance, leading to the eventual triumph of the people.' It was impossible that this material had been 'planted,' since I myself found it in the refuse, and the Bolivian patrol that was with me had never heard of Giap."

Sayle said that he was not certain that the photograph had been taken in Ñancahuazú, and stated: "It really doesn't help clear up the mystery of Guevara's whereabouts."[1]

During the search, the officers and men found cardboard boxes and munitions with labels from the Dominican Republic, clippings from newspapers concerning the habitual itineraries of General Barrientos, and others that were political in nature. Here and there they picked up orders written by the guerrilla Rolando directing the movements of the rear guard.

The company went on to the eastern end of Ñancahuazú where they came face to face with a macabre spectacle: the scattered remains of those who had died in the encounter on March 23. From the waist up the corpses showed white bones, bright and clean; the

---

[1] *Granma* (Havana, April 23, 1967).

tight pants had kept off the birds of prey. Hunks of waterlogged human flesh were working loose from the clothes and following the current downstream. A few days before, the guerrillas had passed this way and had seen the same sight.

Sánchez's company continued on, following the course of the stream so as to make contact with Captain Calvi's unit and begin recovering the corpses; when it was almost dark they contacted the platoons that were guarding the eastern mouth of the ravine in the vicinity of the Calamine House. From this point on, both units made the house that had been bought by the guerrillas their command post. At dawn the next day, they began the task of picking up the corpses in sacks and boxes that served as coffins. This long, pathetic task was accomplished amid signs of sorrowful indignation on the part of relatives of the men who had fallen, and their comrades in arms. Once this work had been done, the bodies were buried with military honors. At the end of the day, Colonel Augusto Calderón appeared in the new command post, and congratulated the officers and enlisted men for recovering the corpses, with special commendation for Major Sánchez's work.

On Thursday, April 6, a large group of Bolivian and foreign journalists arrived in the zone; entering the former camp sites of the guerrillas, they amply fulfilled their task of informing the public. They verified that the subversive organization dated back approximately a year and a half. The well-known French journalist Jean Lartéguy, on observing how effective the defenses of the guerrilla organization were, expressed his admiration for the bravery of the military unit that had entered the Ñancahuazú Ravine.

On Saturday, April 8, Sánchez's company received orders to explore the Iripití Ravine, some miles north of Ñancahuazú, a task that it completed the next day, without coming into contact with the enemy. At seven o'clock on Monday, the tenth, Lieutenant Luís Saavedra again marched to Iripití and Lieutenant Lafuente was given the mission of moving to Tiraboy, to the northeast. At midday, groups of very excited soldiers appeared in the command post at the Calamine House.

"Ambush . . . ambush! The lieutenant is wounded down on the river bank," the young conscripts of Lieutenant Saavedra's patrol shouted.

Once they had gotten over their nervousness, Warrant Officer

Sáenz and several privates explained that Saavedra's patrol had been the victim of a new ambush. After taking the measures that the situation seemed to require, Major Sánchez went to a military post in Pincal, south of Ñancahuazú, so as to be put in touch with the command of the Fourth Division in Camiri. He informed the command of what had happened and asked for instructions. Colonel Rocha ordered him to gather together the reserves stationed in Pincal, make a forced march to the zone of the ambush, and pin the enemy down there. Following the orders given him, Sánchez returned immediately to the Calamine House, where at four in the afternoon he advanced with his troops along the edge of the river toward Iripití, with the object of coming to the aid of his men, under fire since morning.

The ups and downs of the struggle also filtered back to Che Guevara's command post. At this juncture he was at the Bear Camp, to the north of the original positions in Ñancahuazú. He was hoping that any enemy attack would come from the south, and on seeing that the army was approaching from the east, from Iripití, he chose to set up an ambush in this zone so as to stop the army's advance. Preparations were made, and plans were hastily drawn up, following very closely the model of the ambush of March 23. At 10:30, the first part of the action against them began. The command post, established in a clearing in the woods, was not far from the spot where the fight took place; it was barely ten minutes' walk away. The courier gave Guevara the news of the encounter with the enemy patrol and the acquisition of other spoils of war; he also asked for immediate medical aid for El Rubio, who had been seriously wounded (he was later to die from the wounds he had received). Che gave orders to the group commanders to mobilize their forces and sent doctors to the place where the fight was going on.

Meanwhile, Major Sánchez's unit was proceeding with extreme caution. At that moment—4:30—a small Cessna of the Bolivian air force carrying Colonel Rocha flew over the zone; after recognizing the infantry troops, it launched a flare, waggled its wings in salute, and disappeared toward its base. But no combat plane followed it as the unit engaged with the enemy had desperately hoped. This lack of aerial support, the cause of which was unknown to the combatants, was due to the fact that all military airplanes had been pulled back to La Paz by order of General Jorge Belmonte Ardiles, the Commander in Chief of the Bolivian air force, who doubted that the guerrillas represented a real danger.

By this time the preliminaries of the second encounter of the day had begun. The auxiliary force continued its advance. Surprisingly, the troops began to receive heavy fire from automatic weapons and rifles from the wooded shore of the river and the surrounding heights; this fire was returned by the army unit. Around five the fighting grew more intense. The government force had greater firepower, but the guerrillas knew the zone and fired more accurately. Warrant Officer Cornejo, carrying a machine gun in the vanguard, was the first casualty. The fire grew heavier, and the shouts of the wounded soldiers mingled with the guerrillas' voices:

"Surrender, soldiers, we won't kill you! Surrender!" There were also anguished moans from the soldiers, all shouting to Major Sánchez that they were wounded and needed help.

The combat went on mercilessly. Sánchez and Ayala continued to fight. Cornejo died at the height of the battle.

Major Sánchez and Lieutenant Ayala fought hard, shouting orders and trying to rally their troops. As Lieutenant Ayala was firing a mortar, he received a bullet in the chest that pierced his lung. The wounded man began to shout for the Major. At this disconcerting moment, several soldiers in the rear guard and their commanding officer retreated; others surrendered, so that the Major and two soldiers were left to defend themselves. The guerrillas recognized the officer whom they had heard about after the engagements of the days immediately preceding, and told him to surrender. Luckily for him, instead of shooting him several insurgents who had come down from the heights crept up on him and took him by surprise, subduing him after a brief struggle. Then Inti came over to him and said:

"Ah, you're Major Sánchez, the one that ruined our plans. We'll see now . . . "

Guerrilla Rolando appeared and also recognized him. He shouted:

"This is Major Sánchez; we've got to kill him . . . " Then he shouted to him threateningly: "Make your company surrender or we'll kill you."

Other guerrillas approached and ordered him to surrender his men. Major Sánchez refused. They asked him several times to cooperate so as to "avoid more bloodshed." At one juncture Sánchez shouted to his men to fall back. Long before this, the whole rear guard of his company had done exactly this, without waiting for orders to that effect.

Later, there were more or less violent discussions and altercations between Major Sánchez and his captors. The officer asked for attention for his wounded and guarantees for his soldiers, as well as the assurance that he could pick up his dead. Once tempers cooled, aid was forthcoming. Several dead and wounded were picked up out of the river, and the prisoners were grouped around their commanding officer.

Lieutenant Ayala and the rest of the wounded begged for help from their commanding officer, and the prisoners shouted for him not to abandon them. Major Sánchez had only words of consolation for some and words of encouragement for the others. He asked insistently for aid for his wounded. It was an hour before two guerrilla doctors arrived; they first aided Lieutenant Ayala, whose wounds were the most severe. The army men were later to relate that the insurgent doctors looked after this valiant officer attentively. Once the wounded had been cared for and the dead had been picked up, the prisoners were taken to a nearby ravine where they were subjected to an interrogation mingled with threats and offers to take them into the guerrilla ranks.

Through Pombo the news of the fight arrived at the guerrilla center located in the Bear Camp, where Major Guevara was. Pombo told what a hard-fought battle it had been, spoke of the resistance offered by the commanding officer of the army troops, and described how many arms and how much equipment had been captured. Che ordered the doctors to immediately begin their work, starting with the wounded of their own band, gave instructions on the proper conduct toward the prisoners, ordered his vanguard and rear guard to gather the booty together, and decided to move from the guerrilla zone to a point farther north.

It was a sad sight for the prisoners; the wounded groaned constantly and the rest of the men were exhausted, hungry, and cold. Major Sánchez, with the permission of his hosts, ordered his soldiers to light a bonfire, ostensibly so as to dry their clothes and fight against the damp cold of the night air; but his hidden purpose was to give some sign of life to the other platoons that he was sure would come looking for him. There were threats from one or another of the guerrillas, but these were cut short by Coco, who seemed to be in command at the moment. Voices grew less harsh, and a dialogue began, at times rough and at times friendly. Coco, Inti, Ñato, Rolando, the ex-miner Moisés Guevara, two others who said they belonged to the MNR and the PRIN, and a few Cubans, took part in this colloquy with the soldiers. They discussed the plans of the guerrillas, the ideals of the Army of National Liberation of Bolivia, the "present government's policy of handing everything over [to the imperialists]," the reasons that drove the guerrillas to "go up in the mountains and fight face to face with the army and the government, which are indirect instruments of imperialism," and various other subjects. The doctors returned to ask if there were any wounded with fractures; they went back to their posts and then returned a few minutes later to put casts on those who needed such attention. Ñato, a fat Bolivian guerrilla born in Beni, took a few photographs of Major Sánchez, from the front and in profile, using a camera with a flash attachment. Cups of coffee were served to the wounded and the commanding officer. Coco gave the Major back his personal weapon, a revolver, "as homage to his courageous behavior in that day's encounter." Sánchez took advantage of this moment of almost cordial expansiveness to bring up what had happened during the action on March 23, in which Lieutenant Amézaga and others lost their lives. The Major said recriminatingly: "You're murderers and thieves."

Coco asked: "Why do you say that?"

"Because you killed Lieutenant Amézaga and others and stole their personal effects."

"That officer came here to fight. He had the choice of killing or being killed, just as we did. He killed one of our men and wounded two others. We had to kill him so that he wouldn't kill any more of our comrades. As for Vargas the guide, whom we recognized immediately, I'll tell you that we didn't mind killing him at all: he was a traitor. Wait a minute . . . "

Coco withdrew for a minute, came back immediately, and said:

"We aren't murderers or thieves. We're engaged in a fight in which, to our regret, we may kill or be killed, because we are fighting for a great cause. I'll give you another proof that we aren't what you think we are." And as he said this, he handed him Lieutenant Amézaga's wedding ring: "Please see that this gets to his family. As for his watch, I'm sorry I can't give it back to you. We need watches badly and they aren't easy to get."

The conversation went on. There were a few moans close by. They were the death rattle of Lieutenant Ayala, who had fought heroically that day; he died at 11:30. Despite the care he had received and the emergency operation performed on him to save his life, his right lung had been fatally injured. When Major Sánchez tried to take his ring off, a guerrilla took it. Sánchez therefore called Coco over, and the guerrilla chief went up to a group of his comrades and told them to wait and see what "the center" had to say about what happened to the ring. Meanwhile, the Major had his men stir up the fire, to keep up their hopes of being rescued by their comrades. This trick, however, didn't work.

Moments later, some guerrillas threatened to shoot Major Sánchez and asked him what his last wish was; he told them once again what he had told them before: it was his wish that his body be given to his men so that they could take it to the nearest army camp.

"Why do you insist that that's the only thing you want?" they asked him.

"Because I don't want the same thing to happen to my dead body as happened to my dead comrades in Ñancahuazú."

"But that wasn't our fault," the guerrillas replied. "We told Major Plata that time that he could come back the next day to get his men's bodies."

Around 12:30 A.M. on April 11, the prisoners were told that they would be freed in a few minutes. Major Sánchez insisted on taking all his dead and wounded with him.

"How do you think you can solve this problem if you don't have enough men to take care of it?" Coco asked.

"The warrant officer and the men that aren't wounded will take care of it," Sánchez replied.

The decision was accepted, and he was also given instructions on how to make litters out of branches. At 4 A.M. the guerrillas hurriedly ordered the soldiers to get ready to march; apparently they hadn't been watching the time. Someone—a Cuban—said to them:

"You'll have to be on your way before dawn. We're planning to get out of the zone in the morning, or at the latest, early in the afternoon. Hurry. We don't want your comrades and your planes to kill both us and you."

Before they started on their way, the guerrillas again offered to let Major Sánchez join their ranks, along with his men, a kindness that was again refused. Then the guerrillas gave him back the ring, watch, flashlight, money, and papers that they had confiscated from him. They asked the rest if they had anything to claim. One soldier said that they had taken ten Bolivian pesos that he had hidden in a pack of cigarettes, and the guerrilla chief gave him back the amount he had asked for. At 5:30 Coco ordered them to take the wounded down to the river bank. Then he gathered the soldiers together and told them:

"Well, soldiers: you are our brothers. If your superiors order you to fight, or force you to fight, come ahead and don't be afraid: we won't do anything to you if you throw down your arms and raise your hands at the first shout. You'll leave again just as you're going back now." Then, after a pause: "We aren't taking your uniforms because you might get cold. We'll keep your boots though, because we need them badly; the army will give you others as soon as you get back; we have no place to get them at the moment. Only Major Sánchez is to keep his."

They immediately made them take their boots off; there were seventeen pairs. The handful of taciturn young warriors set off, following the shores of the Iripití River, those slightly wounded trying to match the marching rhythm of their comrades, the soldiers carrying dead or seriously wounded comrades on their backs, Major Sánchez carrying the dead body of Lieutenant Ayala. They often had to relieve each other of their strange burdens. The dawn fog enveloped the odd caravan as if it were a mourning veil, amid the calls of the first birds.

Behind them, the guerrillas, each smoking a cigarette, slowly followed the sad cortege. They accompanied their conquered adversaries for about a mile and a half, then said good-by:

"This is as far as we go; good luck." With a certain irony, they added: "Let's hope we see each other again, because we'll still need the arms and ammunition we get from you."

The guerrillas, about twenty of them, scattered in groups of four or five. A few of them followed after the soldiers for a few more paces. As they started off again, the guerrillas discovered a soldier hiding in the brush. They called to him to surrender and asked him where he came from. The soldier answered that he belonged to Major Sánchez's company, and that he'd fallen asleep after hiding out the afternoon before. Finally the guerrillas simply said to him:

"All right, go on with them."

After having gone on a half mile or so in this fashion, the returning column met a military unit that had come in search of them. With the troops were Captain Hugo Padilla, an information officer of the Fourth Division, Captain Humberto Villarroel, a parachutist, and Captain Alfredo Calvi. Obeying Major Sánchez's prudent advice after a very emotional reunion, both units continued to the command post at the Calamine House. During the march there, the ex-prisoners learned that units of the army had reconnoitered the heights of Iripití the night before, coming close to the place where the fighters had camped, and that a patrol in command of Lieutenant Eduardo Galindo had gone past the spot where the ambush had taken place without his men seeing the bonfire. "The only thing we saw in the thick darkness," these men said, "was a whole bunch of winged, luminous points of light like glow-worms." These were nothing other than the miniature flashlights that the guerrillas were in the habit of using. This confusion favored the rebels, for if the guerrillas had been discovered and attacked by the army platoons, their fate might have been different: the army had precise instructions not to take any prisoners whatsoever, and to shoot to kill. These strict orders came from the Military High Command.

The battle of Iripití was the most costly of the war for the army. Lieutenants Luís Saavedra and Jorge Ayala, Warrant Officer Raúl

Cornejo, and seven soldiers were dead; eighteen men had been taken prisoner. But on the other hand, the army was able to confirm the presence of known militants of leftist parties among the guerrillas.

Major Sánchez went by jeep from the command post on the Ñancahuazú River to the town of Lagunillas, where he made a detailed report on the action to his immediate superiors of the Fourth Division. From there he went in a Cessna belonging to the military to Camiri, where he gave the same report to Generals David Lafuente and Juan José Torres, the Commander of the army and the Chief of Staff of the armed forces, respectively. Sánchez gave these military authorities the insurgents' first official communiqué, which he had come by during his brief captivity; it is not known whether it was left purposely for him or came into his possession by chance. Later he gave a very detailed report to the chief of the Second Section (the Intelligence Service) of the armed forces, Lieutenant Colonel Rocha, and other members of this section, accompanied by CIA agent Eduardo Gonzáles. Then, after receiving the felicitations of President Barrientos in Camiri, the officer enjoyed a brief leave in the interior of the country, as did the other officers who had distinguished themselves in the fight against the guerrillas.

It is important to emphasize the general behavior of the guerrillas toward prisoners and civilians.

More than once military units fell into enemy ambushes where they could easily have been wiped out. The rebels, however, almost always preferred to avoid all unnecessary killing and bloodshed. At times they called out to the soldiers from the dense mountain thickets, telling them to return to their bases and making it clear to them that they had no intention of fighting against them and even less intention of killing them. At other times the guerrillas decided to surprise the army while keeping casualties to a minimum. The object was to indoctrinate them politically, calling upon them to resist all subsequent orders to attack. One case from among many occurred when Major Rubén Sánchez Valdivia was taken prisoner on the afternoon of April 10. In the thick of the battle the rebels had him at their mercy, but they preferred to use a trick to take him prisoner. They slipped behind some rocks, surprised him, and disarmed him with no recourse to shooting, even though Rolando was pointing a machine gun straight at him. And the junior officers, noncommissioned officers, and privates taken prisoner along with their chief were also treated properly, as far as was possible in the circumstances.

The guerrillas' prisoners never denied that the rebel doctors used every means they had to attend to the many wounded government troops or to save their lives, even at the risk of exhausting their scanty reserves of medicine. Whether this was done as a matter of political tactics or out of humanitarian feelings is another question; in either case, this conduct was the general rule with the guerrillas.

According to the Bolivian magazine *Primera Plana*, General Alfredo Ovando Candia had expressed the opinion that one of the causes of the guerrillas' defeat was the fact that they let their prisoners go. The magazine quoted Ovando as follows: "It was undoubtedly bad tactics on the part of the guerrillas to allow some twenty men to go back to their bases. The guerrillas should have done them all in or else not have left a single trace behind so as to remain undiscovered for some time more, during which time they could have planned their operations better."

It must also not be forgotten that all the guerrillas' theories and all their manuals obliged them to treat prisoners and civilians as kindly as possible. Armed struggle against government forces was inevitable and necessary, and in the course of such operations it was a matter of kill or be killed. Guerrilla warfare is a new way of fighting a revolution that may or may not be right, but it is a part of today's violence. Nonetheless there are two factors that are an essential part of the theory of guerrilla warfare: first, that revolutionaries are not motivated by hatred for soldiers because soldiers are part of the people, and second, that shock waves from the struggle serve to make the people conscious of the revolutionary cause.

Obeying this policy of enlisting the sympathies of the people, the insurgents normally did not commit abuses against life and private property, except when forced to do so by exceptional situations of extreme necessity, or as reprisals against supposed informers. During the Camiri trial there was the picturesque case of a witness for the prosecution who accused the guerrillas of having ransacked his farm and stolen, among other things, 120 pigs. One of the lawyers for the defense immediately asked him how many vehicles would be needed to cart away that much booty. The witness answered, amid justified general disbelief, that at least three trucks would be needed. This reply alone was enough to confirm the falsity of the allegation, since in that part of the country logistics of this kind would have been extremely difficult.

Another fact that shows how faithfully the guerrillas carried out their policy of respecting government or private property is that they never committed acts of sabotage against the oil wells, the pipelines, or the railroads in their area of operations.

At one point it was officially announced that the rebels paid enormous sums for the things they bought because they used counterfeit money. Not a single piece of counterfeit money was ever called to the attention of the authorities.

One piece of behavior characteristic of the Cuban guerrillas, which was noticed by their Bolivian comrades, and by journalists and observers, was their enormous fondness for photographs and meticulously kept campaign diaries. Though this is, of course, a regularly observed practice of combatants of any army, for reasons of security these documents must be destroyed when it is probable that they may fall into the hands of the adversary, for they are documents that are invaluable to the enemy. This basic rule—not to leave such clear traces in the power of the enemy—must be strictly observed, especially by conspirators or revolutionaries, but it was never put into effect in the rebels' camps, so that the army and the security services obtained information about the whole immense guerrilla network, including the identity of guerrilla agents and connections both inside and outside the country. The innumerable photographs, magnetic tapes, film, and minutely kept diaries were so many threads which led the authorities to discover the warp and woof of much information previously unknown to them. Even Che Guevara committed this obvious error; this is incomprehensible in the case of an experienced revolutionary.

It must be emphasized that the press could not fulfill its professional task by accompanying the military units, despite having asked for permission and having tried to do so as a *fait accompli*. In the course of the prisoners' bitter night, a few special correspondents and photographers attempted to enter the Iripití ravines, but a military order dictated by prudence eliminated such a possibility. As a consequence, journalists and photographers in Camiri and Lagunillas had to limit themselves to reconstructing the details of the action by relying on information offered by the actors in the drama.

11

The Visitors
Must Leave

The bloody action at Iripití was barely over when Guevara, on April 11, proceeded to an overall strategic evaluation of the guerrilla war that had now definitely begun, and to a detailed tactical evaluation of the guerrilla *foco* in particular. The conclusions were not very encouraging. Everything had become more complicated than had been foreseen. The reality did not match the plans that had been drawn up; new plans, therefore, had to be adopted.

Among other measures, he resolved to try once more to evacuate the visitors—Bustos, Debray, Chino, and Tania—and take advantage of this opportunity to get supplies and drugs, the reserves of which were almost exhausted. Before temporarily abandoning the camp, the guerrillas proceeded to hide everything that was not indispensable for the march in caves or subterranean storerooms: arms, munitions, part of the medicine, documents, photographs and negatives, books, dollars, cameras and film, tape recorders, typewriters, clothing, blankets, etc. Ñato was put in charge of this operation. Presumably, Guevara's initial project of "making Ñancahuazú a stronghold"—contrary to all his theoretical teachings—was abandoned for the dynamism and mobility that should characterize the sort of struggle in which the guerrillas were engaged.

On the twelfth he notes in his diary: "At 6:30 I assembled all the fighters, except the four I expelled, to hold a little memorial service for Rubio and point out that the first blood shed was

1) Che and other guerrillas in camp around January 1967. Chino is at Guevara's left.

4

2) The Ñancahuazú Ravine, where the guerrillas first went into action against the Bolivian army, March 23, 1967. 3) (l. to r.) Three deserters: Vicente Rocabado Terrazas, Salustio Choque Choque, and Pastor Barrera Quintana. 4) Che and Chino.

5

Pombo

Benigno

Urbano

Inti

Dario

Sb. 10.000.—
(DIEZ MILLONES DE BOLIVIANOS)
POR CADA UNO VIVO

RECOMPENSA

Sb. 10.000.—
(DIEZ MILLONES DE BOLIVI
POR CADA UNO VI

ESTOS SON LOS BANDOLEROS MERCENARIOS AL SERVICIO DEL CASTROCOMUNISMO
ESTOS SON LOS CAUSANTES DE LUTO Y DOLOR EN LOS HOGARES BOLIVIANOS
INFORMACION QUE RESULTE CIERTA, DARA DERECHO A LA RECOMPENSA

Ciudadano Boliviano, Ayúdanos a Capturarlos Vivos en lo Pos

NOTA.— Pueden usar barba o llevar otros nombres falsos

5) Tania in the camp at Ñancahuazú. 6) Mario Monje Molina, Secretary of the PCB's pro-Soviet wing. 7) Reward poster circulated after Che's capture and death.

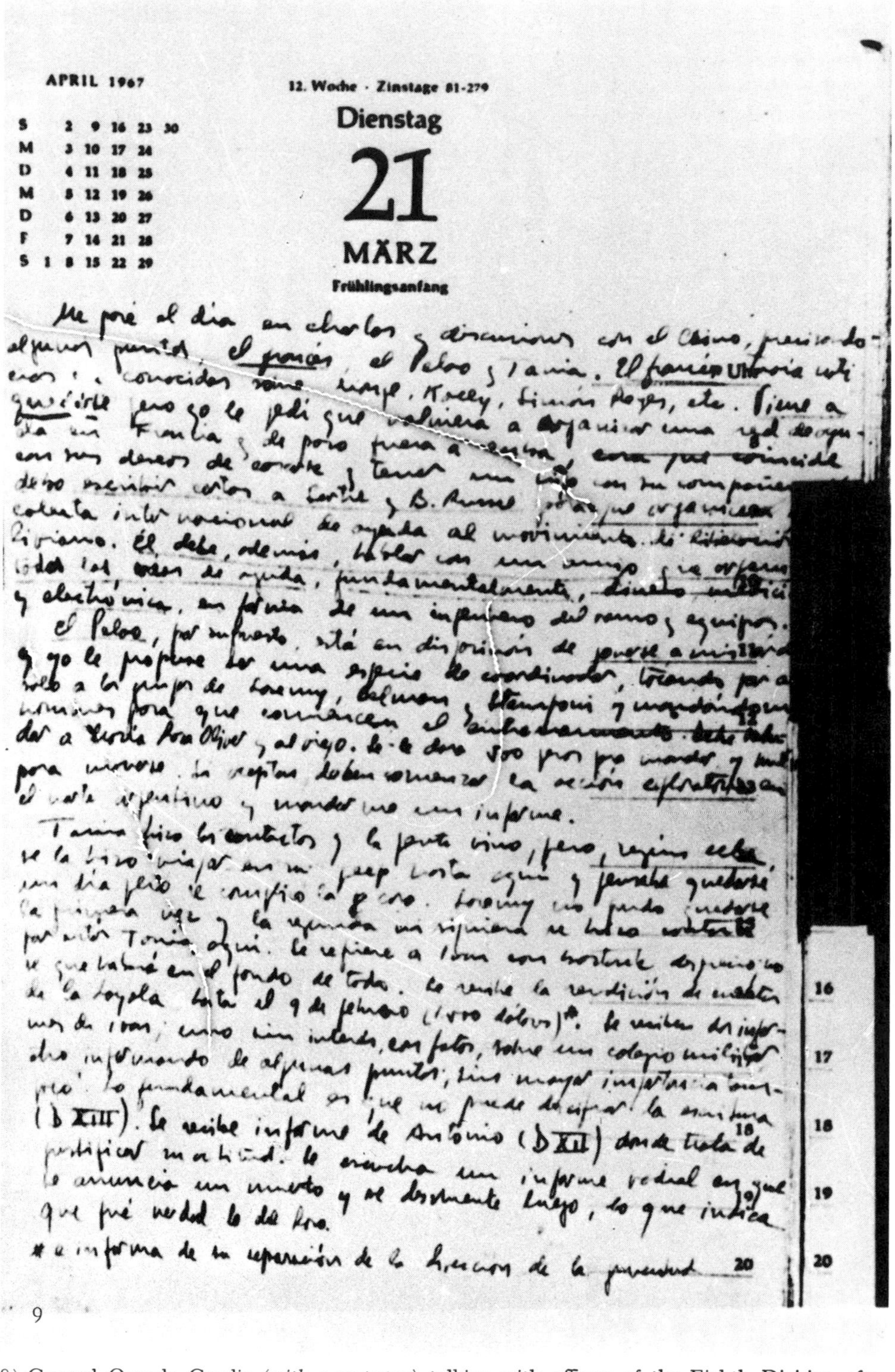
APRIL 1967

12. Woche · Zinstage 81-279

Dienstag

21

MÄRZ

Frühlingsanfang

Me pasé el día en charlas y discusiones con el Chino, precisando algunos puntos, el francés, el Pelado y Tania. El francés traía noticias ya conocidas sobre Monje, Kolle, Simón Reyes, etc. Viene a quedarse pero yo le pedí que volviera a organizar una red de ayuda en Francia y de paso fuera a Cuba, cosa que coincide con sus deseos de casarse y tener un hijo con su compañera. Debo escribir cartas a Sartre y B. Russell para que organicen una colecta internacional de ayuda al movimiento de liberación boliviano. Él debe, además, hablar con un amigo que organizará todas las vías de ayuda, fundamentalmente dinero, medicinas y electrónica, en forma de un ingeniero del ramo y equipos.

El Pelado, por supuesto, está en disposición de ponerse a mis órdenes y yo le propuse ser una especie de coordinador, tocando por ahora sólo a los grupos de Jozamy, Gelman y Stamponi y mandándome hombres para que comiencen el entrenamiento. Debe saludar a María Rosa Oliver y al viejo. Se le dará 500 pesos para mandar y mil para moverse. Si aceptan, deben comenzar la acción exploratoria en el norte argentino y mandarme un informe.

Tania hizo los contactos y la gente vino, pero, según ella, se la hizo viajar en su jeep hasta aquí y pensaba quedarse un día pero se complicó la cosa. Jozamy no pudo quedarse la primera vez y la segunda ni siquiera se hizo contacto por estar Tania aquí. Se refiere a Iván con bastante desprecio; no sé qué habrá en el fondo de todo. Se recibe la rendición de cuentas de Loyola hasta el 9 de febrero (1500 dólares). Se reciben dos informes de Iván; uno sin interés, con fotos, sobre un colegio militar; otro informando de algunos puntos, sin mayor importancia tampoco. Lo fundamental es que no se puede descifrar la escritura (D XIII). Se recibe informe de Antonio (D XII) donde trata de justificar su actitud. Se escucha un informe radial en que se anuncia un muerto y se desmiente luego, lo que indica que fue verdad lo del Loro.

* Se informa de la separación de la dirección de la juventud

9

8) General Ovando Candia *(with newspaper)* talking with officers of the Eighth Division after Guevara's death. 9) A page from Che's diary.

10

10) The CIA agent, Gonzáles.

11) The laundry at Valle Grande which was used as a morgue. 12) Bodies of guerrillas killed at Vado del Yeso.

12

13

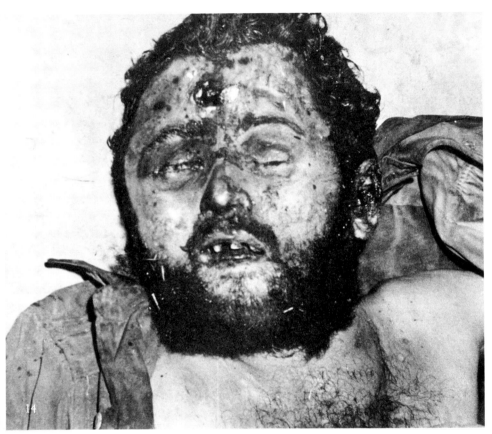

13) Captured guerrilla arms found in caves near Vado del Yeso. 14) Chino's body.

15) Che in death.

16) (*l. to r.*) Régis Debray's father, Debray, and Gustavo A. Sánchez Salazar. 17) Debray in prisoner's uniform.

18) Sketches of guerrillas made by Ciro Roberto Bustos

Pombo   Urbano   Ricardo

Alejandro   Miguel   Rolando

Marcos   Pacho   Benigno

Moro

Médico

Chino

Pedro

Ñato

Camba

Andrés

Isaac Rutman

Inti

Luís   Ramón

Cuban. I brought out into the open a tendency to be scornful of the Cubans that I had observed in the vanguard and that I had noticed yesterday when Camba showed that he trusted the Cubans less and less, because of an incident with Ricardo. I made a new appeal for integration as the only possibility of developing our army, and said that its firepower and morale were improving, but that its numbers were not increasing; on the contrary, the number has diminished in the last few days.

"After storing all the booty in a cave that had been put in good shape by Ñato, we went out at 14:00 hours, but slowly. So slowly that we made almost no progress, having to sleep in a little watering place when the march had only just begun.

"The announced number of army dead is eleven; it appears that they found another one or that one of the wounded died. I started a little course on Debray's book."

Guevara resolved to get Bustos and Debray out first through Muyupampa, sixty-three miles south of Ñancahuazú. The place selected was within a sector that had already been officially declared a military zone and was very carefully watched by civilian authorities, the police, and military units, all dependent on the command of the Fourth Division. Guevara thought that Bustos and Debray, as journalists, would have enough proof of their status to be allowed to pass through the region. As can be seen by subsequent events, this decision was wrong, the fruit of an unrealistic estimate of the situation, explicable only because of the guerrillas' lack of information from the outside. As a consequence of this decision, Bustos and Debray were practically handed over to the government forces. (Let it be said parenthetically that in a confidential meeting in Cochabamba in March, 1967, the then Minister of National Defense, General Hugo Suárez Guzmán, announced that there was a French writer with the guerrillas. Moreover, in circles close to the intelligence services there was a certainty that "where the Frenchman was, there Che Guevara was sure to be," a conviction that to some sources confirms the efficient cooperation offered by the CIA.)

Guevara had in mind for the evacuation of Tania and Chino a plan for a safer route, one which was to be put into execution in the days immediately following. (Chino—who suffered from progressive myopia—had been given the task of making contact with the revolutionary organization of Peru, beginning in that country another guerrilla attack which was to be synchronized with the one which was to take place in Bolivia in October, 1967; but this occurred too soon for the reasons already discussed. Tania, in turn, was the prime agent for urban contacts in Bolivia, and at this time was suffering from an increasingly severe nervous depression and a sore leg.) The plan to get the two of them out was drawn up with great care, in the conviction that if either of them fell into the hands of the government forces there would be grave repercussions for the guerrilla movement. Apparently the itinerary they prepared was by way of Monteagudo-Padilla-Sucre, toward the northeast, a route that Tania had followed fairly often. The number of precautions taken turned out in the end to work to their disadvantage. Neither now nor at any other time could Tania and Chino abandon their companions, and they were forced to share their bad fortune until they died in the last encounters.

The three principal groups—the vanguard, the center, and the rear guard—numbering only thirty-nine men because of the many desertions, moved out at two o'clock on the twelfth. Che's diary reads as follows:

"A monotonous day. Some things were brought from the refuge for the sick, which gives us food for five days. Someone went to get cans of milk from the upper cave, and it was discovered that twenty-three cans were inexplicably missing, since Moro left forty-eight and no one seems to have had the time necessary to take them out. Milk is one of the factors making for vice. A mortar and the machine gun were taken out of the special cave in order to reinforce the position until Joaquín comes.

"It is not clear how to carry out the operation but it seems best to me to get everybody out and operate a little around the area of Muyupampa and then retreat north. If it is possible Danton and Carlos will still head for Sucre-Cochabamba, depending on circumstances.

"Communiqué No. 2 for the Bolivian people is being written and Report No. 4 for Manila, which the Frenchman is to take with him."

On the sixteenth they went back to the little hamlet of Ipitá, buying food in the shops there. On the seventeenth, Che made a decision that was to have an adverse effect on the course of the fight: he ordered the rear guard, under Joaquín, to stop and wait for his return in Iquira, where they had camped and spent the previous night. This was done because there were many men in poor physical shape due to illness and lack of food. Braulio, Marcos, Pedro, Wálter, Ernesto, Polo, Víctor, and those expelled by Che formed part of this group. The latter—Pepe, Eusebio, Chingolo, and Paco,[1] all Bolivians—were only waiting for a chance to leave the guerrilla sector; all their arms had been taken away from them, and they were made to do the most disagreeable chores around the camp. For reasons of security and because Tania was ailing, he ordered her, Alejandro, Moisés, Serapio, and the doctor, El Negro, who belonged to the center group, to stay with the rear guard. Seventeen guerrillas in all remained behind. When put into effect, the plan failed, and from this point on Joaquín's section was never again to be in contact with the main body of guerrillas to the day it was wiped out in Vado del Yeso, August 31. On this point Camba declared:

> The defeat was more or less caused by errors on the part of Che himself. In the first place, he [made a mistake by] separating Joaquín from our group for reasons that couldn't be helped (sicknesses) and in order to get Debray and Bustos out of the guerrilla sector as soon as possible; he was hurrying because Debray insisted on leaving quickly. Then Che decided that Joaquín should stay with some of those who were sick, among them Tania, establishing a position for him to stay at, with eighteen men, so as to be able to find them on his return; but things did not turn out that way in practice. When we returned we couldn't go back to that same place, and so Joaquín was abandoned to his fate; we didn't meet up with them again until they fell at Vado del Yeso.

The center group, with Che in command, and the vanguard, headed by Miguel, continued on toward Muyupampa, using the highway that leads to El Mesón as the axis of their march. At 5 p.m. or thereabouts, on April 19, they surprised a person being guided by two native children down the steep hillsides of the Incahuasi from

---

[1] Paco was deceived by Moisés Guevara when he signed up to join the guerrillas; therefore he was resentful and unwilling to work. But he was loyal to his companions in the cause up to the time he fell prisoner on August 30.

the nearby hamlet of Yacumbay. The protagonist[2] of this encounter says:

". . . a figure suddenly stepped out of a maize field. At first it looked like a woman in an army uniform carrying an M-1 carbine. But it was a man. He took the boys' horse by the bridle and in a steady, serious tone without any trace of violence said:

" 'You are under arrest.'

" 'No,' one of the boys replied nervously.

" 'Yes, you are under arrest,' the man insisted in the same tone of voice.

" 'No,' the boy repeated, now smiling and without any sign of fear.

"The man turned toward me, looking like someone who had been interrupted in his work. He was slim and short with a mop of hair that fell to his shoulders and a policeman's cap like the ones worn by Bolivian soldiers. He had little hair on his face but had a wispy moustache and a small, pointed beard. Behind him I soon saw another man heading toward me. He was small but huskier and had a thick, black beard. His big grin was reassuring but it could have been due as much to a sense of his own ridiculous looks as to cordiality. He was an Oriental, a Chinese or Japanese. He walked up calmly without fingering his submachine gun. Smiling, I said:

" 'Hello, gentlemen. I have spent a good deal of time trying to find you!'

" 'Hello,' the Oriental replied amiably, continuing to smile and exhibiting a perfect set of white teeth through his black beard. His uniform, which matched his companion's camouflage suit for dirtiness, was the olive green of Bolivian army rookies. He, too, wore a policeman's cap, plus a pair of thick, black-framed spectacles.

"He saw me getting ready to use my camera and stopped me.

" 'Please, no pictures,' he said. 'Come with us.'

"He spoke perfect Spanish with a Bolivian accent. His tone was both pleasant and firm. He motioned to a road leading into a wood between the high, dried stalks.

"The other guerrilla took the boys' horse by the bridle. They

---

[2] George Andrew Roth, "I Was Arrested With Debray," *Evergreen Review*, No. 51 (February, 1968), p. 45 ff.

entered the wood and then stopped. More armed men appeared. I caught up with the boys, who were laughing as though they had played a good trick, and saw a man who couldn't have been more than twenty-five coming toward me. He, too, was in a camouflage suit with an automatic rifle hung from his shoulder. He spoke to me politely.

" 'Please hand me your cameras and get off your horse.'

"I obeyed and took my horse by the bridle as we went through a fence of tree trunks. He motioned me to tie up my horse and indicated a path leading to a little clearing.

" 'Wait there,' he said. 'The chief is going to come and speak to you.' "

This strange visitor was the Anglo-Chilean journalist-photographer George Andrew Roth, and his captor the guerrilla, Luís, a graduate engineer of the Universidad Mayor y Autónoma Tomás Frías, of Potosí. They had a long talk together about the guerrillas, and the journalist was invited to have a meal with them. Roth continues:

"Just as I finished, I saw striding toward me a big pale man of thirty or thirty-five with a bearded angular face that made him look something like Abraham Lincoln.

" 'I'm the commander of this guerrilla outfit,' he said. 'I have a few questions to ask you. Please sit down here.' (He motioned to some big rocks about six feet from Luís.)"

At the request of his captors Roth handed over his personal documents, his notebook, his cameras and film, and other belongings. They proceeded to check his identification and to submit him to a long interrogation. He remained in a kind of captivity for something less than twelve hours. They seemed never to trust him completely. They were decidedly reticent with him because on coming into contact with the guerrilla patrol he immediately asked for Che, whose presence he had heard of from an army source and perhaps from friends in the Peace Corps. Guevara writes of Roth in his diary: "The Englishman is a bona fide journalist (unless he's from the FBI)." Nonetheless, they were very cordial toward him, ate with him, and had lively conversations with him. Besides those mentioned, he made the acquaintance of several other Bolivians and foreigners, who were introduced to him by their *noms de guerre*; he had an interesting exchange of ideas with Julio, a doctor from Beni, and Loco, who has not been identified. Roth said that this latter, like all the men, had an "unhealthily pale face" and "looked like a man subjected to exhausting physical trials." He also saw the peasant Fernando, a guide and an army informant whom he had met some days before in the hotel at Lagunillas, mingling with the guerrillas, but the two of them pretended not to know each other. Some days later this same peasant sold Che a horse.

Despite the unremitting cold, Roth slept for a time and was waked with the news that he was to leave the zone along with some other persons. He continues:

" 'These men are journalists like you. I present Mr. Frutos [*sic*] and Mr. Debray.'

"We shook hands."

The three of them were then told that they would be left on their own in Muyupampa, and from there could make their way to Sucre. Roth's documents, his notebook, and all the belongings that had been taken from him were returned to him, though the guerrillas asked him to leave them a few rolls of film. In his notebook the guerrillas put down a few notes in the guise of an "interview"; Roth thought he had a scoop, dictated by Che himself.

The three of them were also each given copies of Communiqués Nos. 1 and 2 of the Army of National Liberation of Bolivia.

While all this was happening to Roth, more important events were taking place elsewhere. Muyupampa had been recently reinforced by military units and personnel from the Department of Criminal Investigation, and for a month civilian police had been going in and out of the jurisdictions of Camiri, Boyuibe, Monteagudo, Lagunillas, and Muyupampa. At nightfall on the nineteenth peasants warned the authorities of the presence of guerrillas a mile or so from town. The security forces of the DIC consisted at that time of ten men, among them the regional head of the division, Guido Benavídez, and Lieutenant Néstor Ruíz of the army. Once the peasants' report came to their attention, each of them headed a group of five men and went out to find the insurgents. Before they had gone even a half mile down the road Benavídez's group was taken prisoner; the men in the group were taken into the brush, disarmed, interrogated, and finally set free about 6:30 on the morning of April 20.[3]

The other group of guerrillas, meanwhile, took Roth, Bustos, and Debray down close to the road about three miles from Muyu-pampa, a spot they reached around three in the morning on the twentieth.

"Good-by, get out the way that seems best to you; we must leave," was the guerrillas' laconic farewell.

In the intense cold that gripped them, especially Roth, who had only light clothing, they did as best they could to pass the first hours of this day that was to turn out to be so unfortunate for them. As the first rays of sunshine fell on them, they took the road that led them to Muyupampa. At 8:30 they appeared, unarmed, in the narrow streets of this town whose 1500 inhabitants live in adobe huts, where they were immediately arrested by soldiers and agents of the DIC, among them Benavídez. This was a real event in the life of the re-mote, godforsaken town, and the break in the routine caused a great to-do.

The three men were immediately taken to the City Hall, and their documents, credentials, money, notebooks, and all their personal effects taken away from them. They were then submitted to a routine preliminary investigation.

Among Bustos' effects the authorities found the 2000 Bolivian pesos and the 2000 U.S. dollars that Guevara had given him, and confiscated them. They also confiscated Debray's billfold with $170 in tens and twenties, Bolivian pesos, and French and Swiss francs. In his confession Bustos declared that Guevara had given the same amount in Bolivian pesos to Debray as he had to him. Debray roundly denied before the military court that he had received any

---

[3] The account of this episode given later by Guido Benavídez has a certain tropical sensationalism about it. In one place he says: "For more security they made us walk twelve miles back into the mountains." And on relating their "escape" from the place to which the guerrillas brought them, he says that it took them "an hour and fifty-five minutes to get to Muyupampa." (*El Diario*, November 23, 1967.) Running twelve miles through mountain brush in an hour and fifty-five minutes would break every Olympic record.

money from any of the guerrillas or that he had brought any money in to them from the outside, as persistent rumor later had it. In any case, neither during the trial nor at any other time were these sums of money put in evidence. Nor was there any mention of what had happened to the money.

A new chapter in the lives of the three men opens here. For Roth it lasted only two and a half months, for he was set free July 8, 1967; but in the case of Bustos and Debray, no end is in sight, since they still have thirty-year sentences to serve.

At the end of March, 1967, George Andrew Roth, an Anglo-Chilean freelancer who was just completing an assignment in Santiago, Chile, for the London *Daily Express*, had planned to go to London via Buenos Aires, Lisbon, and Zurich. It was at about this time that the first news of a guerrilla *foco* in Bolivia began to circulate. In Chile, as in other countries, the first information was vague and contradictory. But Roth smelled a story and on March 30, he went to Buenos Aires, where he exchanged ideas on the subject with friends who were newspapermen and others who belonged to the Peace Corps. His suspicions that there was a story to be gotten grew, and he decided to go to Bolivia. To finance his trip he agreed to send material back to his colleague Moisés García, of *Time-Life*. He made the trip on a regular flight of the Lloyd Aéreo Boliviano and on April 5, landed at Santa Cruz de la Sierra, where he spent the night. The next day he arrived at Camiri, the nerve center of the army's campaign against the guerrillas. He presented himself to the military authorities, put his documents in order, and began a painstaking trip through the whole so-called Red Triangle, including farm areas, hamlets, and small towns: towns such as Lagunillas, Gutiérrez, Tararenda, Pirirenda, Abapó, Carahuatarenda, El Espino, etc. He accompanied the military patrols as they moved about, suffered the same privations they did, endured the relentless cold at night, drank "polluted water with insects buzzing in it," and ate "the sickening C-rations provided by the Americans." But his principal desire was not fulfilled, for no guerrillas appeared anywhere. There were only rumors that they were in such and such a town buying food and medicine and lecturing the population. On April 10, accompanying troops that were marching in the rear guard of Major Sánchez's troops, he entered the now-famous ravine of the Ñancahuazú River, where he admired the stony grandeur of its steep cliffs. He arrived at the Calamine House and entered the different camps abandoned by the guerrillas. Turning over ashes, searching through nooks and crannies and along the paths, he found, among other things, scattered, scorched papers, part of the diary of the Cuban, Braulio, and a piece of paper with an order for the guerrilla Rubio. He also came across photographs of some of the first wounded in the action at Iripití. Once daylight was gone, he returned to Camiri, passing through Lagunillas, and then headed for La Paz. In the airport at Cochabamba, one of the authors of this book, who is also regional editor of *El Diario* in that city, interviewed him and signed a contract for some of his photographs. At that time Roth gave two addresses in La Paz, one of which was the Peace Corps. On the following day, April 13, this material, which was a scoop, was published on the first page of the oldest Bolivian newspaper. All this work on the story, in spite of its value, still did not satisfy Roth's ambition to write an authentic story on the rebels. This was why he returned to Camiri immediately—on April 17—to try to do a story on the guerrillas, if possible within the guerrilla area. That same day he went to Lagunillas along with some foreign photographers and journalists. On the recommendation of people in the area, he hired the same guide who had previously brought the army information. He rented a mule and got ready to leave, but the military authorities prevented him from going any farther than the territory under their control. Despite this, he managed during the night to slip through the military's guard and started out with his guide and another person. The trip was painful, but after stumbling about all night, on the following day they arrived at a peasant shack whose occupants sold him something to eat. When he was ready to go on at midday, his guides would not go with him and told him to go on with two young native boys as guides. This was on April 19. The rest of the story, up to Roth's arrest in Muyupampa, has already been told. Thus the restless and painstaking journalist only partially accomplished his objective, and wasn't even able to see Che. His scoop remained in the hands of the military authorities, perhaps lost forever among the many other documents left on dusty office shelves or sold to some intelligence organization.

12

The Statements of Bustos and Debray

Differences in the treatment of Bustos, Roth, and Debray were noticeable from the moment that the three suspicious-looking foreigners were arrested. There seemed to be a preconceived plan to treat Debray with particular acrimony and violence, and efficient members of the FBI and the CIA appeared to have had a hand in this plan. Bustos and Roth continued to be held in Muyupampa, while Debray was transferred the very afternoon of his arrest to the little village of Choreti, where the airport nearest Camiri was located. The army used a helicopter rented from the Bolivian Fiscal Petroleum Deposits and piloted by Captain Pinto. At three o'clock the helicopter landed directly in the patio of the military barracks under extraordinary security measures. It was met by Major Rubén Sánchez Valdivia, who did not know the identity of the passenger.[1]

This transfer operation seemed to have been intended to foil any attempt to rescue the prisoner if he had been transferred overland; we have evidence that the guerrillas knew immediately what had happened to their ex-companions. Bustos and Roth were taken overland to Choreti under the watchful eye of Lieutenant Néstor Ruíz, according to the latter.

---

[1] The young Frenchman later told Sánchez that he had heard about him from the guerrillas after the events of April 10, when Sánchez had fallen prisoner.

Perhaps using this procedure in Debray's case can be understood in the light of the Bolivians' knowledge of his trips to Cuba and Bolivia, his travels throughout Latin America, his intellectual background, and his literary, political, and sociological writings. In "A Message to My Friends," first published months later by the prestigious Parisian weekly *Le Nouvel Observateur* and published in English in February, 1968, in *Evergreen Review,* Debray wrote:

> They [the men from the CIA] had a complete file on me, a *curriculum vitae,* a record of where I had been and what I had done over the preceding two years, who my friends were, etc. As for the guerrilla movement itself, they knew practically all there was to know. They already had three prisoners in their hands, two of whom were deserters, and a number of documents left behind in an abandoned guerrilla camp (the diary of a guerrilla); by the time three weeks were up they had even shown me two photographs of Che.

And Madame Debray told Lee Hall, an American journalist: "In less than forty-eight hours following the arrest of my son, President Barrientos already had a dossier on him from the CIA on his desk."

The initial statements made by Debray and Bustos show their different reactions to being questioned and explain the different treatment they received. The statements are extremely important in that they belie the often reiterated but false statements that Debray was the one who betrayed the fact that Che was the leader of the guerrillas.

Extracts from these interrogations—made from copies of transcripts of the tapes—read as follows:

THE INTERROGATION OF RÉGIS DEBRAY

April 20:

Colonel Eladio Sánchez, then Chief of Staff of the Fourth Division, and Colonel Alberto Libera directed the interrogation. Neither of them knew who Debray was or what he had been doing with the guerrillas. The questions concerned generalities: the number of combatants, the quality and quantity of their armament, the names of their leaders, the presence of Che Guevara, etc. Since Debray's replies were evasive, Libera began to rough him up, trying to get satisfactory information out of him. In the face of this, Debray admitted that he "was sent here by Maspero to write an article on a political meeting. It was a very important article. I didn't interview Che; I don't know him. One of the guerrillas told us that Che would arrive in three days, but we didn't see him; we waited, but nothing happened. As the interview with him didn't come off, we decided to leave the zone."

April 21:

Colonel Federico Arama of the armed forces and Major Roberto Toto Quintanilla of the intelligence service of the Guardia Nacional de Seguridad Pública (National Guard for Public Security) and a confidant of the Minister of the Interior arrived, accompanied by "Doctor" Eduardo Gonzáles of the CIA, a Puerto Rican or Cuban exile, who was to have control of many future events. At about ten o'clock Debray was again interrogated. His face and body bore the marks of the beating he had received at the hands of soldiers of the Fourth Division. The CIA agent informed him that Fructuoso had confessed that Che Guevara had been in Ñancahuazú and asked him to confirm the Argentinian's story. The exchange went as follows:

DEBRAY: I don't believe Señor Fructuoso has said that Che Guevara is with the guerrillas. We were together and he knows perfectly well that that isn't true. I don't believe that he said that.

CIA: Do you know Coco and Inti Peredo?

DEBRAY: I don't know any Coco or Inti Peredo.

CIA: Do you know Tania?

DEBRAY: I have no idea who Tania is. I once met an Emma Laura Gutiérrez. But I don't know whether they call her Tania.

CIA: Señor Debray: we're asking you to help us so we can help you. You won't get anywhere with all this fooling around that you're doing, I promise you.

DEBRAY: I don't know anything. (*He has a slight smile on his face.*)

CIA: Will you permit me to tape your statement, Señor Debray?

DEBRAY: Well, if I say no, it'll be yes; I prefer to say yes because I know that that's the way it's going to be . . .

The above conversation was already being secretly taped; the recording machine was now placed in front of the prisoner. The interrogation continued:

CIA: We would like you to begin to tell us everything you know. We would like you to tell us: where did you write *Revolution in the Revolution?*

DEBRAY: Well, you know where I was before. I was in Cuba for six months as a professor of philosophy at the University. I wrote *Revolution in the Revolution?* as an essay, and I don't think it's a guerrilla manual at all, because there are much better ones than that.

At this point the interrogation was suspended. During the night, Debray was again beaten. Libera fractured his right hand when he went to punch Debray in the head and the blow instead landed on the headboard of Debray's bed.

April 22:

Another interrogation in front of the same people.

CIA: We don't want to hurt you, Debray, but we want to tell you that Señor Fructuoso has declared that you were the only one who talked to Che Guevara and that they isolated him [Bustos]. We want to ask you to collaborate with us so you can go free soon.

DEBRAY: I already told you that I don't believe that Señor Fructuoso said that he was with Che. Fructuoso and I were together, and he knows, as I do, that we didn't get to meet Che, and that's why we came out of the mountains.

The representative of the Ministry of the Interior took over:

QUINTANILLA (*handing Debray a map*): We want you to show us where the paths from the central guerrilla camp to the Calamine House are.

DEBRAY: It's quite true that I went along some paths. But I don't know where it was I went. I was following a guerrilla and looking at the ground so I wouldn't fall. I don't know if they have secret paths. I didn't go out with the guerrillas.

QUINTANILLA: You think we're stupid. What's happening is that you think you're a smartass and we'll have to treat you as one. If you don't tell where the paths are you'll see what'll happen.

DEBRAY: I've already said that I don't know where the paths are. I've already told you everything I learned in Ñancahuazú. I don't know anything. I'm a journalist; I came for an interview I never got. In order not to waste time waiting for nothing we left the zone. I don't know anything.

CIA: How many times did you speak with Che Guevara?

DEBRAY: I don't know Señor Guevara. I didn't speak with Che.

In view of the negative results, the interrogation was suspended.

THE INTERROGATION OF BUSTOS

April 21:

Gonzáles (CIA), Arana (armed forces), Quintanilla (National Guard for Public Security), and others interrogated Bustos. At this point the investigators did not know that Carlos Alberto Fructuoso, as he was identified on his forged passport, was really Ciro Roberto Bustos. He was uncooperative and at first talked less than Debray. This conduct led journalist Lee Hall to write: "An Argentinian Communist, bungling, half-defiant, Bustos seems to typify the irresponsible journalist-guerrilla."

The Argentinian painter said that he had been invited to visit the zone, but that he knew absolutely nothing about the guerrillas. He said he was a civil engineer doing studies for a company.

April 22:

The interrogation began:

CIA: Señor Fructuoso: Señor Debray has confessed that you were with Che Guevara and that you were the only one to talk with him. You can hear this tape-recorded information in a few minutes. We want to see how sincere you are about collaborating with us.

FRUCTUOSO: I don't know Che Guevara. If Debray has told you he saw Che, it's probably because he did see him. We were together, and I don't believe what he says is true.

CIA: Do you know Coco Peredo?

FRUCTUOSO: I don't know any Peredos, although I heard the men in the forest talking about them. I don't know who they are or what they do.

CIA: We should like you to think seriously about your family. We're ready to help you. We're going to let you think about them until tomorrow. We want to tell you that the security of your wife and daughters is in good hands. Good-by, Fructuoso.

FRUCTUOSO: Good-by. (*His face has a rather desperate look on it and tears betray him.*)

April 23:

Eight o'clock. They bring him various books, packages of cigarettes, biscuits, jam, and other presents.

CIA: Señor Fructuoso: we believe you've thought over what we said yesterday. You have a chance to save your family and yourself. We can bring your family to La Paz to live with you, but we need your collaboration. All we want is the truth. You know, don't you, Señor Fructuoso, that you can't go back to Argentina without gravely risking your security. Can you collaborate with us?

FRUCTUOSO: Well, I'll collaborate with you if you'll tell me what you want from me.

CIA: When we make a promise we keep it. You can trust us, Señor Fructuoso. We're asking you to tell us everything you know.

FRUCTUOSO: First I want to tell you that I came because I'm poor and wanted to earn money. I came to interview Che Guevara, who goes by the name of Ramón.

CIA: Did you meet Tania?

FRUCTUOSO: Yes, I did. I met Tania. She's in the camp.

CIA: Tell us who sent you and when you came to Bolivia.

FRUCTUOSO: Laura Gutiérrez, now known as Tania, contacted Isaac Rutman in Argentina and he's the one who sent me. Rutman attended the meeting of the Tricontinental and I think that that's where the guerrilla movement started.

CIA: What did Che Guevara tell you?

FRUCTUOSO: Well, I was never really alone with Che. Debray was the one who talked to him the most. I didn't talk to him very much because they didn't trust me.

CIA: How many guerrillas are there and who are they?

FRUCTUOSO: I knew the guerrillas by their *noms de guerre*. I didn't learn very much on that score. It's true that Coco Peredo, his brother Inti, and others are there. Coco is the one who has the most authority. I remember their faces perfectly but I can't remember their names.

CIA: Let's talk about Che.

FRUCTUOSO: I saw Ramón in the central camp once. He was always moving around, reconnoitering the land, tracing paths, directing operations; in short, making sure that they wouldn't be taken by surprise.

QUINTANILLA: You're talking to us about paths; we have maps of the region here. Would you mind showing us which paths were the last ones made?

Fructuoso points on the map to a path that the army doesn't know about. He marks it on the map. Later reconnaissance missions found Bustos' tracings on the map correct and of unquestionable value.

FRUCTUOSO: In order to avoid being surprised, they recently opened two paths, one to go from the Calamine House to the central camp without using the ravine, and another from Iripití to the Bear Camp. From Iripití there's a ravine to the same camp, so as to go to the Yuqui.

CIA: Could you write us a report on what you're telling us?

FRUCTUOSO: Of course. But I want to wind the whole thing up by telling you that there's a cache of arms near a lagoon in the central camp. I can't show you the place exactly on the map, but if I were there I could show you the cache.

CIA: That interests us; write everything you remember down and also set everything you've told us down on paper. This is very valuable to us.

FRUCTUOSO: I'll write everything, and not only that; I'll try to sketch from memory the faces of some of the guerrillas I remember.

CIA: Will you start with Ramón?

FRUCTUOSO: Very well. (*He asks for paper and pencil and for the first time sketches Che Guevara, his head partly shaved and smoking a pipe.*)[2]

Five days later, General David Lafuente arrived in Camiri with Bustos' sketches in order to identify the guerrillas. Photostats were made and distributed to various unit commanders and the personnel of the Department of Criminal Investigation.

The three prisoners were treated very harshly. Contrary to clear and express constitutional provisions, they remained incommunicado for two months, without any writ of mandamus from the proper authorities. The psychological pressure and corporal punishment were unexpected. Bustos was the first to have them stopped because of his willingness to collaborate with the investigators.

---

[2] See Appendix III for Bustos' descriptions of the guerrillas.

Both Roth and Debray report being told that the world believed that they had already been shot. Roth recalled the incident as follows:

> The next day other officers showed me cuttings from Bolivian newspapers announcing that we had all been shot.
>
> "You see," they told me, "we can do whatever we want with you. For the whole world, you are dead. We can kill you within the next hour, or let you rot in prison. But don't worry, for you it's different. You will soon get out. In a year, two, three years . . . who can say?"[3]

Lee Hall reports that Debray said to him: "At the beginning I thought that the army would shoot me. The interrogators showed me a newspaper in which I was officially said to be dead. With a smile they said to me: 'Who would it matter to if we should confirm the news?' "

There are also various reports of the physical torture the men suffered. Roth writes that "[Debray and Bustos] suffered physical torture stoically. We were badly beaten for two weeks. After the first beating, Régis was unconscious for two days. They also tortured us morally and psychologically all the time. The beatings didn't stop for a single day."[4]

Debray was undoubtedly the one who was beaten the most frequently. Lee Hall wrote of an interview he had with Debray several months later:

"Colonel Rocha left us alone for a moment. Debray leaned over to me and said in a low voice, 'They tortured me the first three days.' The Bolivian authorities confess that the three men were treated roughly before they were identified."[5]

Lee Hall also noted that Debray "had a scar that was still inflamed on his prominent forehead." Journalists who were at the trial in Camiri months later also said that he still had scars on his face. There are soldiers who say that he was in a coma for more than seventy-two hours after the last interrogation.

At a certain point a Bolivian officer, out of sympathy for Debray's suffering, wrapped him in a military cloak and took him

---

[3] George Andrew Roth, *op. cit.*, p. 92.

[4] *Punto Final* (Santiago de Chile, No. 37: Septiembre, 1967).

[5] *Life en Español* (September 11, 1967).

from the barracks to the Camiri infirmary. On the other hand, in reply to certain statements by General Barrientos reported in the press, Debray told the authors:

> But in the end he [Barrientos] says that three officers saved my life when they wanted to lynch me, among them Major Sánchez. I have always recognized this and said that I owed Major Sánchez a debt of honor. I am very grateful to him. But I must say that I never saw any civilians who wanted to beat me up when I was in Choreti. I was beaten up, many times and very badly; but it was officers and noncommissioned officers who did it, never civilians. They didn't even try to. I must say that there are honorable men in the Bolivian army who acted courageously and most honorably; I can't hide that fact.

There is also a great deal of evidence proving that agents of the FBI and the CIA intervened from the very beginning. "In another aspect of the case, Debray proved to be less hesitant. He believes firmly that his prolonged imprisonment is due to pressure on the Bolivian government by the CIA. 'That's true, I'm sure of it,' [he told Lee Hall]. "When I asked him how he could be so sure, he answered: 'From the sort of questions the American interrogators asked me.' "[6]

This view was confirmed by Colonel Reque Terán in an interview he granted this same journalist: "Colonel Luís Reque Terán, [now] commander of the Fourth Division, whose jurisdiction Debray is under, says that some FBI agents recently interrogated Debray. Colonel Reque Terán refused to reveal what questions the FBI agents had asked him, but supposedly they were about Guevara."

In Debray's "Message" published in *Evergreen Review*, we read:

> Why two months of solitary confinement? In order to allow the CIA (in the guise of Puerto Ricans, Cuban exiles, or Panamanians, all of whom speak English as well as Spanish and are careful not to reveal their identity or their nationality) the time to carry out its mission. By its arrival at Choreti the third day after my arrest, the CIA may well have saved my life! I was then in very bad shape, at the end of my rope, and the excitement of the officers who were venting their anger on me, with no precise goal in mind, had reached

---

[6] *Ibid.*

its peak, since they were amusing themselves at that point by shooting at me, firing between my legs and as close to my head as possible.

The gentleman from the CIA called a halt to such shenanigans, summoned a doctor, and at first treated me with utmost courtesy . . . .[7]

It should be emphasized that the unusual use of physical violence for the most part did not come from, nor was it approved by, the great majority of officers of the Bolivian army. The few noncommissioned officers and officers who did participate were undoubtedly led to do so by too rigid a sense of duty or because of a fiery patriotism, and acted without the knowledge of high officials in the government and the army.

As we have noted, the authorities made no announcement of any kind about the arrests of Bustos, Debray, and Roth. The press kept running up against the most rigorous secrecy in their attempts to secure information on the three men. There was no censorship, but neither was there free access to original sources of information. In violation of clear constitutional provisions, a curtain of silence fell over the men for two months, during which time they were worn out by the travels forced upon them as they were moved from one place to another in the *departamento* of Santa Cruz. They were first handcuffed and flown to the Manchego regiment barracks in Montero, north of Santa Cruz. After that they were transferred overland, usually at night, and the orders to get ready to travel were always peremptory, as if to purposely exacerbate the prisoners. In the beginning, they were kept under strict and continuous guard. Debray was permanently handcuffed and even spent his nights handcuffed to his cot. They were isolated from the world and seldom even saw each other. The only people they could talk to were the zealous and uncommunicative guards. At certain moments, as the guards led them out to the lavatory, they exchanged a few words or hurried monosyllables with each other in English or French. They had to learn to discipline their physiological needs, and Roth remembers that the floor of his cell became, out of necessity, a sewer.

A sergeant-medical aide took care of them, especially Bustos, who suffered from chronic asthma and was spitting blood. Debray was

---

[7] *Evergreen Review*, No. 51 (February, 1968), p. 49 ff.

not as lucky, although he could scarcely walk because of infected feet and legs.

Roth complained about the food, but, as he himself says, they ate the same food as the troops. And they could not have had first-class attention under the circumstances: in the field the army has neither the obligation nor the ability to give its prisoners better attention than its own men. In the Manchego barracks, Roth went on a hunger strike for four days. A humanitarian gesture on the part of the wife of the captain in charge of the barracks put an end to his strike. As he told it:

> Toward the middle of the fifth day, a Sunday, the door opened and two little girls came in followed by a boy of three. They were the Captain's children and they brought me hot coffee in a gleaming white bowl and a spotless plate holding a lovely slice of French bread (real bread!) covered with peach jam . . . I shut the door with my foot so they couldn't see the tears in my eyes while I ate and drank. Thus ended my hunger strike.[8]

After another transfer, this time to a farm owned by the army, the prisoners' situation changed for the better. Their food improved and they were permitted to talk to each other, although they were still closely guarded. They entered into long discussions about movies, art, literature, and philosophy. They exchanged confidences, told why they had come to Bolivia, and shared memories of their families. They faced the winter cold of the *surazo* during the long days and nights by singing sentimental tropical love songs; Bustos, a sensitive extrovert, spoke of his little girls; Debray, the cold and theoretical reasoner, gave himself away by asking them to sing "Guantanamera," which brought back memories of his fiancée Elizabeth Burgos; and Roth, temperamental and explosive, worked off his hostilities.

During this period Bustos was submitted to various interrogations by men sent specially by the Argentinian military intelligence. The details of these confrontations are still unknown.

The CIA agents also made Debray listen to the taped confession of wounded guerrilla Jorge Vásquez Viaña, which had been secretly recorded in the hospital in Camiri. Debray had two reactions to this: First, he decided to confirm the facts about the guerrillas

---

[8] George Andrew Roth, *op. cit.*, p. 92.

that the authorities had obtained from Vásquez; and second, knowing nothing of what had happened after April 20, he suspected that Vásquez had deserted. He did not find out until later that this suspicion had no basis in fact.

At certain times, General Ovando had secret interviews with Debray. The press was not informed of these meetings or of what was discussed. Apparently Ovando tried to induce Debray to tell the armed forces everything he knew about the guerrilla movement and its connections inside and outside the country in exchange for better treatment and a possible reduction in his sentence. As Dr. Roger Lallemand told us later, the General tried to convince Debray that his companion Bustos had agreed to this bargain. But Debray did not believe him, and Ovando's wishes were unfulfilled.

During this time the national press was insisting on some explanation of what had happened to the journalists. Their questions were echoed by the foreign press. Eminent political pundits, journalists, and political, governmental, and cultural organizations all over the world began to be concerned about the prisoners—especially about Debray, who was better known because of his intellectual background —and these sources asked for an impartial tribunal to pass judgment. Pope Paul VI, indirectly, and Charles de Gaulle, in a personal letter to President Barrientos, expressed their concern about Debray.

The international pressure was so forceful that the government was obliged to show its hand. In the face of contradictory rumors that were circulating about the fate of the three journalists, it was decided to give an American priest, Monsignor Andrés Kennedy, the secretary of the Bolivian Conference of Bishops and a chaplain in the armed forces, the secret mission of seeing the prisoners and of giving the world news of their whereabouts and condition. The priest went to the El Torno farm, landing in a helicopter near the farmhouse. This was the prisoners' first contact with the outside world since their arrest.

On June 21, General Ovando Candia informed the press that Monsignor Kennedy had talked with Régis Debray, and added that his whereabouts were still a "military secret." On the twenty-third, Monsignor Kennedy, in a statement to the press, said that he had interviewed the prisoners, and stated that they were in good health and had not been mistreated. He hinted that they were upset at not knowing what was to happen to them. They had told him that they had been there for more than two months without trial and without even having been formally charged, and added that they were ready to undergo trial as soon as possible. The prisoners later said that this government observer was in a great hurry to return to Santa Cruz. The separate interviews lasted barely ten minutes. Monsignor Kennedy had brought them some old magazines, duly excised and passed by the censor. As he said good-by to the priest, Debray gave him a short message for his mother, who was in La Paz. Debray's mother never received this little note, and she told the authorities that Kennedy had not given it to her and had apologized for losing it.[10]

---

[10] It has never been explained why the government sent Monsignor Kennedy on this errand, since he was an American citizen. It is ironic that one of the most serious charges against the guerrillas and the prisoners was their status as foreigners meddling in the internal affairs of the country. Kennedy's mission, however noble it may have been, was also a case of meddling from the outside, aggravated by the fact that other Americans were helping in the fight against the guerrillas and men from American agencies conducted the interrogations. A Bolivian clergyman could have handled this delicate mission just as well as Monsignor Kennedy.

13

Jorge Vásquez Viaña

On April 27, Jorge Vásquez Viaña, called Loro, one of the most outstanding of the Bolivian revolutionaries, was wounded and taken prisoner in the vicinity of Monteagudo. He had been wandering about in the area, all alone and lost, since April 22, trying to make contact with his group.

Nicolás Montaño, a native of Monteagudo, has this to say about the guerrilla's capture: "I observed strange tracks around my field three days before the Day of the Cross. I decided to follow them. Once I located the guerrilla, I told the police officer on guard at Monteagudo." They went to the place together and surprised Vásquez, who was stretched out in the grass hiding, armed with a submachine gun. Montaño fired a shot at him, which made a path through his buttocks to his intestines. "Just as I was about to kill him, the police officer snatched my gun and we were able to capture the guerrilla alive."[1]

After receiving first aid in Monteagudo, the wounded man was transferred to Camiri, where he entered the hospital of the national petroleum agency (the YPFB) on April 29.

Jorge Vásquez Viaña was born in La Paz on January 5, 1939, to a distinguished Bolivian family. He was the son of the famous

---

[1] *El Diario* (May 5, 1967).

writer and historian Humberto Vásquez Machicado and Elvira Viaña Canedo. He completed his primary studies in the La Salle school in La Paz. Later—in 1957—he traveled to Munich to study geology. In 1958, he and his brother Humberto organized a society of Bolivian students in Germany, which later became the Association of Bolivian Students in Europe, of which he was elected the first president. His interest in political studies and his ties with various groups of intellectuals strengthened his Marxist convictions, and he became one of Marxism's principal popularizers among Latin American young people. He was also a sensitive painter. In Germany he married Rosa Zaunseder and they had three children: Jana, Tupac, and Antonio. On his return to Bolivia in 1962, he entered the Bolivian Communist Party and was made an editor of its official newspaper, *Unidad*, and a member of its military commission. In order to have some knowledge of rural life, he worked as a teacher in the school in the native community of Collana, in La Paz. Along with several of his comrades, among them Coco and Inti Peredo, he went to Cuba in 1965 for indoctrination and military training. In July, 1966, he returned to Bolivia, and in August or September of that year he began to prepare the Bolivian guerrilla movement. He worked tirelessly helping to set up an operational base, and after helping recruit guerrillas in the urban centers, he joined the central camp of Ñancahuazú just before the first engagements. The deserter Choque Choque spoke of his iron discipline, his intelligence, and his leadership within the camp. He gave lessons in guerrilla theory and practice to his comrades. He was highly respected by his fellow revolutionaries, and those who knew him well say that if it had not been for his death he might have been the Bolivian leader of the revolutionaries—and perhaps the number one guerrilla if Guevara had eventually carried out his decision to leave the country.

"The patient came in on a stretcher with a projectile in his left leg, a sutured wound; he is being prepared for surgery," the first sheet of Vásquez's chart at the YPFB hospital reads. While he waited for the operation he received two transfusions of 2000 cc. each. He went into the operating room at 3:15 and came out at 6:20 with permanent rectal and duodenal catheters, which indicates how serious his condition was. The wounded man had asked to be operated on without an anaesthetic to show his stubborn and inseparable interrogator and guard, Major Ivez Alarcón, that he would not be intimidated and that no violence could force him to make statements that would prejudice the interests of his fighting comrades. The operation, performed by Dr. Jorge Baldivieso Zambrana, saved his life. In the following days he received other transfusions, medication, and attention, all of which were adequate. "He never asked for anything, there was never a complaint from him, not even when he was delirious," said Nurse Lola Omonte, who took care of him. He remained in the hospital until May 7. At the end of his chart on that day is the following entry: "Eleven P.M. The patient was taken out on a stretcher to an ambulance by Dr. Antúnez and army officers . . ." He was taken to the military hospital at Camiri.

A few days before being transferred from the YPFB hospital, Vásquez Viaña was visited by Dr. Manfredo Kempff Mercado, a Senator in the national legislature and a friend of the family. He was accompanied by Deputy Rodolfo Luco. Part of the exchange went as follows:

KEMPFF: Why have you gotten yourself involved with these problems?

VÁSQUEZ: Because there's lots of thievery, lots of exploitation, lots of injustice. Our country is being handed over to imperialism on a platter.

KEMPFF: But at the time of the MNR the situation was worse and you didn't fight with guerrillas.

VÁSQUEZ: Yes, but there were no gorillas[2] then.

KEMPFF (*after a moment of reflection*): If your father could see you, I assure you he wouldn't like it.

VÁSQUEZ: My father, sir, was also a guerrilla in his time. He defended Bolivian oil. I think he would be proud of my fighting. I'm fighting to prevent our country from being turned over to foreigners.

Senator Kempff withdrew, promising Vásquez to do everything in his power to better the situation. The wounded man told him not to bother.

---

[2] "Gorillas" refers to Bolivian officials who sided with foreign interests. —*Trans.*

In the days that followed, Vásquez again submitted to repeated interrogations, but did not give an inch despite the physical pressure brought to bear on him. Unconfirmed reports have it that he suffered fractures at the hands of his interrogators.[3] An official of the army sent to Camiri later reported that a CIA man said of Vásquez: "He's too intelligent and brave to be allowed to live," and recommended that he be killed off in any way possible.

At this juncture Vásquez was visited by a CIA agent—the so-called "Doctor" Eduardo Gonzáles—who took advantage of the wounded man's extreme weakness to deceive him as to who he really was. He said that he was a leftist journalist from Panama and showed fake credentials. Gonzáles showed that he was thoroughly acquainted with the guerrilla organization, the Bolivian contacts, and some other details, and the mention of these led Vásquez to trust him. The interview was tape-recorded. Thus the CIA and the Bolivian army secured one more piece of evidence that Che was in the country and got other information of interest to them.

The La Paz paper *Presencia* confirmed the interview, although it did not identify the international agent, doubtless because it did not know who he was:

> He was in the hospital of the YPFB camp, where a clever detective, passing himself off as a lieutenant of Castro's and taking advantage of the wounded man's serious condition, managed to worm the great secret out of him. Vásquez revealed that Che was in Bolivia and was to all intents and purposes the leader and organizer of the guerrilla group in the southeast. "I was with him in Ñancahuazú and was wounded and captured later, and I don't know any more about him," was one of Vásquez's phrases. He added: "Debray must know where he is now."[4]

Doña Elvira Viaña learned about the tragedy that had befallen her son on May 3. She went immediately to Camiri, begging the military to allow her to see him. One of the nuns at the hospital told Jorge that his mother was in Camiri, and he sent her word to go back to La Paz because they were going to kill him. She was finally allowed to see him, but only through the door of his room; this was her final

---

[3] In a statement he had prepared for the trial in Camiri, journalist Ralph Schoenman claims that Vásquez Viaña had all four limbs fractured.

[4] *Presencia* (August 6, 1967).

farewell to her son, for the next day the threats she received made her leave Camiri.

It was impossible to get information out of Vásquez without resort to devious means; even Ivez Alarcón, who had learned his business in Fort Gulick, Panama, could not break his will. It is said that in a moment of indignation Vásquez spat on a high official who was pretending to be paternal and trying to provoke him into committing an indiscretion. FBI and CIA agents, who harassed him continually with their tape recorders, saw the difference between an idealist and a mercenary.

One night a high official arrived in Camiri and ordered Vásquez shot. A volunteer was sought for this mission and more than one army man offered to do the job. But the officer entrusted with the mission did not carry it through because Vásquez was secretly transferred to the hospital in Choreti and then brought back again the next day.

After having lived through several attempts on his life, on the morning of May 27 he was taken in a jeep to Choreti, where he was placed under the guard of Lieutenant Torres Torres. In this tiny town, Warrant Officer Florencio Siles Villarroel signed a report that Vásquez had "escaped" by making a hole in the wall. Nonetheless, reliable sources say that early in the morning the bloody body of Vásquez, wrapped in an old military coat, was loaded into a helicopter at the Choreti airport. On the twenty-ninth the command of the Fourth Division announced that the prisoner had escaped from the military hospital in Camiri.

Political enemies and detractors of Vásquez later circulated the rumor that the stubborn revolutionary had fled from the guerrilla camp, and that after he turned himself in to the military authorities, he was taken by FBI agents to the United States, where he was said to be living.

The mysterious disappearance of Jorge Vásquez Viaña gave rise to all sorts of conjectures and comments. The least believable of these is probably the official version of his "escape," since his condition allowed him no sort of unusual physical effort. A few days after his disappearance, Colonel Humberto Rocha, the Commander of the Fourth Division, said that Vásquez had crossed the border into Paraguay and "would be captured in a few days." Months later—on October 4, 1967—the new commander of the division, Colonel Luís Antonio Reque Terán, in answer to a question, told a delegation of alumni of the Universidad Mayor de San Andrés in La Paz who were attending the trial in Camiri as observers that "Jorge Vásquez Viaña escaped from the hospital in Camiri and disappeared with the sentinel who was guarding him." The strange thing is that there were never any sort of criminal charges brought against the soldier who deserted in the face of the enemy, not to mention his having disappeared with a prisoner. Moreover, he was never identified.

In August, at the beginning of the trial of Bustos, Debray, and four Bolivians implicated with the guerrillas (one of whom was Vásquez Viaña), the judge ordered "the Bolivian citizen Jorge Vásquez Viaña, a student of geology, to present himself before the Supreme Tribunal of Military Justice, within ten days"; Viaña, naturally, could not appear, but a permanent seat was reserved for him at the defense table in front of the judges' bench. Its emptiness was eloquent: a symbolic accusation about an event that will continue to be wrapped in mystery until those responsible decide to shed light on it.

As the trial began, the correspondent of *Presencia* in Camiri had the following conversation with the military prosecuting attorney, Colonel Remberto Iriarte Paz:

JOURNALIST: Could you tell me if you have any information on the whereabouts of Jorge Vásquez Viaña, who will be tried in absentia for rebellion?

PROSECUTING ATTORNEY: I don't have any information on Vásquez; all I know is that he escaped from the hospital in Camiri.

JOURNALIST: Well, I have information that allows me to assure you that Vásquez will appear before the Military Court on November 2.

PROSECUTING ATTORNEY: Well, you certainly are well informed!

The prosecuting attorney did not catch this irony on the part of the journalist until later: November 2 is the Day of the Dead.

Later Jorge's older brother, Humberto, a student of economics, was accused of having been one of the guerrillas' city contacts. His home, where he lived with his mother and sisters, was searched by order of the police, under the pretense that he was hiding a secret radio transmitter. As a result Humberto Vásquez took refuge in the Mexican embassy and went to Mexico after three months of political asylum.

Vásquez Viaña's mother was befriended by many people, among them the columnist Politicus (Alberto Bailey Gutiérrez), who is a co-director of the newspaper *Presencia*, and the deputy for the district of Cochabamba, David Añez Pedraza. The former put pressure on the authorities to clear up the mystery of the Vásquez Viaña case, and the latter did everything possible to get the government and the military to shed light on what had happened to Vásquez. It was all to no avail. Faced with the complete lack of results from his efforts, Añez Pedraza let it be a matter of record for public opinion and for the High Tribunal of Military Justice that "perhaps for the first time in the judicial history of Bolivia, a dead man will be judged and condemned."

14

The Guerrillas:
April to September

While the military trial was going on in Camiri, the guerrilla struggle went on without a letup. Military and rebel forces went after each other in a long chain of violent engagements in which there was much bloodshed.

Paradoxically, the battles of Ñancahuazú and Iripití marked the beginning of the end for the guerrillas. The untimely discovery of the central *foco* was a rude shock since the revolutionary war was still in a preparatory stage and the equipment was still being readied. And Ñancahuazú was only meant to be the logistic nucleus: apparently Guevara's plan was for the real zone of operations to be north of the Río Grande and the area of Río Rositas, crossing the Cochabamba-Santa Cruz highway—this was the reason he had led the fifty-day march through that region. But this plan was not to have been put into operation until October or November—that is, at least seven months after the battle at Ñancahuazú. Top military authorities agree on this. But imponderables hastened events, bringing on, as Major Olmos of the Eighth Division put it, "the fortunate failure of the subversive uprising because of the indiscretions of Marcos, who was the number two guerrilla."

Once the nerve center at Ñancahuazú had been discovered, the guerrilla command lost one of its essential elements: the initiative. Even though the army was taken by surprise and had not had adequate anti-guerrilla training, its superiority in number of combatants, arms, and other resources gave it sufficient time and space to make its preparations in the following months. Meanwhile, it could hold its positions and control enemy movements as well. The insurgents, on the other hand, merely drifted along on the tide of events. After April 17, one of the guerrilla group's three principal sections—the rear guard led by Joaquín—was operating entirely on its own, having lost all contact with the main group. The command was shifted and as a result there was no operational coordination. The principal supply center was abandoned and, what is worse, there was no contact with subversive groups outside the country. According to the guerrillas themselves, all contact with urban centers was lost after March 23. The situation worsened after April 20, because the command now had to improvise.

On the morning of the twentieth, after Bustos, Debray, and Roth were arrested in Muyupampa, a platoon of armed men— "emaciated and filthy"—turned up near the town. The townspeople, afraid of being attacked, decided to deal with them through a committee made up of the sub-prefect Justino Curcuy Gonzáles, Dr. Mario Cuellar, and the parish priest, Father Leo Schwartz. The committee arrived at the meeting place near the Ayango ranch at eleven o'clock, bearing a white flag. After extending friendly greetings, the priest asked: "What do you want and why are you engaged in armed struggle?"

The leader of the rebel platoon explained the purpose of the uprising, and outlined its immediate and long-range objectives. The conference lasted for almost three hours while government planes carefully patrolled the skies above the zone. The discussion was completely cordial as opinions were traded back and forth. Finally, the guerrillas explained that they had come to the town to get supplies and medicine, but that when they saw armed civilians they had given up their plan so as to avoid a clash. An agreement was reached, a list of the foodstuffs and medicines that the committee would bring back to the guerrillas was drawn up, and the guerrillas agreed to pay whatever the bills amounted to. The committee was to return to the meeting place around 6:30 P.M. if nothing untoward happened; but if there were any sort of clash, the guerrillas' advice was that "it would be better for you not to return." Before leaving, the insurgents asked about the three journalists who had been their companions until that morning. They were told that they had been arrested but were being treated well, and that one of them had received medical attention from the doctor on the committee. The committee withdrew, promising to bring the articles the guerrillas requested at the appointed time. Guevara noted in his diary: "Inti spoke with them. They came seeking peace but a nationwide peace for which they offered to be intermediaries."

On returning to Muyupampa, the emissaries told the military authorities what had happened; the military did not allow them to fulfill the agreement that they had made with the guerrillas. Instead, at 5 P.M. planes from the Bolivian air force bombarded the area in which the meeting had taken place.

In Che's diary the entry for the twenty-first says that in Taperillas they heard on the radio that three mercenaries had been killed —an Englishman, a Frenchman, and an Argentinian. "This uncertainty must be cleared up so as to mete out an exemplary punishment," he wrote. That same night the rebel group visited "veteran Rodas," the stepfather of Epifanio Vargas, the army guide who had died at Ñancahuazú, and gave him "an explanation which seemed to satisfy him."

On the Monteagudo-Muyupampa road that same night, Joaquín's group—which had been separated from the main group for several days—seized a power wagon belonging to the Bolivian Fiscal Petroleum Deposits in Caripite and a truck belonging to César Manrique which was taking supplies to Muyupampa. When the army learned of this, they sent out units to pursue the guerrillas, but no contact was made.

On the twenty-fourth and twenty-fifth there were armed encounters in El Mesón,Ití, and Taperillas, near Muyupampa. Villanova Sánchez Cerro, the chief of the National Guard for Public Security, the civilian guide Luís Beltrán Vargas, and the army bloodhound Tempest died in the action. The military communiqué which announced this stated that the guerrillas had four dead and several wounded, who remained in the hands of the armed forces, though it did not state what had happened to them until later. The army reported that Rubio was among the guerrilla dead, but this was incorrect since Rubio had died on April 10 in Iripití. The guerrilla killed was Rolando.

On the twenty-sixth two sentinels were surprised by a guerrilla on the highway entering Ticucha, near Taperillas. The sentinels were shot, and the guerrilla—who almost certainly was the aforementioned Vásquez Viaña (Loro)—got away.

On April 27, Jorge Vásquez Viaña was wounded and taken prisoner near Monteagudo. On the twenty-ninth the guerrillas in Joaquín's group went back into the mountain fastnesses of Ñancahuazú, making their way through the army encirclement. They picked up some provisions which they had hidden and which somehow the army had not turned up when it had searched the camp.

In his analysis of the month of April, Guevara noted that the death of Rolando was a severe blow, "since I was planning to leave him in charge of the eventual second front." Further on he writes:

> On another plane: we are still totally isolated; sickness has undermined the health of some comrades, obliging us to divide our forces, which has taken away much of our effectiveness. We still have not been able to make contact with Joaquín. The peasant base continues to make no progress although it may be that through planned terror we will succeed in getting the neutrality of some; support will come later. Not a single person has enlisted with us, and, apart from the deaths, we have lost Loro, who disappeared after the fighting in Taperillas . . . there is no mobilization of the peasants, who except for the tasks of securing information, are something of a bother. They are neither quick nor efficient; we can do away with their help.

On May 8, in another encounter with the main group in El Pincal, fifteen miles north of Lagunillas and forty-two north of Camiri, Second Lieutenant Henry Loredo Arze, and Sergeants Alfredo Arroyo and Luís Peláez died, and Privates José Villarroel and Rodolfo Pinto were wounded. On May 15, the insurgents appeared at the farm of Oscar Otero, in Tiraboy, to get food supplies.

On the sixteenth a military patrol came across a guerrilla camp in the region of Pirirenda. There were two clashes: one at dawn in La Manga, and another in El Platanal, late in the afternoon.

By now the army was almost completely in control of events. The physical inferiority of the guerrillas, due to sickness, lack of food, and excessive physical effort, was a known fact.

During this time, Guevara copied into his diary a report he sent to Fidel Castro, one of the paragraphs of which reads:

> . . . we have arms for one hundred more men including four 60 [mm.] mortars and ammunition for them, but not a single peasant

has been taken in. We suffered four casualties, Benjamín, Carlos, Bolivians drowned in accidents, Félix (J. S. G.) and Rolando (S. L.), killed in combat. The last loss is very important. He was the best man in the guerrilla group.

On May 26, Pepe, who had been expelled from the main group and was staying with Joaquín's group, deserted and gave himself up in El Espino to troops who were part of a company under the command of Captain Armando Pacheco. The captain went to Camiri and nervously announced that his troops were surrounded. The army later stated that Pepe had died in combat, but in reality he had been killed when he had given himself up. He had complained of the bad treatment he had received from the Cuban guerrillas, and stated that he wanted to get even and was willing to indicate the precise places where arms had been hidden in Ñancahuazú. He revealed that he had been in Cuba and Vietnam and had fought with the guerrillas in Peru. He asked the army to spare his life, but they did not believe his story, taking him for a contact or for bait left by the guerrillas. He was later killed, and his body exhibited in Camiri.[1]

On May 28, after taking over the town of Caraguatarenda, about eight miles from Gutiérrez, the guerrillas went on to Cararaca and spent the night in Pueblo Nuevo. On May 30, there was a violent two-hour battle around a grade crossing on the railroad line from Yacuiba to Santa Cruz. Second Lieutenant Eduardo Velarde and Private Wilfredo Benegas died, and four soldiers from the Ranger Regiment were wounded.

That same day at 8 P.M. an army patrol which had been brought in in an "Alligator" truck was ambushed in Muchiri, a station on the same railroad line about seventy miles south of Santa Cruz. This led to the suspension of railroad services on that line at the army's request. It was supposed that the guerrillas, who were now short of food, intended to attack a convoy so as to get supplies.

On June 4, Marcos and Víctor, members of Joaquín's group, died in an ambush near the La Laguna camp as they were coming

---

[1] His real name was Julio Velasco Montaño; he was born in Oruro, was thirty-two years old, married, and the father of four children. He had been a director of a miners' union in a San José mine and was also a militant of the pro-Chinese wing of the PCB.

back from *góndola* service bringing in a supply of corn. Pedro managed to escape alive.

On June 5, there was a heavy exchange of fire from both banks of the Río Grande, in the Abapó region. One soldier was wounded.

On June 6, Colonel Edmundo Rocha was relieved as Commander of the Fourth Division operating against the guerrillas, and replaced by Colonel Luís Reque Terán. The new commander immediately took on the task of mounting "Operation Cynthia," whose object was to destroy the guerrillas—or at least push them northward, outside the sector under his command.

Around June 7, the guerrillas attacked the farm of Dardo Hassenteufeld in Taperillas, fifteen miles from Monteagudo, presumably in order to get supplies. On the tenth, the army suffered two casualties north of Ipitá, Privates Antonio Melgar (dead) and Eladio Arias Garnica (wounded), and officially announced that "in the ambush that caused three casualties among the Reds operating north of Ipitá, the guerrilla nicknamed Inti, whose last name is Peredo, the brother of Coco, was killed. The watch that belonged to this revolutionary is in the chief command post. Said personal belonging may be claimed in our offices by the family of Roberto Peredo." The communiqué was false: Inti would be one of the five guerrillas to escape alive.

During the afternoon of June 26, the army suffered five casualties in La Florida, forty-two miles southeast of Valle Grande: three dead and two wounded. The guerrillas suffered two casualties: one dead and one wounded.

On Thursday, July 6, Che Guevara personally led a battle worthy of the movies in Samaipata (a town of 2500 inhabitants)—a hastily planned and precisely executed action with as much suspense as a Hitchcock film. The unexpected action surprised the army and caused public opinion to leap to the wrong conclusions, for the battle was really no more than the last swipe of a cornered cat's paw. The guerrillas' surprising appearance took place in a zone outside of the Fourth Division's area of operations, for Samaipata was within the jurisdiction of the Eighth Division, under Colonel Joaquín Zenteno Anaya, with headquarters in Santa Cruz. The attack on Samaipata showed that the rebels were being slowly but inexorably forced out of the Ñancahuazú nucleus toward the northeast. The Fourth Division, even though it had not managed to wipe out the guerrilla *foco* entirely, nonetheless had succeeded in driving it out of the Division's jurisdiction and forcing it onto a terrain where it could more easily be destroyed.

Sickness, fatigue, and lack of food made increasingly severe inroads on the band. One thing was especially depressing: their leader's health was getting worse and worse. Since the middle of June Guevara had not moved except on mule- or horseback; he was suffering from rheumatic arthritis and he had had several violent attacks of asthma, aggravated by the fact that there was no appropriate medication on hand. All this entered into the decision to attack Samaipata so as to get supplies and look for some way of communicating with urban contacts and sympathizers.

Cochabamba, the geographic center of Bolivia, is linked by asphalt highway to Santa Cruz, the capital of the east of Bolivia, three hundred miles away. Samaipata is between the two cities, 222 miles from Cochabamba and seventy-eight from Santa Cruz. At 6:15 P.M. on July 6 the guerrillas arrived at the combination farm and sawmill of Las Cuevas, located ten miles to the east of Samaipata on a road just off the main highway and owned by a German national named Enrique Stenderg. Almost immediately they stopped a truck on the highway, and minutes later stopped a bus on the regular Cochabamba-Santa Cruz line, carrying a group of students. Another vehicle that pretended not to hear the guerrillas' orders to stop finally did so after getting bullets in its tires. From this moment on all travel on the highway was stopped. Though the passengers were naturally nervous, there was no violence of any kind; the guerrillas asked only that they obey orders.

At 7 P.M. the guerrillas instructed the owner of the sawmill to telephone authorities in Samaipata that they were going to take the town that same night. They motioned to the passengers and drivers to stay in a group around the bus station and not to try anything, leaving them in the care of six of the guerrillas: Coco, Aniceto, Pacho, Julio, El Chino, and a sixth, all under the command of Ricardo. Guevara himself did not take part in the action, but rather directed it from an advance post in a place called Peña Colorada, from which he and others could control all movement on the highway.

At 8 P.M. two guerrillas got into the truck and another five got into the bus and sat down as passengers. At 8:10 the two vehicles, each driven by a guerrilla, went on at moderate speed toward Samaipata, passing slowly in front of a Bolivian Gulf Oil Company pumping station located on this stretch of the road.

Samaipata is not on the main highway, but on a branch road, less than half a mile south of the highway. At the intersection of the branch road and the main highway there is a police booth, commonly known in Bolivia as a *"tranca,"* with a table in front of it where food, cigarettes, soft drinks, and such are sold.

The telephone call from Las Cuevas seemed not to have completely convinced the authorities in Samaipata, for, somewhat lazily, all they had done was increase their usual security forces—there were not enough men to really ward off an armed invasion. The authorities' incredulity is somewhat explained by the fact that up to this time the guerrillas had been operating a long distance away from Samaipata and the public had become bored with stories of their appearing in the most unexpected places and doing the most extraordinary things.

The authorities held a sort of conference of notables and came in a body to the stand in front of the police booth. At 11:45 a truck and a bus came from the direction of Santa Cruz, going no faster than is usual at that spot. As the traffic police got ready to perform their routine check on the vehicles, the guerrillas, hiding their arms, secretly crept into position around the authorities, the passengers, and the townspeople, who were all standing there in a group. Suddenly the whole group began to jostle and shove, without anybody guessing why. The tumult lasted only a moment, until the people realized that they had been surrounded and were under the hostile vigilance of a fully armed group of guerrillas. The daring coup was beautifully synchronized and not a single shot was fired.

The passengers and the curious onlookers, now prisoners, remained there under strict vigilance while most of the attackers trooped off toward Samaipata. They took the authorities with them, using the truck that had brought them to the police booth and a light truck belonging to the Bolivian Gulf Oil Company that they found parked nearby. They went directly to the Infant of Prague pharmacy and got the proprietor out of bed. They drew up a huge list of drugs, medicine of all sorts, and clothes, paid the sum of one thousand Bolivian pesos and went off toward the school, which at the time was being used as a barracks for the few soldiers stationed in the area. Second Lieutenant Vacaflor, one of the authorities in tow, identified himself and he and all the men with him were allowed in. The guerrillas loaded their vehicles with arms, munitions, clothes, blankets, and various equipment. They ordered the officer and warrant officers to undress, so that they couldn't follow them immediately or give orders that they be pursued.

The speed of events paralyzed the tired young conscripts wakened from sleep, and only one of them tried to resist. It was a modest private, José Verazaín, who was the only one to appreciate the situation for what it was; a watchful guerrilla immediately shot him down.

Once they had what they wanted from the town, the rebels went back to the police booth. They bought fresh food and canned goods, paying sixty pesos for the former and twelve hundred pesos for the latter, then immediately went off in the direction they had come from, taking Second Lieutenant Vacaflor and nine privates with them as hostages. On the outskirts of Las Cuevas they gave the drivers of the vehicles money to repay any damages done, and freed the military hostages and the others detained there. After telling the soldiers not to try to follow them or there would be immediate reprisals, they disappeared in the darkness. At 12:30 A.M. this lightning command operation was over, its only victim a humble soldier.

Two days later, on July 9, the armed forces had two encounters with Joaquín's group and as a consequence the rebel camp of El Dorado was occupied by the army.

The next day the guerrilla Serapio died. According to the deserter, Paco, his group

> had gone up the Yuqui or the Iquira in the middle of the stream so as not to leave tracks. The march was very painful because the whole group was exhausted from the heavy loads they were carrying. The one who suffered most was Serapio, because some time before Joaquín had inadvertently kicked him in the foot and the injured foot had swollen, so that he was walking with a cane. During rest halts they ordered Serapio to go on ahead so as to gain time, because he was lagging too far behind. One time, Pedro and Eusebio followed him after a bit, intending to help him carry his knapsack. When they

were just about to catch up with him, Serapio motioned to them and shouted for them not to come any farther because the army had set up an ambush there. The army fired at Serapio, and he fell dead, but he had saved the whole group from falling into the ambush.

On Sunday the twenty-third, Chingolo and Eusebio deserted from Joaquín's group and were arrested in Chuayaco, five miles to the west of Monteagudo. They were taken by surprise as they were bathing in a stream and claimed that they were peddlers who had come to a local religious fiesta to sell their goods. Members of Major Sánchez's unit, who had found them, submitted them to a brief routine interrogation from the bank of the river. The military patrol was about to continue its march when a chance circumstance gave the two deserters away. One of them, submerged up to his waist in the water, raised a hand to his face to chase away an insect, thus showing his forearm and the back of his right hand, which were covered with deep scratches. These natural tattoos are found on anyone who has to hack his way through thick brush and in those days were characteristic of the guerrillas. The marks were noticed by the Major and his soldiers, and the two deserters were immediately taken to Lagunillas and then to Camiri. They confessed that they had deserted the revolutionary camp and were intending to turn themselves in to the authorities in La Paz. Their first depositions gave the army facts which enabled them to follow the trail of the guerrillas more closely. Despite their eagerness to cooperate, Chingolo and Eusebio suffered various indignities at the hands of some soldiers of the Fourth Division. Obeying a violent impulse, Colonel Luís Antonio Reque Terán traced the prisoners' silhouettes with bullets, wounding Eusebio in the right shoulder.

Although Eusebio testified for the prosecution during the trial at Camiri, he is still imprisoned. Chingolo, for his part, would later serve as a guide to help locate the caches, camps, and defensive constructions of the rebels; he finally joined the army, where he still is today.

On July 30, there was an encounter with Che's group near El Filo, north of the Río Grande, where the military's casualties were four dead and six wounded. The guerrillas lost two men—Raúl and Ricardo—and had one wounded.

On August 9, the army surrounded the group commanded by

Joaquín in the Iñaú hills, in the zone of Taperillas, and would have been able to catch and destroy them completely had it not been for the cooperation given the guerrillas by a peasant named Vicente Soto, who was also a sometime guide for the army. Once warned, Joaquín engaged in a brief fight and then ordered his men to retreat by scaling a cliff, the only way out not controlled by the army. The guerrilla Pedro offered to cover their retreat and did so until his .30-caliber machine gun ran out of ammunition. His suicide mission over, he was mortally wounded as he began to retreat and follow his companions. His decision to fight on gave the group time to escape from the troops encircling them. Pedro's disappearance was deeply regretted by his comrades, because apart from being a dedicated revolutionary and a loyal comrade, he was extremely kind, a fact which had earned him the nickname of "God's Bread." In this action Tania, who was growing sicker and more nervous by the day, miraculously escaped dying or being taken prisoner.

On the morning of August 10, it was reported that three guerrillas had been seen at Mairana; Inti was believed to be one of them. In the afternoon it was reported that twenty rebels were operating at a place called Las Cruces. On the twelfth, the company led by Eduardo Galindo captured a suspect by the name of Agapito Chuquimia in Palermo. At the end of the month of August, a vehicle carrying a platoon of twenty-seven engineers from the Pando battalion had an accident in the zone of Masicurí Bajo, in which a noncommissioned officer, Ademar Muriel, and a soldier, Rómulo Rivero, were killed and several were injured. It could not be determined whether this was sabotage or an accident. The men in the unit all agreed that two soldiers and a medical corpsman had been taken prisoner by the rebels.

Near a pass called Puerto Mauricio leading to the Río Grande was a hut belonging to the only people around, a family of peasants: Honorato Rojas, his wife, and several small children. The army discovered that Rojas was in the habit of supplying food and medicine to a group of rebels marauding in the neighborhood, and by making serious threats they forced him to cooperate and tell them everything he knew about the guerrillas' movements. On Tuesday, August 29, Lieutenant Pedro Barberí sent a medical sergeant and a private to see that Rojas complied with their orders. On the thirtieth at 6 P.M. an exhausted soldier came running to Captain Mario Vargas Salinas, who was in the neighborhood with a military contingent transporting supplies, with the news that a group of insurgents had arrived at Puerto Mauricio around eleven o'clock. Captain Vargas immediately went into action. He addressed his soldiers, exhorting them to defend their country against "well-armed foreigners and killers, who have both defects and perhaps virtues, but are neither invulnerable nor invincible." At 8 P.M. they started out toward the Río Grande.

They walked through darkness, crossing five fords on the Masicurí before reaching the Río Grande. At 2 A.M., they picked up the local mayor, Evaristo Caballero, and a peasant called Don José (who along with Rojas were later to be invaluable to the army) at the first ford; they arrived, after a short rest and a nine-mile march, at the next-to-last ford early on Thursday, August 31. A few moments later, medical corpsman García came looking for Captain Vargas to report that the guerrillas had arrived at Rojas' farm the afternoon before.

Joaquín's group had fallen into the trap. Two days before, they had gone to visit their friend Rojas to get supplies and to ask him to guide them across the river since he was familiar with the area. In the magazine *Sucesos* García told his version of the guerrillas' visit.

According to García, the dogs began to bark, showing that strangers were approaching, and Rojas said fearfully: "It's them."

García immediately got undressed and got into the bed, pretending that he was sick. The rebels entered and, on seeing a stranger in Rojas' bed, asked who he was.

Rojas explained that it was a neighbor he knew very well who was trembling because he was suffering from malaria. The guerrillas took pity on him and promised to take him to see their doctor, Braulio, the next day so that he could take care of him.[2]

They then asked Rojas where he had been and told him that this time they really needed him because they absolutely had to ford the Río Grande immediately.

The military column meanwhile went on once more. The vanguard received the order not to go as far as Vado del Yeso but to

---

[2] In fact, Braulio was not a doctor.

stop a few hundred yards away so as not to enter the sector the guerrillas were guarding. As day was breaking, the patrol led by Captain Vargas—thirty-one soldiers and two civilians—arrived at the appointed place. It was 5:45 A.M. Vargas reported events as follows:

> A little farther on, we met Honorato and his wife and children. They tried to run away, and I made them understand that they were to go back home and wait for the guerrillas, who had said they would be back so that Rojas could take them across the Río Grande at a ford he knew of.
>
> I managed to convince him. I gave him instructions to choose Vado del Yeso, where the river narrows and is turbulent and dangerous. He promised to do so, as long as we would spare his life. We agreed that he would put on a white shirt so that he would be easily recognized.
>
> We went to Vado and I chose the best position in the place: in front of the pass in the form of a horseshoe.
>
> Lieutenant Barberí and I got our men in position on both banks of the river. If luck was with us, this time we would be the ones to surprise the enemy.

They waited until nightfall, suffering from the mosquitoes, the stifling heat, and thirst, but there was not a sign of life from the guerrillas. At 5:20 Mayor Caballero gave the alarm.

"We all tried to see," Captain Vargas said, "and in the distance I saw a black knot of people that looked as if it wasn't moving. We tried to calculate how many men were coming, and disagreed on the number . . . while the guerrillas advanced toward Vado del Yeso . . . They stopped once to hurry Tania along—we recognized her by her graceful figure—because she was lagging behind."

Braulio was on point, studying the ground for possible footprints, but the soldiers had had the foresight to erase their footprints with branches. Something attracted Braulio's attention, but Rojas took it upon himself to convince him that the footprints were old ones. "We could recognize the guide," Vargas continues, "when they came within a hundred yards of us. We were about to face the terrible situation of having to fire against all of them, with our guide in the group. But luckily the guerrillas said good-by to him a few yards before they got to the ford. Honorato Rojas had more than kept his promise."

Braulio was the first to go across, with a machete in his right hand and a submachine gun in his left. With the water up to his calves, he stopped to drink in the middle of the stream, looked all around, and continued to walk toward the other side. Lieutenant Barberí begged Captain Vargas to fire, but the Captain told him he wanted to make sure of his target first.

"The guerrilla point arrived on the sandy shore, looked over to where we were, but saw nothing suspicious, and turned off toward our right. I spied him between some dry branches and saw that he was raising his machete as a signal for the others to come ahead." His comrades started across in Indian file. The last in line was Tania, with a knapsack over her shoulder and her blue pants rolled up to her knees. When the group got to the middle of the river, where the water was up to their waists, the soldiers began to fire. Those not hit by the first shots returned the fire in all directions, unable to locate any definite target. Braulio, who had come face to face with Private Antonio Vaca, finished him off with one shot, but another soldier fired right at Braulio's face and left him stretched out on the ground. Too late, the guerrillas realized they had fallen into an ambush. In the stream, a multitude of little red spots turned into liquid purple streams gliding along on the surface of the water. Tania waved a bit of white cloth as a signal that the guerrillas would surrender, but the only answer she received was a hail of bullets. Joaquín managed to get back to the bank from which his group had started to cross the river; he ran along the bank trying to escape but was soon riddled with bullets. The dead, the wounded, the arms, the knapsacks, and other objects were dragged along by the current. The soldiers shot at every visible object, fearing that they might lose the quarry.

Paco let himself be carried downstream a few dozen yards. The doctor, Ernesto, swam over to join him. Both protected themselves by hiding behind some large rocks, watching their dead or wounded comrades being swept past them by the current. In a few minutes they were discovered and the soldiers fired on them. Paco was hit twice, once in the right forearm and once below the left shoulder in the armpit. Ernesto shouted to the soldiers to cease firing so that he could take care of the wounded, making signs that they were ready to surrender. His plea seemed to be answered, for several soldiers advanced cautiously toward the river bank, shouting to the two guerrillas to come back up out of the river with their hands up. Ernesto did so, but Paco could not raise his arms because of his wounds and the weight of his full knapsack on his back. Ernesto then helped his comrade out of the water, but they were immediately separated and pushed, kicked, insulted, and trampled upon. Ernesto, who was hurriedly trying to give first aid to Paco, was recognized by some sergeants from the place where he lived (the *departamento* of Beni), and they too began to hurl invective at him. Ernesto replied angrily, the shouts died out, and the soldiers began beating him up again. Someone shot at him and ripped his arm to pieces. At that moment, witnesses say, an officer shouted from the opposite bank of the river to bring the prisoners over.

Once they were on the other side of the river, the two prisoners were made to stand in front of the corpses that had already been picked up and were ordered to identify them. Paco did so, for despite having two wounds, he was in better shape physically than Ernesto. A short time later, the latter fell to the ground complaining of sharp pains. A sympathetic corpsman took him to a quiet spot and, because he lacked adequate medicine, gave him only hasty first aid. It was night now, and Ernesto's moans were heard continuously. Some soldiers and an officer finally took him to the river bank and killed him with a burst of machine-gun fire.

The action had lasted only fifteen or twenty minutes, but the entire rebel group had been wiped out—except for Paco, who was taken prisoner. The soldiers had thought that they had been fighting Guevara's group, but Paco had disabused them of this illusion when he identified the corpses of his comrades: Joaquín, the leader of the group; Braulio, the second in command; Alejandro, the chief of operations of the guerrilla command; Polo; Wálter; the Bolivian doctor Ernesto; and Moisés Guevara. The bodies of Tania and El Negro were washed away by the current.

The only thing of Tania's that could be recovered was her knapsack. Almost all its contents were more or less intact, and a meticulous search turned up her identity card—issued in the name of Laura Gutiérrez Bauer—personal documents, a notebook, and a list of names and addresses that the authorities presumed were those of city contacts.

Some versions of the encounter, among them that of Captain Vargas, who said that he had left Puerto Mauricio at eleven the next day, agree that Guevara's group came to the ford at eleven that night. Vargas added that with this ambush, the days of the main group were numbered. Señor Guevara listened to the reports announcing a [government] victory, but he refused to believe them, and for a long time insisted on looking for the rear guard led by Joaquín.

León, the prisoner with the memory of an elephant, told us that the Cuban leader insisted on shrugging these reports off, supposing that they were wishful thinking and propaganda for the armed forces.

Nonetheless, the Bolivian guerrilla Camba, who was with Guevara during this period and is now a prisoner of the armed forces, has a different version. Here is a dialogue extracted from a tape he made for the authors:

Q: How did you hear of what had happened in Vado del Yeso?

A: The first news came over the Voice of America. We heard a communiqué talking about how effective the armed forces were in the fight against the guerrillas and announcing that all of Joaquín's group had been killed. This was the first news we had.

Q: What did Che say?

A: At first he didn't believe it. The report gave no names or details. Then he said that it could be propaganda. He said that the whole group couldn't have been killed unless they had been surprised while they were asleep. Almost all of us wouldn't let ourselves believe the news. Later we heard details on Radio Altiplano [in La Paz] and then we began to believe it. Joaquín's whole group had been killed. At first Che didn't say a thing and seemed not to have any reaction at all. Later he told us: "It appears that he's dead. He fell into an ambush, which makes me hope that there were some survivors, because they couldn't all have been killed together." But when Radio Cruz del Sur reported finding Tania's body, that confirmed the whole thing and he told us that we were slipping, even though we were entering a new phase. And he added: "Yes, we're slipping; we can't deny it."

Q: What did he mean by slipping?

A: He was referring to the fact that there had been casualties instead of people joining up. Because the peasants, instead of giving us the help that we were hoping they would, or at least moral support, were afraid of the army and fled from us. This was what he, in particular, and the rest of us as well, meant by slipping. From the political point of view we had gotten absolutely nowhere with the peasants.

Q: The influence of the guerrillas on the peasants was negative?
A: Yes, it was negative.

Joaquín's group had suffered both from physical hardships and from low morale, for he did not have enough authority to stop the permanent altercations and misunderstandings among his subordinates. There were recriminations and quarrels over anything and everything. Tania, who was suffering from severe anxiety and had terrible nightmares, was a handy target for these fits of rage. They criticized her continually, accusing her of being the cause of their separation from the main group. Those who were most severe on her were Joaquín, Alejandro, and Braulio. More than once Tania begged them to kill her, bursting into helpless tears, or pleaded for them to leave her behind somewhere so that she could surrender to the army or try to escape to a safe place. It is reported that during one discussion Joaquín and she came to blows. Toward the end it appears that they kept an extremely close watch on her, because she was always accompanied by Joaquín or Alejandro as they marched along.

Hunger and exhaustion had reduced the group's ability to act. Joaquín himself seemed to be completely exhausted, lagging behind his comrades sometimes as much as a whole day's march.

The battle at Vado del Yeso was the first meaningful victory for the armed forces. It also marked the end of "Operation Cynthia," which had been planned by the Fourth Division. Even though this unit had not taken part in the battle, Vado del Yeso was the result of pressure from the Fourth Division on the rebel band so as to clear it out of their area of operations. The Ñancahuazú area was now free of enemy units and once again fully in the government's control.

For the first time names and details about the guerrilla casualties were known because almost all the dead bodies remained in the hands of the military forces. In the previous sporadic encounters it had been impossible to have certain proof because, as official reports announced, the guerrillas rarely abandoned their dead or their wounded. They clung to this principle, at whatever sacrifice and within the limits of the possible, up until the very end. In extremely grave situations, the guerrillas were obliged to finish off their own comrades at their request or on their own initiative so as to avoid their falling into the enemy's hands; some guerrillas preferred to commit suicide.

Encouraged by their victory on August 31, the units of the

Eighth Division spread out farther and farther toward the south and southeast from their base of operations in Valle Grande. The intensive search for Tania and the other guerrilla who had disappeared during the encounter at Vado del Yeso also continued. On September 3, there was a minor clash in El Palmerito, on the Río Grande. The Rangers of the Fourth Division were left in possession of the body of a guerrilla who, once he had been taken to Choreti to be identified by Ciro Roberto Bustos, turned out to be El Negro. Therefore, it was not a rebel patrol that participated in the clash, but only this guerrilla who had escaped some days before in Vado del Yeso. According to the version of events written up by Captain Vargas, El Negro was hiding in a tree when he was shot in the wrist and his cry of pain led him to be discovered. The army had no casualties.

On this same day, September 3, the command of the armed forces announced that at 3:30 P.M. there had been another encounter in the zone of Masicurí Bajo, in which the army had had two casualties: Private Benito Gutiérrez was killed and one other soldier wounded. The army reported: "Red casualties: five dead, which have not as yet been identified. There is no evidence that any of the guerrillas were wounded."

On September 7, the military command announced publicly that the body of Tania had been found: "Today, Thursday, the body of Tania was found on the shores of the Río Grande and will be taken to Santa Cruz." According to the campaign diary of an officer who had taken part in the recovery of the body, it was found in an advanced state of putrefaction on September 5 about five miles from Vado del Yeso, and was immediately taken to Valle Grande where an autopsy was performed. Chaplain Captain Manuel Laredo offered prayers for the body, which had been wrapped in a white sheet. The piety of the German nuns in the Christian School in Valle Grande moved them to provide a modest coffin and a place in the public cemetery.

Army chiefs, civilian officials, a military platoon, and a great number of curious onlookers attended the funeral services; photographs of the ceremony were published in the press. It was reported that Tania had been given military honors, but the President of the Republic and the Commander in Chief of the armed forces categorically denied that this was the case and assured the public that the funeral had been no more than a simple humanitarian act.

Although Tania had no relatives in Valle Grande, lighted candles and flowers appeared from time to time at the place where her remains were buried. These tributes took place at night, and a military commander ordered a special guard to watch over the tomb of the "Red," so as to discover what "guerrilla contacts" were making such offerings; thus far they have remained anonymous.

On September 9, President Barrientos arrived in Valle Grande and later went to the zone where the latest encounters with the guerrillas had taken place to offer his moral support and his compliments to the men on the front lines. Insistent rumors—which have not yet been fully verified—had it that the guerrillas had burned down Honorato Rojas' hut for having betrayed Joaquín's group as it was crossing the Vado del Yeso, and that the President had ordered that the family be paid for the damages out of gratitude for the cooperation that they had given the army. At the same time, General Barrientos ordered that loud-speaker announcements be made and leaflets be dropped urging the guerrillas to surrender, guaranteeing that their lives would be spared, and promising those who were Bolivian that they would be allowed to live a normal civilian life once again.

On September 11, the President announced a reward of 50,000 Bolivian pesos for the capture, dead or alive but preferably alive, of Che Guevara, thus changing his official opinion that Guevara was "keeping Camilo Cienfuegos company." Guevara, on learning the price put on his head, had this to say in his diary about Barrientos: "One must have brains to govern. Words aren't enough. He is a stupid man." On another occasion, when he learned of the President's proposal to invade Cuba, Guevara had written of Barrientos: "He is talking nonsense, as usual."

From August 31 on there was intense activity in the whole sector covered by the tactical groups of the Eighth Division, which had mounted "Operation Parabano" to push the rebels south of Valle Grande. The main body of guerrillas was boxed in and had to confine its incursions to the zone between the Río Grande and the Masicurí, making sporadic appearances in the small hamlets of the region. During this time there were many reports of the real or imagined appearance of guerrillas over the whole large area, obliging Tactical Groups 1 and 3 of the Eighth Division, whose headquarters were in Valle Grande, to mobilize their scattered troops for a real witch hunt. The troops had to move about constantly, sometimes in answer to what proved to be false alarms and at other times to arrest suspicious characters or to verify unexpected appearances of the guerrillas, who subsequently disappeared as if by magic.

At one point, the insurgents tried to cross the Río Grande and go south so as to return to the basin of the Ñancahuazú, but the stubborn watchfulness of the units of the Fourth Division did not allow them to do so. The insurgents were definitely trapped. The Eighth Division was putting pressure on them from the north and northeast, and on the south the Fourth Division was having no trouble containing them at the shores of the Río Grande. It was a real cul-de-sac. But still, the only way out was to turn back toward the northeast, in the zone of Higuera, San Antonio, Abra del Picacho, Alto Seco, and El Churo. Possibly they were trying to gain an area better suited to their needs in the triangle formed by the confluence of the Río Grande and the Mizque.

During the second half of September the situation was critical for the remaining guerrilla combatants. The military had spread out in a huge circle which grew smaller and smaller as they closed in, so that the guerrillas had little chance to move about. The reports from the government forces were increasingly optimistic. The rebel group had only a limited area in which to operate, and official sources announced that it would soon be liquidated and its leader captured.

All this resulted in an unusual mobilization of the left in the cities. The urban agents of the Army of National Liberation sought contacts and the order trickled down like dust to the people emotionally and politically tied to the rebels: "Save Che."

A few dissident members of the orthodox Communist parties managed to make contact with rebel agents in the city of Cochabamba. Some of them stated that they could get a trained group ready to reinforce the sector still controlled by the insurgents. But the rebel agents believed that any effort in this direction was useless, and explained that this same project had been studied earlier, when some seventy men had been ready to carry out such an operation.

A new proposal was then put forward: to open another guerrilla *foco* somewhere in the *departamento* of Cochabamba or in Alto Beni, this latter being already part of Guevara's plans. But once all the aspects of both proposals had been analyzed, it was concluded that it was materially impossible to put them into effect. The die had already been cast.

In the first hours of dawn on the morning of September 22, the guerrilla group arrived in the community of Alto Seco, followed a little later by Che Guevara himself. Everyone in the town was asleep and nobody realized what had happened until dawn. The townspeople treated the guerrillas fairly cordially, so that the visitors stayed in the town for about forty-eight hours. As the townspeople tell it, there were about twenty-five or thirty men in the group. They set up a sentry post within the town and took positions around it. They broke into a house and cut the only telephone line connected with the *Corregidor*, the local political authority. They bought medicine, a fair amount of clothing, a few pairs of shoes and boots, transistor radios, and supplies with which they prepared their breakfast. They tried to pay in foreign money, but at the insistence of the shop-keepers, they paid in Bolivian money. They did not pay anything, however, for the things acquired in the house of the *Corregidor*, which was hidden on the outskirts of the town. "Your husband is the *Corregidor*. The government pays him. Let the President pay him," they are said to have remarked to the *Corregidor*'s wife, Sara Calza-dilla.[3]

The guerrillas came and went constantly during their stay in the town. Guevara was seen only on a very few occasions. On the afternoon of the twenty-second, he gathered the townspeople together in a little square and gave them a brief speech on the general state of the country and of the Bolivian peasantry in particular. He explained the purpose of the guerrilla uprising and the reason for the presence of Latin American citizens among the combatants, but nothing dispelled the inexpressive silence of his audience. He talked with many of them, being rude to some and affectionate to others. He played with the children and asked them questions about their studies and their daily

---

[3] Correspondent Edwin Chacón in *Presencia*, October 4, 1967.

routine in this isolated little hamlet. And every time he could he slipped in a little lecture explaining Communism. But only rarely did he come out of his command post, located two hundred yards or so from the edge of the town. Apparently his illness and exhaustion obliged him to rest most of the time.

Coco also addressed the townspeople, vehemently attacking the government of General Barrientos and American imperialism.

In one of the many conversations that the visitors had with the natives, one of the peasants asked a guerrilla if he could join the group, and received the following reply: "Don't be silly; we're done for . . . we don't know how to get out of here."[4]

Beginning on the morning of the twenty-third, the rebels abandoned Alto Seco in successive groups. The last group left on the twenty-fourth. Guevara departed on muleback.

The schoolmaster of the town, Wálter Romero, had several opportunities to talk with the guerrillas. Moro went to his house to rest and sleep for a few hours, and later commented with feeling on the softness of the modest bed. During a conversation with Romero, they spoke of Barrientos' offer to spare the lives of the last guerrillas. Moro said that this didn't interest them: "We're fighting for our ideals," he concluded. A few days later Wálter Romero asked his pupils to write a composition on their "experience with the guerrillas." The children had quite different impressions: some stated that the "men with the beards" were Communists, atheists, and destroyers of freedom, and others wrote of their admiration for Che and his comrades. One of them wrote: "Che Guevara is the Francisco Pizarro of our time."[5]

On Monday the twenty-fifth the guerrilla group appeared in Abra del Picacho. In the interview which the authors had with the guerrilla Camba, the following appears:

Q: When was the last time you saw Che?

A: The last time was September 25. I didn't talk with him that day, as I had done other times. We were with him that day in Abra del Picacho. The town was having a fiesta. Those of us in the vanguard arrived first. The townspeople were dancing; they invited us to

---

[4] *Ibid.*

[5] Mery Saavedra Flores in *Confirmado Internacional* (La Paz, February, 1968).

have some *chicha*.[6] Che arrived a half-hour or so later. He asked us what was going on. We told him. Then he came in and had *chicha*. Meanwhile those of us in the vanguard went on. He stayed there. He always came along behind us. Che remained in Abra del Picacho for about an hour and a half, and then went on.

Q: How did Che treat the peasants?

A: He had very few dealings with them. The ones who were supposed to do the political work were Inti and Coco; that is to say, he left this to Bolivians. Sometimes he chatted with the peasants—in the little town of Alto Seco, for example. He talked for a long time to the people who lived there. He was very amiable and expansive. Before that he didn't talk much with townspeople because he didn't want his identity to be known. He only talked when it was necessary; that is to say, when he had to cure peasants, or take their teeth out. Then he would be very outgoing and would take care of them. His specialty was working with teeth. The doctors in our group were Julio and Morogoro.

At 10 P.M. on Tuesday, September 26, the company of Lieutenant Eduardo Galindo Grandchand received information that "the Reds were marching in the direction of Higuera–Abra del Picacho." That is to say, they were entering the lion's mouth.

Lieutenant Galindo asked for permission to pursue the enemy closely, but that permission was denied. The Commander of the Tactical Group undoubtedly did not want to expose Galindo's company to the danger of a night march. The order came through some hours later, however, and the company (thirty-nine men) started off at 6 A.M. on the twenty-seventh in the direction of Higuera, a hamlet situated on the Río Pirainambí, a tributary of the Río Grande, some forty-two miles south of Valle Grande. At eleven in the morning the unit arrived at some hills about two miles from Higuera. At first they saw what appeared to be groups of men, women, and children approaching the town. Another observer thought that it was a military patrol advancing toward the town from the opposite direction. All this produced an instant of indecision in Galindo's company, but at the first shots they realized that they had come up against the enemy vanguard. The encounter began at midday and lasted two and a half

---

[6] *Chicha* is a popular fermented beverage made of corn, pineapple, etc. —*Trans.*

hours. It was obvious from the beginning that the government troops were the stronger force. The rebels were pursued about two miles, at the end of which all resistance ceased. There were three guerrilla dead: political commissar Coco, Miguel, and Julio. The three guerrillas seemed to be the only casualties on that side; the army had no casualties at all. The defeated guerrillas abandoned a large quantity of equipment in what had been their camp. The precariousness of the guerrilla situation was evident from their ragged clothes and their worn-out, broken-down footwear. In the six knapsacks the army recovered were numerous important guerrilla documents.

There was no official announcement on the precise circumstances in which Coco died. It was later learned from confidential guerrilla sources that this leader of the vanguard received a very serious wound moments after the fight began, at about 12:40. Aided by a companion, he dragged himself along for some six hundred yards. At this point another guerrilla tried to help him. But on seeing that any effort was useless and that his comrades were running the risk of being wounded or killed, he asked them to finish him off; as they paid no attention, he shot himself.

The three bodies were taken to Valle Grande, arriving at 5:30 in the afternoon of the twenty-seventh. After being identified and shown to journalists in the Señor de Malta hospital, they were buried in the local cemetery.

When he learned of his brother's death, Inti, who had been with Che's group, had a serious emotional shock from which he did not recover for several days. He wandered about in confusion, kept himself apart from the others, and was disconcertingly silent. The first thing he did when he had recovered from the shock was to portion out among the guerrillas the money that had been given him when the rebel cell was organized in Ñancahuazú.

A short time later two more rebels fell into the army's hands. León surrendered about seven and a half miles from Pucara on the twenty-seventh; on the twenty-ninth Camba, a convinced and militant Communist, deserted and was taken prisoner after having resisted fiercely.

While the army was winning this new victory, the Military High Command decided to send new troops to Valle Grande, the center of the current operation. On the night of September 25, the Second Ranger Battalion, seven hundred men trained for months by American instructors, left the city of Santa Cruz for Valle Grande. Platoons from this unit would soon deal the revolutionary movement its mortal blow.

The isolated clashes and occasional skirmishes between the government troops and the insurgents in the Fourth Division's sector gave the impression that the guerrillas were very active. It seemed as if they were closely observing the third of the three "golden rules" of guerrilla warfare: constant mobility. As we have seen, what had really happened was that the insurgent force had been separated into two groups. Che led the principal group (the vanguard and the center), and operated in the south, in the Muyupampa–Monteagudo sector. Joaquín led the rear guard, and, at the beginning at least, operated a little farther north, fruitlessly trying to find the main group. When he saw that this was useless, he moved a few dozen miles farther north, in the region of Ipitá–El Pincal–Ñancahuazú. A relatively large stretch of mountains with tangled brush and no easily accessible roads separated the two groups.

Jorge Vásquez Viaña and a companion, who had been, in April, on a specific mission in the area bordering Monteagudo, were separated from the other groups and frequently clashed with political authorities and local police units. This confused disposition of the guerrilla troops, with no central command, was what gave them a certain appearance of carrying out tactical missions everywhere at once.

We referred above to the thousand-and-one crises faced by the insurgents, especially those caused by the fact that medicine and food reached them sporadically. The problem of food became exasperating as time went by. The peasants were sharp businessmen and for a time they did a booming business since the rebels, in accordance with the guerrilla principle of getting the civilian population on their side, paid generously for all the merchandise they bought. In the days when they were prowling about in the vicinity of Samaipata, there was one baker who sold out all his wares in a few hours, making a 500 per cent profit. During the critical times in August, the guerrillas paid $.83 (U.S. money) for half a pound of bread and $10 for a chicken.

We learned how desperate this food situation was in an interview we had with the guerrilla Camba:

> Well, at times we had a very bad time of it. When the engagement began we had a few days when we were short of food. But we never went more than five days without food supplies. We always had something to eat once a day. But on the whole we weren't short of provisions. Of course, we had to limit ourselves. We couldn't get enough food for the kind of work we were doing. As a result of the long marches we made we were weak, exhausted, sick. But when we finally got food, we rested a few days, and they treated us with vitamins so that we'd be somewhat healthier again.

The life of the army in the field was no bed of roses either. The detachments quartered in large or small towns were relatively comfortable, but the small units detached from the main groups to pursue the enemy and commanded by junior officers were habitually exposed to hunger and exhaustion in their fight against both a human enemy and a hostile nature. The campaign diaries of these young officers eloquently reflect their great suffering.

This calls to mind a story, perhaps apocryphal, about a civilian anti-guerrilla group. Leaders of the farmers in Cochabamba organized a detachment of peasants and sent them off to Ñancahuazú. The lack of discipline and the failure of those who had been mobilized to adapt aroused general protest from the civilian population wherever they appeared. They were more a hindrance than a help to the armed forces, and a military commander had to ask his superiors to send the group back where it had come from. The army thus understandably preferred to use its own units.

Guevara himself had to grant that the military units had both great physical endurance and high morale. There are several notations to that effect in his diary. In his monthly summary at the end of April he wrote: ". . . the army (at least one company or two) has improved its tactics: they surprised us in Taperillas and were not demoralized in El Mesón."

15

The Death of
Che Guevara

The unit changed its marching rhythm and fell into the traditional goose step. The authorities and military leaders occupying the official reviewing stand loudly applauded the troops passing in front of the flag. The soldiers in turn held their heads high and paraded by with the martial spirit characteristic of young recruits. People got a good idea of the firepower of each unit in the different squadrons, for they were equipped with gleaming FAL and SIG rifles, the former made in Argentina and the latter in Switzerland, as well as automatic arms made in the United States. The label "U.S. Army" could be seen on the field equipment and on the camouflage suits of the young Rangers, which contrasted with their dark complexions. It was September 24, and this peaceful demonstration in Santa Cruz was being held to commemorate the anniversary of a heroic day of battle in the war for national liberation.

Company B, Ranger Battalion, marching along so smartly, was especially trained for combat against guerrillas. A short time after the guerrilla activity had begun, the company began to receive military instruction from American specialists and Bolivian officers who had studied combat strategy at the John F. Kennedy Center for Special Strategy, a school run by the United States at Fort Gulick, Panama Canal Zone. The abandoned sugar mill of La Esperanza, forty-five miles north of Santa Cruz, served as a training camp to

184

teach the Rangers the repressive tactics that had been used in Vietnam, Laos, and the Dominican Republic. Fourteen days after the parade these young soldiers were to take Ernesto Guevara prisoner in the Churo ravine.

At noon on September 25, the officers received the order that put an end to their arduous training. A new phase began that afternoon as the troops were loaded into the heavy "Alligator" trucks and driven to the Río Grande, where they would receive their baptism of fire as they confronted the remaining insurgent force. El Fuerte, Estanque, Pujro, and Abra del Picacho were part of the itinerary and the company finally arrived, on October 4, in the forgotten town of Higuera, which today is famous in Latin America for having been the scene of the death of Che Guevara.

From the heights of Higuera several ravines wander down toward the Río Grande: Jaguey, Churo, Tusca, Higuera, San Antonio. For several days the insurgents had been camped at the meeting point of the first three. The intense movement of the military forces in the neighborhood had put an end to the guerrillas' mobility; their moral and physical strength had been diminishing. Doubtless the daring attack by Lieutenant Eduardo Galindo on September 26, which culminated in the death of Coco Peredo and two other guerrillas, had something to do with their depression.

Around noon on October 7, an old peasant woman from the neighborhood who was looking for a goat that had strayed from her flock discovered the guerrillas' temporary camp. Guevara wrote in his diary:

Eleven months have gone by since our inauguration as guerrillas; the day was spent without complications, bucolically, until 12:30, when an old woman shepherding her goats came into the ravine where we were camped and it was necessary to take her prisoner. The woman gave no truthful information about the soldiers, answering all our questions by saying that she didn't know anything, that she hasn't been around here for a long time; she only gave information on the roads back. From what she says we are approximately one league from Higuera and another from Jaguey and two from Pucara. At 17:30 Inti, Aniceto, and Pablito went to the old woman's house; she has a daughter sick in bed and another half-dwarfed; they gave her fifty pesos so that she wouldn't say a word, but there is little hope that she will do so in spite of her promises.

The guerrillas had lost all confidence. The casual incident upset them and made them nervous. They discussed and analyzed other such events. Most of the casualties on the guerrilla side had been caused by informers among the people in the region. "The peasants are as impenetrable as stones . . . " As a consequence, they decided to abandon the position.

At twilight on October 7, as the sun went down behind the hills, to be followed by a very dark night, seventeen men in a column began marching up Churo ravine. Che writes what was to be the next-to-last paragraph in his diary: "The seventeen of us left under a waning moon. The march was very tiring and we left many tracks in the ravine where we were. There are no houses around, only potato patches irrigated by ditches from the same brook. At two we stopped to rest, since we couldn't go on. Chino turns into a regular old woman when there is a night march."

A little later Víctor Colomi, a peasant, tried to take advantage of the trickle of water running down Churo ravine to water his potato crop. He opened the irrigation ditch, stretched his limbs, and looked for a tree to lean on. Soon he heard footsteps and barely audible voices. He became frightened, hid behind the tree, and saw bearded, emaciated men go by, awkwardly carrying large knapsacks on backs that seemed to bend their starving bodies in two. They were all armed. Three of them went by. Colomi waited and a few minutes later many more passed by: Colomi counted seventeen of them in all.

The peasant knew who they were, for everybody had been talking about the guerrillas and the government had offered a reward for their capture. He had all night to decide what to do since the army had set a curfew for security reasons and had prohibited all movement at night. So it was morning before Colomi sent his son to Higuera, about two and a half miles away, to the commander of the army company established in the zone, Captain Gary Prado Salmón. Not finding him there, the messenger went on to Abra del Picacho, the next town, and told Prado what his father had discovered some hours before. Captain Prado immediately informed Valle Grande, where the command of the Eighth Division was, and prepared for combat, intending to box the guerrillas in and surround them.

Churo ravine runs roughly north and south. Prado placed Lieutenant Carlos Pérez's platoon at the top of the ravine, toward the north, in order to close off this exit. Lieutenant Eduardo Huerta's platoon went to do the same to Tusca ravine, which borders Churo on the east. Prado positioned himself and the rest of his forces where the two ravines meet, a little over a mile south of Lieutenant Pérez's position. The rebels were thus practically surrounded, since all the area was now controlled by army patrols.

At approximately 10:30, at the same time as the break-up of the first watch, a scuffle took place near Lieutenant Pérez's position. The soldiers were the first to fire, and rifle fire and mortar shells stripped the thin foliage from the trees. From the bottom of the ravine, the guerrillas returned the fire with automatic weapons and immediately the army had two dead and one wounded. These casualties cooled the soldiers' enthusiasm and their fire became less intense, tapering off into isolated bursts during most of the afternoon.

The guerrilla band had been in difficulty for several days. The zone in which they found themselves was different from the wild and heavily wooded mountains where they had fought before. Here the vegetation was sparse, thorny plants with thick stems and scraggly trees clinging to the sides of the ravine. At the bottom of the ravine, alongside the narrow stream of water, the vegetation was thicker and leafier.

Guevara had had no medicine for a month. His asthma was constricting his lungs and throat and preventing him from breathing. There were times when he would ask his comrades to beat him on the chest while he lay on the ground or hung from the branch of a tree. Apparently this helped his breathing. Some weeks before, he had sent Urbano to get drugs from the caves at Ñancahuazú. Urbano managed to get to one cave that had not yet been discovered and he brought back all that he could carry. But this supply had been exhausted and the only medicine left was two bottles of a special kind of collyrium with a strong admixture of cortisone. When he was feeling particularly ill—or when they were getting ready for action—Che would inject himself with the collyrium mixture, but this helped for only a very short time.

On the day of the battle in Churo ravine, Sunday, October 8, Guevara had only sixteen men under his command. The men noticed troop movements at the top of the ravine at about ten o'clock and

Che told his men that if the troops attacked before twelve, the situation would be quite serious, but if the action took place around three, or after that, there was a better chance of resisting and getting out of the ravine because of the approaching darkness. The situation was sized up. The guerrillas had noticed the enveloping movement of the army troops, but they hoped that they had not been completely surrounded. Guevara asked for seven volunteers to sacrifice themselves and cover the retreat of the others: all the men in the squadron stepped forward.

In his television speech on October 15 announcing the death of Che, Fidel Castro said: "It is always said that guerrillas are surrounded. We were always surrounded, for example: we had the sea behind us, the plains and the rice fields in front of us, and for a long time our movements took place in an area that in general was only six miles wide and six miles long."

But the position of the guerrilla nucleus in Churo ravine was different. Che's men were at the bottom of a ravine whose heights and exits were held by the enemy. Little more than a mile separated the enemy positions. Moreover, according to official announcements from military sources printed in the newspapers, "Operation Parabano," whose aim was to liquidate the last remaining guerrillas, had mobilized from a thousand to fifteen hundred men in the region.

Che decided to leave a covering force while he and the rest tried to get out by going down the ravine to the southeast, toward the Río Grande. The platoon headed by Inti—which up to now had constituted the vanguard of the group—insisted on being the covering or resisting force. Guevara hesitated and talked the matter over. He had his doubts: Inti and Pombo were two of his most valuable men. Nonetheless, these men firmly expressed their intention to remain and cover the retreat of their leader and his companions. The group was made up of Inti, Pombo, Urbano, Benigno, Darío, Ñato, and Aniceto. These seven men promptly took up positions and the battle began at around 10:30 in the morning. But a burst of machine-gun fire a little less than a mile below them (one of the bullets probably wounded Che) indicated clearly that they were completely surrounded.

Once the first encounter, which was in Lieutenant Pérez's sector, was over, there was relative calm, interspersed with sporadic exchanges of fire. Captain Prado's unit had not yet entered into action:

he had his men dispersed over a wide area and did not think it prudent to order them into the ravine until Lieutenant Huerta arrived. This situation soon changed.

"Captain, the guerrillas are coming down the ravine," a soldier in charge of a heavy machine gun exclaimed, almost shouting.

"Fire at them as soon as you see them," Prado ordered.

A few minutes went by and then the machine gun began to fire. It fired two bursts and the recruit counted one sure hit and two probables. Then there was silence; only the echoes of detonations less than a mile above indicated that the battle was still going on.

The command post was defended by three men. The recruits, enthusiastic soldiers, wanted to fight, but this was hardly possible considering their position at the top of the ravine. They were almost bored. Suddenly one of them roused the others:

"Two men are coming up," he shouted.

"Keep quiet; we'll catch them," another answered.

Two guerrillas were climbing up the side of the ravine trying to reach a position on the heights. They were barely covering themselves behind a screen of brambles and bushes. One of them was wounded; the other, a short, strong, dark man, was holding him up and dragging a submachine gun along the ground.

"Halt! Surrender!" the three soldiers yelled to them, jumping out from where they had been hiding behind some vegetation.

Two M-1's and an FAL were pointed at the guerrillas' chests. The dark man dropped his weapon.

The threats of one of the soldiers seemed to imply violence. And when everything led him to believe that the threats were about to become a reality, the wounded prisoner exclaimed:

"Don't kill us. I'm Che. I'm worth more to you alive than dead."

One of these efficient, American-trained soldiers went up to Captain Prado. "Captain, Captain, we've caught two. One of them says he's Che."

It was about 1 P.M.

Captain Prado and two of his soldiers went down to the place where his men were holding the man who had said he was Che and ordered that the prisoners be tied up with leather thongs and rope.

The Captain realized immediately that he had before him the legendary guerrilla who had dropped out of sight for two years. The man answered the description of Che that the "American advisers" had given during the long months of training at La Esperanza. He asked peremptorily:

"Who are you?"

"I'm Che," the captive guerrilla replied calmly. The other man identified himself as Willy.

Guevara was unarmed; his M-2 had not been used since the first skirmish that morning when a bullet had shot it out of his hands. He had a knapsack over his shoulder, a leather documents case hanging from his belt on the right side, and another of thick canvas on the left side. These contained his campaign diary, books, notebooks, some poems he had written, documents, personal observations, opinions about his subordinates, and a very small number of personal effects. The campaign diary was kept in two notebooks from Germany, with dark brown covers: one was for 1966 and the other for 1967, the first of these with annotations beginning November 7.

A bullet had lodged in Che's right calf and he asked for medical attention. Captain Prado looked at the wound and explained that two of his soldiers were more seriously wounded. Che's leg was simply bandaged to avoid hemorrhaging.

The battle was still going on in other sectors. Prado left two soldiers with the prisoners and gave orders to kill them if the guerrillas attacked the area. He believed that if Che's companions located him, they would try to rescue him. But Guevara said to him:

"Don't worry, Captain; it's all over . . . "

Prado hastened to report to his superiors. Communications with Valle Grande, the headquarters of the Tactical Group to which he belonged, went through radio station GRC-9 in Abra del Picacho. Captain Prado said into the microphone:

"This is Thin Man. Attention, this is Thin Man. I have Papa. Over."

A few minutes went by. The receiver seemed to have gone dead. Then a voice came from Valle Grande:

"This is Saturn. Let me talk to the Thin Man to confirm that you have Papa." ("Saturn" was the code name for Colonel Zenteno.) Prado then confirmed that he had Papa, and asked: "How do you want him?"

"Alive!" he was told. Prado asked for the helicopter to transfer the prisoner, and Zenteno promised to send it. Captain Prado then ordered the prisoners and the wounded to be moved some three hundred yards from where they were. Some soldiers meanwhile piled up brush and straw to make a fire to signal to the helicopter. The wait lasted twenty minutes. Everyone was tense and nervous.

Meanwhile, Prado's men brought in the bodies of two unidentified guerrillas, and set them down very close to the prisoners, who seemed relaxed and resigned to their fate.

The officer and his men came up to the wounded guerrilla chief and talked to him for a few minutes, asking him the expected questions: Why he hadn't fought with the guerrillas in his own country; why he had chosen Bolivia as the place for his experiments. The answers came immediately: "The revolution has no geographic borders. The battlefield should be wherever there is imperialism." When the questions were offensive Che said nothing.

There was almost no firing now where Captain Prado's position had been. But higher up the fight was continuing and the echoes of the shots could be heard clearly. The wounded prisoner, now completely bound, remained impassive.

The characteristic whir of the helicopter was heard even before the soldiers could see it. Soon they could see it silhouetted against the hills as it circled, searching. The soldiers were ready to set the little signal fires ablaze, but at that instant there was a heavy burst of fire: the guerrillas were shooting at the helicopter. Captain Prado thought that the helicopter landing would be very dangerous—the guerrillas might take suicidal measures in their eagerness to bring it down and prevent the transfer of their leader. He told the pilot, Major Jaime Niño de Guzmán, to land in Higuera.

The pilot pointed out that it was too late in the day to wait for Prado in Higuera. He arranged with Prado to take the helicopter back to Valle Grande and return early the next day.

Then began the two-mile trek back to the little town of Higuera, a hamlet where about three hundred people scratch out a living from a poor, rough, gray soil.

Two patrols were left behind to prevent the remaining guerrillas from escaping from the ravine during the night. The first patrol took up a position at the top of the ravine, to the north; the other settled down in San Antonio ravine, the place where Tusca, Churo, and

Jaguey ravines meet. The rest of the men and the prisoners proceeded painfully, carrying the seriously wounded and the dead, both soldiers and guerrillas, on stretchers.

Guevara leaned for support on a soldier, and conversed with another, named Benito Jiménez, who had been slightly wounded in the left knee. From behind, Willy did what he could to help hold him up. Five days later, in Valle Grande, Jiménez was to recall this march: "Che walked along with no signs of desperation. His wound seemed at times to hurt him a lot. He was almost dragging his foot. He talked with me, asking me about my family. But Captain Prado wouldn't let us talk. We couldn't say any more to each other."[1]

At one point Guevara asked for a cigarette. Captain Prado offered him a pack of Bolivian "Pacific" cigarettes made of light tobacco. The guerrilla chief refused one:

"Thanks anyway, I don't smoke that light tobacco."

"What brand do you prefer?" the officer asked.

"Astoria. I smoke dark tobacco."

A soldier offered him a cigarette of that brand. Guevara took advantage of the halt to ask them to untie him.

"Look, Captain, don't you think it's useless to keep me tied up? There's nothing I can do; I'm wounded and defenseless."

Prado gave orders to untie him.

All that afternoon the little town of Higuera had listened attentively to the sounds of battle. Men and women, children and old people, were at the outskirts of the town watching for the arrival of the troops. As the soldiers approached, a woman broke the silence and cried almost prophetically, pointing to Guevara:

"Here he is, kill him! Kill him right now."

Two or three voices were heard agreeing with her.

Higuera is not an important town. It is little more than a cluster of shacks with a couple of alleys as streets. The mud schoolhouse, in the center of town, looks like a shack, with its walls covered with a calcimine that once was white. After making the town the base of its operations, the army had made the school its command post. Colonel Andrés Selić, the commander of the Regiment of Engineers, with

---

[1] From a conversation one of the authors had with the wounded soldier.

headquarters in Valle Grande, had arrived some hours before in the helicopter. The prisoners were handed over to Lieutenant Tomás Toty Aguilera, the officer on guard, and put in two separate classrooms, which served as cells.

Guevara spent his first moments in the classroom reading what was on the blackboards. The schoolmistress of Higuera, Julia Vallejos, found him doing this and they exchanged a few words.

"Congratulations, señorita," Che said. "This is good work. But I'd like to point out one thing to you: there are no accents on monosyllables." His eye for detail had caught the phrase "Tengo fe en Dios" [I have faith in God] with an accent on the second word.

Meanwhile Colonel Selić made radio contact with his wife in Valle Grande and instructed her to visit the ladies of the town and have them gather at the airport the next day so as to avoid the prisoner's being transferred out of Valle Grande. The idea was to put pressure on the government to make this three-hundred-year-old town the site of Guevara's eventual trial.

The night was long for the prisoner, for he was questioned several times. The man from the CIA—"Doctor" Eduardo Gonzáles—who had also arrived in the helicopter, took a special interest in these sessions. They could get no information out of the prisoner.

The officers kept going in and out of the classroom, alternately talking with Che and questioning him. At one point, there was the following exchange between two officers as they looked at Guevara sitting tied up on the floor.

"What do you suppose he's thinking about?" one said.

"About the immortality of the burro, of course," the other replied.

"No," Guevara broke in, "I'm thinking of the immortality of the revolution."

During a visit to Chile the co-director of *Presencia*, Alberto Bailey Gutiérrez, gave a very interesting version of the events of that night. He said that at one point in the interrogations Colonel Zenteno Anaya insulted the guerrilla leader and Guevara responded by slapping Zenteno in the face. In a rage, the Colonel took out his revolver and shot Che in the right arm.

Che's easily visible wound in the arm lends a certain air of truth to the story, but it ignores one fundamental fact: Zenteno Anaya did not arrive in Higuera until the morning of October 9; he didn't even see the prisoner the night before.

Nonetheless, other sources say that the story is true, but that it was another officer, Colonel Andrés Selić, who had been in Higuera since the afternoon of the eighth. Selić did in fact interrogate Guevara, and, according to some soldiers who were on guard at the time, he left the school looking visibly angry after a shot had been heard. However, there is not enough evidence for us to state categorically that this officer actually shot Guevara.[2]

At four in the morning Lieutenants Pérez and Águilar returned to Churo ravine to finish the operation begun the day before.

As dawn broke on October 9, Carlos Guzmán, a young peasant from Pucara who had been supplying the army with provisions, arrived in Higuera and asked to see the prisoner he had heard so much about. His request was granted and he went inside the school. Guevara looked at the peasant's tanned face, noticed that he had two lower teeth missing, and said to him:

"What a shame that we didn't meet each other before. You're missing two teeth; I would have put in new ones for you. You have to take care of your teeth if you want to be in good health." Guzmán looked calmly at the face of the captive, and, as he himself related later, he left the room with tears in his eyes. Then he said to the friends gathered around him: "He has a look that melts your heart."

A few minutes later, the characteristic whir of a helicopter announced the arrival of Colonel Joaquín Zenteno Anaya. The division commander received reports from Colonel Selić and Captain Prado. He looked at the prisoners but did not speak with them. He spoke for quite some time to Gonzáles, the CIA agent. A little later, he and Captain Prado went about a mile in the direction of Churo ravine; Prado showed him the battlefield from the top of the ravine and outlined his plans for finishing off the small remaining guerrilla nucleus.

Meanwhile, the interrogations continued in Higuera. The school

---

[2] Most of the young conscripts and peasants were questioned over and over by journalists, and their stories are vague and contradictory, perhaps because they were afraid, because their memories were faulty, or because they were simply not very observant.

was surrounded by a heavy cordon of soldiers, and peasants loitered in the vicinity.

In the middle of the morning, Guevara had a presentiment of what was going to happen to him. He asked for a plate of food: "Bring me a plate of food. I want to die on a full stomach." In a few minutes he was brought some potatoes with a few slices of mutton.

The night before, Captain Prado had ordered Warrant Officer Villarroel to transfer radio station GRC-9 from Abra del Picacho to Higuera. Villarroel arrived at dawn and installed the equipment in the schoolhouse. Around 10 A.M. the order came from Barrientos to eliminate Ernesto Guevara. It was in code but not in cipher. Later, in one of the corners of the little school, the military officers talked over how to eliminate "the Che Guevara problem." They decided to ask for a volunteer. Before the "sentence" could be carried out, those who received it were prey to an irresistible temptation. They were photographed with the prisoner, who without knowing it, was from this moment on a condemned man.

It was 1:40 in the afternoon of October 9. Warrant Officer Mario Terán came into the schoolroom, which was lighted only through one partially closed window. He came a few steps inside the room, carrying an M-2. Guevara stared at him and Terán took a few steps backward and left the room. The troops waiting outside to hear the shots looked at each other in surprise. Angry voices shouted commands and Terán went back into the room. Suddenly he raised the weapon and fired. A hail of bullets struck Guevara's body. In the last moment of his life, Guevara raised his hands to his mouth and helplessly bit down on his fingers in an attempt to stifle a scream. Then his lifeless body fell slowly against the wall. His eyes, staring from his dirty bearded face, looked serene and full of hope. Ernesto "Che" Guevara was no more; he had passed from legend into myth.

Sergeant Francisco Huanca liquidated Willy, the tireless mining-union official from Huanuni. Simón Cuba died knowing that the sacrifice of his life was an offering to the cause of his comrades in the mines.

The little town of Higuera entered history. A great many of its three hundred inhabitants heard the bursts of rifle fire and guessed what had happened. Since that day, journalists and the curious have been prohibited from visiting this little town.

As all this was happening in Higuera, shots were still ringing out in Churo ravine. Just after they began the new operations, the army troops found two other guerrillas hiding in a cave. In the exchange of fire Antonio and El Chino died. Just before this, the body of Aniceto was found in the position where Inti had been; the body had been just barely covered with brush. Later the bodies of Arturo and Pacho were found.

Once he had died and his material possessions had been divided up among the soldiers, here is the legacy that Ernesto Guevara left to his children:[3]

> To my dear children Hildita, Adeilita, Camilo, Celia, and Ernesto:
>
> If you ever have to read this letter, it will be because I am no longer among you.
>
> You will hardly remember me, and the youngest children will not remember me at all.
>
> Your father has always been a man who acted in accordance with what he thought, and there is no denying that he has been faithful to his convictions.
>
> Grow up like good revolutionaries. Study a lot so as to master the technique that allows man to master nature. Remember that the revolution is the important thing, and that each of us is worth nothing alone.
>
> Above all make yourself capable of responding in your heart of hearts to any injustice committed against anyone in any part of the world. This is the most beautiful quality in a revolutionary.
>
> Good-by forever, children; I still hope to see you again. A big kiss and a big hug from
>
> *Papa*

---

[3] Published in the Cuban periodical *Juventud Rebelde*, Havana.

16

Che's Death:
The Official Reaction

During the last two weeks of September and the first days of October, newspapermen had used the town of Valle Grande—7000 inhabitants —as their center for information. The influx of journalists from Camiri, where they were covering the Debray trial, and other parts of the country, to Valle Grande was caused by repeated reports from official sources indicating that the end of the guerrilla chief and his last followers was imminent. Thus the dramatic military communiqué of the afternoon of October 8—"This is Thin Man, I have Papa"—was picked up by all of the professional news hunters. One of the reporters picked up the army's radio band. On Sunday night, with the report still unconfirmed, it was obvious that a big story was breaking.

Moreover, during that night and the morning of October 9, Señora Socorro de Selić, the wife of the officer who had been sent to Higuera, carried out the mission that her husband had requested with an unusual sense of responsibility. She visited the ladies of the town and invited them to appear at the airport in order to keep the guerrilla leader from being sent away.[1]

---

[1] Some days later the people of Valle Grande demonstrated in the streets of the town, demanding that Che's corpse be kept until the government allocated the funds needed to finance some indispensable public works in that locality.

197

These goings-on, which did not escape the news-hungry journalists, only sharpened their curiosity.

The news of Che's capture spread before it was confirmed officially. In its issue of October 9, 1967, *El Diario* published a dispatch from its special correspondent in Valle Grande reporting the Higuera clash. The story emphasized that wounded guerrillas had been captured. "The helicopter only brought the corpse of the soldier Morales and one wounded man to Valle Grande, although the Command of the Eighth Division reported officially that the 'Rangers' had captured some wounded guerrillas and had the bodies of others." Further on the dispatch added: "Other informed sources said that the troops had captured three guerrillas and had the bodies of two others." On the same day the morning newspaper *Presencia* published a report about the Churo battle: "Three guerrillas were killed, two were wounded—one of them may be Che Guevara—and two soldiers were killed and four wounded in the latest clash which took place yesterday near Higuera, to the south of Valle Grande. The rumor that Che was one of the seriously wounded men whom the guerrillas left on the battlefield comes from a high government source." The article continues: "Last night General Alfredo Ovando Candia, Commander in Chief of the armed forces, said that in yesterday's clash, some seven kilometers to the north of Higuera, two soldiers were killed, four were wounded, and three guerrillas were killed. However, it was learned that two of the guerrillas were badly wounded and had fallen into the hands of the army. A reliable source says that one of the wounded is Che Guevara."

The version of the story which said that there were wounded prisoners became less important as bigger news was released. Eventually, there was no more talk of guerrillas having been taken prisoner; they were all supposed to be dead. Only *El Diario's* special correspondent thought that this situation was strange. In a story from Valle Grande on October 10, he wrote: "The corpses of six other guerrillas will be taken to Valle Grande tomorrow, Tuesday. And nothing more has been said of wounded guerrillas, as there was at the beginning."

The next series of contradictions begins in Valle Grande.

On October 9 there was as much military as journalistic activity; it was extraordinary. At 1:45 P.M. Colonel Joaquín Zenteno Anaya returned to Valle Grande from Higuera and reported: "Che Guevara died in combat yesterday." General Ovando Candia, Commander in Chief of the armed forces, General David Lafuente, army Chief of Staff, and Rear Admiral Horacio Ugarteche, Commander of the Navy, among other officers, arrived there at 1:50 P.M. by air.

Since noon, a considerable crowd of people had gathered at the entrance to the airport. The news of the arrival of Che Guevara's body electrified the population. Men and women, young and old, had an overwhelming desire to see the remains of the guerrilla commander, but a guard kept them back.

At five o'clock the helicopter landed.[2] A small group of soldiers untied the body from the outer platform and carried it to a small truck that drove at top speed through the narrow, winding streets of dirt and stone to the Señor de Malta hospital. Children raced into town behind the vehicle and another restless crowd of curiosity-seekers appeared at the hospital, only to find their way barred by a squad of heavily armed soldiers. Only the newspapermen were able to enter after a great deal of negotiating and demanding.

The corpse was put in the laundry room, which had been turned into a morgue some days earlier as an emergency measure. Guevara was placed on the same concrete bench where Coco's and Tania's remains had lain a few days before. Doctors Moisés Abraham Baptista and José Martínez Casso, two German nuns, and two male nurses partially washed the body, opened an incision in the neck, and injected formaldehyde to retard decomposition.

Meanwhile, police agents watched over the operation and a plainclothesman took fingerprints. When he had finished, Dr. Abraham Baptista told newsmen that he had taken part in an interesting event, and emphasized that he had been impressed by the good condition of Che's feet in spite of the long marches. Dr. Martínez Casso stated that the guerrilla's body had several bullet wounds, "including one through the heart that had caused instantaneous death."

---

[2] It is interesting to note that, according to English journalist Chris Roper, who was an eyewitness, there were wooden boxes on the airfield lettered: "Four charges of napalm for incendiary bombs—FORÇA AEREA BRASILEIRA."

When the doctors had finished their work, the corpse was surrounded by identification experts from the CIA and the Ministry of the Interior, who again took fingerprints and photographs.

The agents from the Central Intelligence Agency who were most active in the Señor de Malta hospital were Félix Ramos and Eduardo Gonzáles. Both had arrived in Santa Cruz on August 5 and registered at the Gran Hotel Santa Cruz as businessmen. They were extremely well-dressed. They spoke very little with the hotel employees, and when they did they kept repeating that they were going to invest money in local businesses. They were traveling with U.S. passports: Gonzáles with No. A8093737 and Ramos with No. O152052. They checked out of the hotel on August 12.

Toward the end of the month, Ramos returned from La Esperanza, with U.S. Major Ralph "Pappy" Shelton, the American adviser to the Bolivian army. This time Ramos was in uniform, although with no insignia or sign of rank, and speaking an English which was much more fluent than his Spanish had been.

The supposed Dr. Gonzáles was in Higuera questioning Che from the night of October 8 on, with no results. Immediately after Guevara's death, the CIA agent minutely examined his corpse, carefully photographing every feature of his anatomy. The fact that Guevara's eyes stayed open was due to the fact that the agent kept forcing the eyelids open while he photographed the eyes, until rigor mortis set in. Several officers witnessed this thorough examination, including Lieutenant Tomás "Totty" Aguilera, who later described it to one of the authors, whom he knew was a journalist.

Gonzáles devoted the following day to carefully and patiently photographing Che's campaign diary and other documents that had fallen into the hands of the military, and then did the same thing with the papers taken from the other guerrillas.

Félix Ramos, a tall, heavy-set, authoritarian man with sparse blond hair, was the dominant figure in Valle Grande. He supervised every phase of the operation: He was at the airport preparing the landing strip for the helicopter, ordering the corpses to be taken to the hospital, keeping the newsmen out and threatening to have two of them, Brian Moser and Richard Gott, expelled from the city. His power was so great that his orders could be revoked only by the Commander in Chief of the armed forces.

The activities of these foreign agents were apparently carried on "without the knowledge" of Colonel Zenteno Anaya, Commander of the Eighth Division, who had jurisdiction over the area they were operating in. At a long press conference in Valle Grande, Colonel Zenteno answered the following question:

NEWSMAN: Are members of the CIA participating in the investigation?

ZENTENO: Until now we have worked exclusively with the aid of Bolivian citizens. I am not aware of the presence of any.[3]

The crowd surrounding the hospital was growing minute by minute. The mass of people was pressing against the armed guards, who were finally unable to hold it back. At that moment the military chiefs arrived. General Ovando spoke to the crowd: "Everyone has a right to see, but wait until the identification of the corpse has been completed." His promise calmed them, and they settled down to wait.

The eyes of the corpse lying on a stretcher were open, and they seemed to be asking what had caused this unnecessary sacrifice. The open lips seemed to be about to smile or to try to say something. The rigidity of death gave Che an air of serenity. He had a Christlike profile. The body was covered with an old, worn jacket of coarse cloth. Later the bare torso was shown to the newsmen and those who came to satisfy their curiosity. The olive-green pants, similar to a soldier's uniform, also showed the effects of the rough marches. The feet wore thick socks made of green wool and worn-out boots, symbols of the hardships, the long marches, and the physical and moral efforts of eleven months of guerrilla activity.

The body had eight or nine bullet holes in the neck, the thorax, and the upper and lower extremities.

Identification was based on fingerprint records sent from Buenos Aires on October 9, and dating back to the time when Guevara took his military physical in Argentina in 1946. León, a captured Bolivian guerrilla, a few days before had also identified the corpse as that of Ramón, the guerrilla leader of Ñancahuazú.

---

[3] *El Diario* (October 11, 1967).

After the corpse had been prepared, General Ovando's promise was kept. For a long time people filed by on their strange pilgrimage. There was an expression of sorrow on their faces. Their looks met Guevara's eyes, which still seemed to have some of the vitality of life. When the curiosity-seekers saw him they stopped talking and observed him respectfully. People fought to get into the hospital until late at night.

President Barrientos had offered 50,000 Bolivian pesos for the capture, dead or alive, of Che Guevara—preferably alive, according to the leaflets—and, since the peasants of Higuera had cooperated in one way or another in his fall, Barrientos decided to give them that sum in a special ceremony to be held in that town.

The crowd gathered awaiting the head of state, who arrived in a helicopter. Barrientos made a speech praising the behavior of the Bolivian peasantry in the anti-guerrilla fight. He then asked his listeners to designate a person they trusted to receive the cash prize. The community decided that the person to receive the money should be Father Schaller, the parish priest from Pucara. The President handed the priest a bundle of money and continued his speech. When the orator finished, Father Schaller asked for the floor and said: "Mr. President, please excuse me, but these people trust me. The package that you gave me ought to contain 50,000 Bolivian pesos, but I can only find 39,000. I request you to clarify this error in front of the peasants."

The President, half-surprised and half-smiling when he realized that an error had been made, said: "It has been a mistake, comrades. I promise you that no later than tomorrow I will send you the 11,000 pesos that are missing."

On October 10, the armed forces issued Communiqué 46/67, in which they officially reported Che's death:

> During mopping-up operations in the zone of Churo ravine, which opens into San Antonio ravine, two other unidentified dead bandits were found.
>
> Army forces working with the inhabitants of the zone occupied

the towns adjacent to the critical areas, where the final actions took place.

Enlarging on our Communiqué 45/67, we are in a position to say that the dead Reds are: Ernesto "Che" Guevara (Argentinian); Arturo (Cuban); Antonio (Cuban); Aniceto (Cuban); Willy (Bolivian); and two unidentified corpses.

During the operations, arms, equipment, and important documents were captured, including Che Guevara's campaign diary.

That same day Colonel Zenteno Anaya held a long press conference in Valle Grande during which he gave a detailed report of the official version of Che's death. He reviewed army movements since the end of September and the events immediately preceding the Churo battle. He was no longer improvising, as he had been when he arrived at Higuera, and he was on firm ground as he gave the official explanation of the "Guevara case": Che "had fallen, critically wounded, and was later taken to Higuera in a coma . . ."[4]

Zenteno Anaya then answered questions from native and foreign newsmen concerning Che's death. Following is part of this very extensive conference:

NEWSMAN: Did Che Guevara confess or was he interrogated?

ZENTENO: That was not possible, since there were no specialized personnel available and his condition was such that he could not be questioned, since he was critically wounded.

The officer denied that Guevara had been executed, and his reply in this case was vehement.

Another question was asked:

NEWSMAN: Surely Che was able to communicate with the soldiers who carried him?

ZENTENO: Those who were in charge of transporting and evacuating Sr. Guevara from the scene of action were unaware of who he was. They were just combat soldiers, so they had no information as to the importance of the person they were carrying.

Yet on that same day and in the same place the Commander in Chief of the armed forces declared that the guerrilla leader had confessed his identity when he was captured: "I am Che Guevara. I have failed." In addition, General Ovando stated that "Che could not be questioned since he was fatally wounded when he was captured."[5]

---

[4] *Presencia* (October 11, 1967).
[5] *Ibid.*

Subsequently, this same officer gave a different version, one which contradicted his statements in Valle Grande. During a press conference held in Rio de Janeiro on November 27, 1967, while he was on vacation, he said that "Guevara received two wounds, one slight and the other serious, that passed through his pancreas and his lungs, causing an internal hemorrhage."[6] (Actually, as has already been noted, there were approximately nine bullets in Che's body.)

Days later, as reported in another dispatch from Rio de Janeiro, Ovando confirmed his more recent statements. The dispatch said in part: "Che Guevara had ample opportunity to talk after he was captured. And actually he talked for several hours. You understand why I can't reveal what he said, don't you? It is for reasons of security. But I can reveal that he was worried about two things: the error of judgment committed by Fidel Castro as a result of his desire for the success of the guerrilla war and the courage of Bolivian soldiers." Ovando added that he personally "had interrogated the revolutionary Ernesto Che Guevara for several hours before the guerrilla leader died. And now that I am on the subject, and in answer to another question, I give my word that Che was not shot as they are going around saying. We found him already wounded in the lungs."[7]

The controversy about the bullet in Che's heart shows another striking aspect of this battle of contradictions. The news that Che died of a bullet through the heart spread like wildlife. This version, which originally came from military sources, struck a new note of confusion in this mass of inaccuracies when it was compared with the original statements. The photographs of the corpse show a black opening a few fractions of an inch below the left nipple. The stories about the bullet in the heart are borne out by the statement one of the doctors who conducted the autopsy made to Max Simons, who quoted him in an Associated Press dispatch datelined Valle Grande, October 13: "José Martínez stated in an interview with AP that the two fatal bullets were fired into the heart and the lungs. However, he added that when he examined the corpse at 7:30 P.M. on the day following the battle the body was still flexible and it was easy to take off his clothes. Guevara must have died five or six hours before he examined the body."

---

[6] Information from the armed forces.
[7] From a Reuters dispatch.

Simons' interview is confirmed by a story which appeared in the October 15 issue of *El Diario* entitled, "There is a medical certificate of Che's death," which said:

> It was revealed that Doctors Abraham Moisés [*sic*] and José Martínez issued a certificate yesterday concerning the death of Ernesto Guevara . . . According to information received by *El Diario*, the document says that Che died as a result of two shots from a firearm. He received one in the heart and another in the lungs. The doctors believe that the bullet in the heart must have killed the guerrilla leader instantly. They also apparently believe that Che died on Monday at 11:30.

Abelardo Sejas, the correspondent for *El Diario* in Valle Grande, told us that Dr. Martínez Casso had informed him that on the night of Tuesday, October 10, he had performed an autopsy on Che's body to extract his internal organs, and that he had verified the fact that there was a bullet wound in the heart. The doctor added that that same night he had tried to make a death mask, but since the wax was not at the right temperature when it was spread on the face, it tore off a large part of the facial epidermis and the eyebrows when it was removed, leaving Guevara completely disfigured.

In addition, there were the assertions of the columnist "Politicus," writing in the daily newspaper *Presencia*:

> To what was said the day before yesterday and yesterday about the twenty-two hours that passed between the capture of the guerrilla leader and his death and the need to explain how and why his death occurred, there has now been added the testimony of Dr. José Martínez of Valle Grande.
>
> Dr. Martínez stated that Che died around 1 P.M. Monday from a bullet that passed through his heart, killing him instantly. He saw the corpse some five hours later and found it still flexible. . . .
>
> What Dr. Martínez said gives new weight to the theory that is circulating in other countries and that is spreading more and more rapidly: that Che was "finished off," to use the term some employ, or that he was "executed," as others put it.
>
> And this even affects the details. For example, it was said at the beginning that one of the fingers had been amputated for subsequent identification. But then two fingers were spoken of. So things were never clear.
>
> The same can be said of the explanation of the deaths of two

more guerrillas—making a total of seven who fell—when actually we knew of only five who had died. It had been said that two men were taken prisoner with Che, but this was never reported officially. It would also be good for the fate of these men to be clarified and for it to be known if they really were taken alive or not.

The director and the resident physician of the Señor de Malta hospital, Doctors Moisés Abraham Baptista and José Martínez Casso, respectively, denied the newspaper reports in the following letter dated October 17 and sent to *El Diario* and *Presencia*:

In the issue of *Presencia* dated Friday the thirteenth, No. 3408, and the one dated Sunday the fifteenth, No. 3410, and in the Saturday issue of *El Diario*, No. 21,693, we are mentioned as informants concerning the death of Ernesto Guevara.

We have read these articles with real astonishment, since they are completely untrue. As doctors who attended the examination and autopsy of Mr. Guevara, we cannot allow poorly informed journalists to speculate in print in our names.

If we have released any information about this event, it has been consistent with the death certificate and the autopsy report, which are in the hands of the military authorities and which surely, by now, are public knowledge. . . .

We have made absolutely no statements in regard to the manner and the exact time of Sr. Guevara's death, since this information was reported to the military authorities at the proper time.

As for the "bullet in the heart" that was said to have caused the death, we wish to clarify this because neither of us said such a thing, since we found in the autopsy that there was no wound in the heart and that death was produced by the hemorrhage caused by wounds in the lungs.

We hope, gentlemen, that you will publish this letter since our professional reputation has been placed in question as a result of said newspaper reports and because the press is characterized by nobility, and that you will thus end the speculations of which we have been made the object.

Another cause of confusion was the way Guevara's corpse was mutilated. First it was said that his thumbs had been cut off for purposes of identification. In order to put an end to these rumors,

President Barrientos gave the press a written statement which said, toward the end: "The last step that my government will take is to carry out the fingerprint test with the amputated finger, which will be placed at the disposal of the technicians." Obviously he was speaking of a single finger. Nevertheless, a few days later Argentinian federal police experts said that they had received "two hands submerged in a colorless liquid that smells like formaldehyde."

Official spokesmen for the armed forces reported that Che's body was buried "somewhere in Valle Grande" at dawn on October 11. Zenteno Anaya released this information in Valle Grande; Ovando and Lafuente confirmed it in La Paz. It was also learned that the corpse was removed from the Señor de Malta hospital at 4:30 in the morning.

However . . .

Attorney Roberto Guevara de la Serna, Che's younger brother, arrived in Santa Cruz from Buenos Aires on the morning of October 12 in a small Cessna airplane accompanied by reporters from *Gente* magazine and Argentinian TV. In Santa Cruz he asked Colonel Zenteno Anaya for permission to see his brother's remains. The Colonel replied that he had no orders from the High Command to comply with this request, and he advised Guevara to go to La Paz in order to arrange for the proper authorization. Roberto Guevara asked if those arrangements could be made by telegraph or telephone in order to save time. Colonel Zenteno Anaya told him that since it was a holiday those services were not in operation. As a result, Guevara traveled to La Paz for the purpose of seeing General Barrientos and General Ovando.

Ovando received Roberto Guevara, but not the reporters who were accompanying him. When he requested authorization to see his brother's remains he received this reply: "If you want to, go ahead, but you may not arrive in time. The armed forces have cremated his body." The news of the cremation was also released to the press by General Ovando's aide, Captain Oscar Pano.

Meanwhile, Barrientos announced that he did not believe that Guevara would be able to see his brother's body in Valle Grande "since it had not been possible to avoid decomposition." And in Valle

Grande, Zenteno Anaya gave the following version of the matter: "We told Sr. Guevara that in accordance with the rules of the armed forces and orders from superior officers, Che's body had been burned."

Roberto Guevara returned to Buenos Aires on October 13 without having succeeded in what he set out to do.

It does not seem entirely likely that the body was actually cremated. We are not familiar with the military rule referred to by Colonel Zenteno Anaya—and applied in a very peculiar way—and it would, in any case, be contrary to well-known precepts of civilian law. Besides, in a state that constitutionally "recognizes and upholds the Catholic, Apostolic and Roman religion," the authorities would not violate the dispositions contained in paragraphs I and II of Canon 1203 of Canonical Law that consider cremation an act contrary "to legitimate and not only Christian, but also natural feelings of humanity and piety . . ."

There have been very few cases of this type in Bolivia. One of them was Second Lieutenant Julio Quintanilla Zuazo, who was killed in the battle of Mandeyapecua. His heroic behavior on the field of battle and his family's connections made it possible to obtain the ecclesiastical and military authorization for the cremation of his body so that the ashes could be sent to La Paz. The process of cremation with improvised means lasted approximately three days. The smoke and odor which are characteristic of this operation permeated a large area.

In Valle Grande, on the other hand, the same phenomena were not observed. And the circumstances would necessarily have been the same, since there are no crematory ovens in Bolivia nor any special facilities for carrying out the operation. If the body had been burned, it would have been noticed by the inhabitants of Valle Grande and by the nearly one hundred newsmen who maintained a constant vigil, day and night, in order not to lose a single detail of what was happening in the Señor de Malta hospital and in the town as a whole.

This leads one to believe that there was no cremation, or if there was, it was very far from Valle Grande, in some isolated rural area. It is more logical to assume that the body was buried in an unknown location.

On October 16, in the following communiqué, the armed forces announced that the case concerning Ernesto Guevara's death was closed:

COMMUNIQUÉ

1. As the people of this and other countries were informed in the documents released by the Military High Command on October 9 and subsequent dates concerning the battle which took place in La Higuera between units of the armed forces and the Red group commanded by Ernesto Che Guevara, as a consequence of which the latter, among others, lost his life, the following is established:

a) Ernesto Guevara fell into the hands of our troops critically wounded and in full use of his mental faculties.

After the battle was over he was taken to the town of La Higuera, more or less at twenty hours on Sunday, October 8, where he died as a result of his wounds.

The transfer of the corpse to the city of Valle Grande took place at 16 hours on Monday the ninth in a helicopter belonging to the Bolivian Armed Forces.

b) Doctors Moisés Abraham Baptista and José Maria [sic] Casso, acting in accordance with their positions as director and resident physician of the Señor de Malta hospital, respectively, certified the death (Attachment 1) and formalized the autopsy ordered by the military authorities of Valle Grande in Attachment 2 that is attached.

c) With relation to the identification of the deceased and the authenticity of the diary that belonged to him, the Supreme Government of the Nation requested the cooperation of Argentinian technical bodies who sent three experts, one handwriting expert, and fingerprint experts, who confirmed the dead man's identity and certified that the handwriting in the campaign diary captured by our troops coincided with that of Ernesto Che Guevara. Attachment 3 shows the corresponding certificate.

d) The campaign diary and notebooks are documents that contain the account of the activities from the date of his arrival on October 7 and the opinions of this subversive leader of the members of the bands that he formed and the elements who collaborated with him both in this country and abroad. As a result, these are documents of exclusively military use.

2. Therefore, the Military High Command declares that no further report relating to the death of Ernesto Guevara will be made.

The death certificate, the report on the autopsy, and the identification by the Argentinian police will be found in Appendix VI.

A few days later the question of the cremation was reopened by General Ovando Candia in Rio de Janeiro, where he was vacationing. A UPI dispatch dated November 28 quoted Ovando as saying: "Guevara was not cremated. He was buried in a place which remains a Bolivian state secret." He added: "We refused to let Roberto Guevara see the corpse because we knew that he intended to deny that it was his brother."

On November 29, the Vice-President of the Republic, Luís Adolfo Siles Salinas, commenting on Ovando's most recent statements, made a point of mentioning that he was satisfied that Che's remains were not burned, but had been buried in a Christian fashion; he added that in his opinion the body ought to be returned to the family.

In a press conference on December 1, General Juan José Torres, acting Commander of the armed forces, said that General Ovando's statements concerning the burning of Che's body had been misinterpreted by the press in Rio de Janeiro. Ratifying the official version of the cremation, he stated that "it took place in Valle Grande, and his [Che's] ashes were buried somewhere in Bolivia."

On December 2 a Reuters dispatch from Rio de Janeiro said: "General Ovando again repeated that Che Guevara's corpse was not cremated and that it was buried in a place that will be kept secret."

According to an interview published at that time in O *Jornal*, Ovando stated: "I do not know what my government's intentions are with respect to the future destination of the mortal remains of Che Guevara. As far as I am concerned, I suppose that at some future time they may be given to his relatives, as would be proper."

At a press conference on December 5 in La Paz, General Barrientos pointed out that "the Commander of the armed forces never said what has been read in the newspapers." He indicated that Ovando had made a very clear statement, saying that Guevara's corpse "before being burned was buried [sic]."

Finally, in Montevideo, Ovando said, according to a Reuters dispatch, "that Che Guevara's ashes are buried."

The responsibility for the official contradictions was once again attributed to the ineptitude or bad faith of the journalists, this time to those of the Brazilian press. But in spite of everything, the final resting place of Che Guevara's remains is still unknown.

The way in which Che Guevara died[8] and the uncertain circumstances that surrounded his death shocked the entire citizenry. Friends and enemies, admirers and detractors, and critics of Guevara's personal convictions were all affected by a collective guilt. Whether produced by an error of command, an error of execution, or an error of reporting, the fact was that a feeling of guilty doubt spread throughout the Bolivian population and was even felt abroad.

Major Guevara was not a prisoner of war, even though the entire area of guerrilla insurgency had been declared a military zone, and so, strictly speaking, the norms established in the Geneva Convention for the treatment of prisoners of war were not applicable. However, its principles could have served as a moral guide for the handling of the case.

Shot, executed, murdered, or "finished off"—whatever particular personal interpretation is given to the facts—there is a human truth which rises above any subjectivism: a man, a sick and wounded prisoner, was killed without any semblance of justice when he was in the hands of those whose duty it was to jealously guard his physical safety. Beyond any moral law and over and above any legal scruples, the truth is that an elementary rule of war had been violated; a prisoner is always sacred.

The murky official reports gave rise to the wildest rumors and news stories. The doubts raised affected many people, especially young army officers who could not afford to have an uncertain shadow floating over their future. Rumors and news stories, inside and outside the country, pointed to several military figures as those responsible for Guevara's death. The names of Colonel Selić, Captain Prado, and Lieutenant Totty Aguilera were mentioned—none of whom actually had had any part in the criminal deed. But it is not important to name the actual author of the killing, because he was someone obliged to obey orders given by his superior officers. It is the high government officials who must tell the whole truth and say who the order came from.

Meanwhile, a spiritually tortured mother stepped forward to attempt to dispel the suspicion that certain irresponsible and poorly

---

[8] Much the same can be said about the death of the guerrilla Willy, who was finished off in the same or similar circumstances as Che.

informed foreign reporters had allowed to fall on the name of her son. In an open letter sent on November 18, 1967, to "Xavier," columnist for the daily newspaper *Presencia*, Mrs. Adela Salmón de Prado said:

> I always read your articles with great interest, because I believe that I see in them love for TRUTH and JUSTICE. That is why I am turning to you now, as an afflicted mother looking for help, even though that help is only of a moral nature.
>
> My son, Captain Gary Prado Salmón, was the person who commanded the unit that fought with and captured the guerrilla leader Ernesto Guevara. He, honorable and patriotic soldier that he is, always careful of the good name that his children ought to be able to use with pride, conducted himself bravely and, after capturing Guevara, turned him over alive in Higuera to his superior officers as a prisoner, which was his duty. More than two hundred people who live in the village of Higuera can testify to this fact.
>
> Nevertheless, an insidious story, with photographs, claiming that Prado had killed Guevara was published widely in the Bolivian press and in other countries (I have evidence of the fact that it was published in Chile, Argentina, Venezuela, France, Italy, and Germany), blaming him for a deed which he would never have been able to commit.
>
> The authorities have said nothing to disprove this monstrosity. After some days had passed, the Italian journalist Franco Pierini wrote, among other things, in the magazine *Siete Dias* of October 31, 1967, published in Buenos Aires: "It was not the commander of the Rangers, Gary Prado Salmón, as many believed, who gave Guevara the *coup de grace*. Gary Prado Salmón, on the other hand, replied indignantly that 'he was a soldier, not an executioner.'" But now it turns out that precisely that magazine which returned my son's honor to him HAS BEEN FORBIDDEN by the military authorities, who have not allowed even one issue to circulate in the country.
>
> I have waited in vain until now for a clarification from the General Staff, and their silence has impelled me to write you.
>
> Is it just that they say nothing in the face of such a great calumny, and that they allow the name of one of their best officers to be stained, knowing that he can say nothing because he is bound by military discipline?
>
> Do real leaders evade their responsibilities, dishonoring a subordinate so that colonels can appear free of guilt?
>
> If this is not so, then why aren't they willing to tell the TRUTH,

or at least why won't they do something to clear the good name of a member of the army?

I, as a mother, do not want honors, promotions, or rewards for my son, who has known how to do his duty. But I do want them to act with JUSTICE and in the name of TRUTH to say publicly in Bolivia and the whole world that Captain Gary Prado Salmón captured Guevara and turned him over alive to his superior officers, returning immediately, with the true sense of responsibility of an officer, to fight by the side of his soldiers against the guerrilla nucleus that still remained, and that Captain Prado had nothing to do with that death. What happened to Guevara after he turned him over is something that he is completely unaware of.

I thank you in advance for anything that you can do for my son, and I sincerely congratulate you for the brave campaign that you are carrying out through the respected daily *Presencia*.

Yours sincerely

[Signed]: *Adela Salmón de Prado*

The Bolivian press was never given an opportunity to hear an authoritative statement from a responsible official source concerning the details of Che Guevara's death. It was United States' reporters, with their special connections, who were accorded that privilege. It has became general knowledge in foreign press circles that President Barrientos gave a detailed account of the Higuera events to U.S. Ambassador Douglas Henderson, and that Henderson, in turn, repeated it at lunch to Mo García and Paul Montgomery, American correspondents based in Latin America.

Subsequently, Juan de Onís, another American journalist, had a long interview with one of the CIA agents who was in Valle Grande. He obtained even more details of Guevara's last minutes than his colleagues possessed. Moreover, through a special concession made by the head of public relations of the High Command, he was the only one who saw Guevara's complete diary, having signed a written promise that he would not make professional use of the material.

On October 11 the Bolivian Congress congratulated the President of the Republic, the Commander in Chief, the officers and men of the armed forces, as well as all those who fell in the struggle, for their defense of national sovereignty against the "Castro-Communist aggression." For this purpose that body held a formal meeting attended by the President, his full ministerial cabinet, the chiefs and officers of the armed forces, foreign diplomatic representatives, ecclesiastical authorities, and other personalities.

The representatives of the opposition presented a substitute motion for the original majority proposal, in which only the armed forces were acknowledged and not the President, and no type of political support was given to the regime in power. In addition, the opposition, while it condemned the guerrilla revolt, expressly stated its repudiation of any other kind of external aggression as well, including aggression of an economic nature. When the proposal was defeated, the opposition walked out of the congressional chamber.

The Vice-President of the Republic, Dr. Luís Adolfo Siles Salinas, expressed the majority sentiment of both houses and was thanked by Generals Barrientos Ortuño and Ovando Candia.

Five days later, at the request of Senator Howard Baker, the United States Senate publicly expressed its gratitude to the Bolivian armed forces because "the free peoples of this hemisphere owe them a great debt of gratitude" for their determined anti-Communist actions. Mr. Baker also asked for an increase in United States economic aid to Bolivia.

Once the guerrilla insurrection had been crushed, the Bolivian government and armed forces received several messages of this nature from Bolivian and foreign groups and personalities.

However, Major Guevara and the "patriots of the Southeast" who fought under his orders also received a number of public tributes in Bolivia and other parts of the world. In Bolivia, the feeling of sorrow over the death of the great Latin American revolutionary was expressed in striking ways in intellectual circles and within student and worker organizations. The act that aroused the greatest controversy and opened the way to the most contradictory reactions—both support and censure—was the resolution of the Federacíon Universitaria Local (Local University Federation) of Cochabamba, adopted unanimously on October 13. After maintaining a minute of silence as a posthumous tribute to the "revolutionary of America, Major Che Guevara," the following statement was approved:

First—To declare university-wide mourning for the death of Major Ernesto Guevara inasmuch as he is a symbol for the youth of the world in the struggle for the people's liberation and for the establishment of social justice. Second—To declare Major Ernesto Guevara a Bolivian Citizen and Patriot, since his struggle incarnates the most noble ideals of humanity, and since our people suffers the most inhuman oppression and the most crushing subjugation. Third— the FUL will issue a document in tribute to the leader of the Latin American Revolution, Ernesto Guevara, in addition to sponsoring a public ceremony on Saturday, the fourteenth of this month. Fourth —To declare that the celebration of Students' Week will continue with almost all of the scheduled events, with the exception of the gala dance which will be suspended indefinitely, but all of these events will be given an air of mourning which will express the deep feeling of sorrow that the youth of Bolivia and the world feel.

17

The Last Guerrillas

The dramatic adventure of the guerrillas in Bolivia did not end with Che's death.

When the first shots sounded in Churo ravine on the morning of that Sunday, October 8, Guevara had calmly proceeded to outline his battle plan. He gave his final orders to the group that was to cover his withdrawal, said good-by to each of its members, and gave them this last instruction: in case the groups were broken up or dispersed as a result of the impending battle, the survivors were to meet two days later at a certain point on the Río San Lorenzo, a little to the north of the place where it joins the Río Grande.

We already know what happened to the unit commanded by Che. Six guerrillas died with him in Churo ravine and in Higuera between the eighth and the ninth of October, and four were able to escape: Moro, Eustaquio, Chapaco, and Pablo.

The group which was to cover the withdrawal clashed almost immediately with the troops commanded by Lieutenant Pérez. When the first shots were exchanged, Aniceto, shot in the mouth, fell and died a few minutes later. This group had minor skirmishes with the army until the middle of the afternoon of the same day.

The original battle plan and the subsequent development of the battle did not permit the remaining rebel fighters to regroup. At the end of the battle they were divided into two very small units: the four survivors from Che's group, and six of the seven who had been, ironically, sent on an almost certain suicide mission: Inti, Pombo, Urbano, Benigno, Darío, and Ñato. We don't know how the first group managed to escape from the enemy, but the one commanded by Inti broke through the encirclement that same night after a sharp clash in which four soldiers were killed. This miracle was possible thanks to the lack of watchfulness of the government troops after Che's capture, which caused them to lessen their pressure and not pursue the defeated enemy.

On Wednesday, October 11, military planes dumped leaflets on the zone occupied by the guerrillas, offering them the opportunity to surrender "in view of the fact that the avenues of escape are blocked" and in order to avoid further bloodshed. In spite of this there were two clashes on the following day. The first occurred at 5 A.M. near Pujro, forty-five miles to the south of Valle Grande, and two soldiers died; the second took place at 11 P.M. near El Naranjal, and two more soldiers and a civilian guide were killed and one person was wounded. The army found several rifles, five knapsacks, and some medicine at the scene of the second action.

On Friday the fourteenth, Moro, Eustaquio, Chapaco, and Pablo were all killed. The first guerrilla was Cuban, the second Peruvian, and the last two Bolivians. The battle, according to official reports, lasted four hours—from six to ten—with no army casualties. It took place in the zone of El Cajón, twenty-three miles to the southwest of Valle Grande and six miles northwest of Pucara.

Señora Fabiola Campero de Arana, the mother of the guerrilla Chapaco—Jaime Arana Campero—and a member of a distinguished Tarija family, went to Valle Grande with her daughter on October 16 in a Bolivian air force plane. "Crying constantly, she begged that she be permitted to see her son's grave so that she could place a cross on it," wrote the *Presencia* correspondent, "but he [Colonel Joaquín Zenteno] replied that he had already placed a cross on all the tombs." The lady explained that she had not seen her son since he had gone to Cuba to study five years before; from the university certificates that he had sent her, she had learned that he had graduated as an engineer but he had never written her again.

The odyssey of Inti's group was longer and ended more happily for its members—with one exception.

The six men walked through the forests for fifteen days trying to elude their pursuers. Then one night they encountered a peasant who, after selling them food and supplies, reported them to the military authorities. At that time they were in an area with very little vegetation, but they had enough time to take refuge in a region with a fair amount of cover while the army patrols combed the vicinity. After midnight they tried to leave their hiding place but ran into a post with double sentinels, who were killed before they could react. Even though the shots alerted the rest of the troops, the rebels were able to escape in the predawn darkness.

A few days later they reached the vicinity of Mataral, approximately forty-two miles to the north of Valle Grande and 105 miles to the east of Santa Cruz. Their pursuers left a town called Casas Viejas on November 11 and pushed them east toward Angostura. The group's destination was a point on the Cochabamba–Santa Cruz highway where they hoped to find some help or means of escape. On the fifteenth, government troops discovered them in their hiding place near the spot known as La Cabaña, about two miles to the southwest of Mataral. After a brief clash, Ñato was critically wounded, a bullet in his spine. Since the insurgents were forced to abandon the area in the face of the strong enemy attack, and since he couldn't stand the intense pain, Ñato repeatedly asked his comrades to kill him. One of his comrades carried out the wounded man's plea, fulfilling the promise that the survivors had made to each other to avoid falling alive into enemy hands.

The armed forces communiqué that referred to this last encounter said:

> At 11 hours today a unit from the Officers' Training School under the command of Second Lieutenant Castellón encountered the last group of Reds who are trying to escape the encirclement in a ravine about two miles northeast of Mataral.
>
> During the action one bandit was killed, and his corpse is being taken to Valle Grande for identification.
>
> The army had no casualties.
>
> Its troops are continuing the pursuit.

The fleeing guerrillas were able to escape to the southwest of the highway, turning north again a few days later and following the

Río Pulquina, obsessed with the idea of reaching the main highway. It was in this area that they met peasants who said they were supporters of the MNR, and who protected and aided the guerrillas in every way. They provided them with new clothes and gave them farm work. Pombo, the easiest to recognize because of the dark color of his skin, spent his days in a tunnel with an exit at both ends, dug especially for him.

At that time a steady stream of Communist sympathizers and militants came along the road to Santa Cruz, possibly hoping to help the fugitives. The guerrillas bought a lightweight truck and with the aid of friends were finally able to reach Santa Cruz, where they could get more help and could have some hope of being able to escape.

During the first two weeks of January, 1968—after a few days of rest—Inti went to Cochabamba in disguise on a regular flight of the Lloyd Aérea Boliviana, and a few days later the rest of his comrades joined him. Meanwhile, the press and the military authorities reported that the last guerrillas were in the region between Mizque and Aiquile, respectively 151 and 174 miles to the east of Cochabamba. As a result this zone was closely watched, and supposed rebel liaison men were arrested, among them the former agrarian leader Edmundo Camacho.

The group's stay in Cochabamba, a city with 140,000 inhabitants, went completely unnoticed and was marked only by the delight of their political friends and a simultaneous fear of what the authorities might do if they were found. They felt so free that one Saturday afternoon the Cuban guerrilla Pombo, no longer able to stand being shut inside, decided to go out, get a haircut, and walk about the downtown section of the city like any other carefree and peaceful stroller.

After this point the guerrillas' trail became obscured, at least for the armed forces and the state security agencies. They were unaware of the fact that the fugitives had begun to gather in the mining centers of the Oruro district, where anti-government feeling is always high. The plans for leaving the country were arranged by Chilean leftist forces and some Bolivian Communists, following orders from Havana. Pombo was to tell, after his arrival in Cuba, of the deep division in the Bolivian Communist Party and how it was the dissident Bolivian Communists who aided the guerrillas unconditionally.

The preparations continued until February 8, when the march to a point on the Chilean border, ninety-nine miles west of Oruro began. Six days later a loud publicity bomb exploded. The news was in a telegram sent at 2 P.M. to the Prefect of the Department of Oruro and the Commander of the Second Division by the magistrate of Sabaya canton, a little village lost in the snows of Carangas province. The dispatch announced the following:

> Six guerrillas reached Sabaya at 2 A.M. today; two Bolivians and four foreigners, all well-armed. They say they have come from the interior of the country and are on their way to Chile. Fifty peasants said that they were unable to capture them because they were carrying automatic weapons and they feared for their lives. We need weapons to stop them. They are still here at this moment. They do not have personal identification papers.

The town of Sabaya is thirty miles from the Chilean border. The surviving guerrillas had thus reached the doorway to freedom and were almost safe, while the search for them was going on in other parts of the country. They had appeared in the most unexpected place. The general belief was that they were trying to escape over the border to Brazil, Argentina, or Paraguay. It would not be difficult to imagine the authorities' surprise at the failure of their security forces.

As soon as the report was received there was feverish political, military, and police activity. Less than an hour after receiving the news, three Bolivian air force planes took off to carry out aerial reconnaissance over Sabaya and neighboring regions. At 9 P.M. motorized vehicles carrying First Camacho Artillery Regiment troops were on their way to the emergency area, which was declared a military zone. Preparations were made in La Paz to mobilize troops from the Ingavi Regiment and in Cochabamba paratroopers of the CITE were getting ready.

The authorities were convinced that the strangers in Sabaya were the last five guerrilla survivors of Churo ravine, and thus, on the following day, they dropped leaflets calling for the fugitives' capture over the entire Sabaya region and distributed them throughout the country. The leaflets offered a reward of 10,000 Bolivian pesos for each one, "alive, if possible," of the "mercenary bandits serving Castro-Communism," whose photographs identified them as Pombo,

Benigno, Urbano, Inti, and Darío, the first three Cubans and the last two Bolivians.

The air force immediately launched Operation Sabaya, commanded by Colonel Francisco Barrero, Prefect of Oruro; Colonel Cardenas, Chief of the Third Section of the army; and Colonel Amado Prudencio, Chief of the Second Division. They released the following communiqué: "Yesterday morning a group of six bandits, presumably the survivors of the Higuera combat, appeared in the vicinity of Sabaya. Army units are operating in the zone to destroy this anti-social group." The chief of the Army General Staff, General Marcos Vásquez Sempértegui, pointed out to the press that the air force was carrying out a plan designed to trap the last remaining guerrillas.

Meanwhile the torrential summer rains poured down on the whole area bordering Chile. The downpour made the roads in the plateau province of Carangas practically impassable. Innumerable vehicles were stuck in the mud in a long column from Oruro to Sabaya. The truck in which the guerrillas were traveling also got bogged down fifty-four miles outside of Sabaya. But on the morning of February 13, the five men who composed the group were able to obtain other means of transportation to reach the small town although they had to pay 300 pesos, a sum that was much higher than the usual fare. A few miles from Sabaya this vehicle also got stuck.

Actually, this "group of bandits" did not include all of the guerrillas who had originally broken through the encirclement and escaped the pursuing government forces. Those who were now on the road to Sabaya were the Cubans Pombo, Urbano, and Benigno, and their Bolivian guides Estanislao Villca and Epifanio Aguilar, who were familiar with the area. They all carried white knapsacks and dark-colored jackets.

One of the five, Estanislao Villca, a native of Sabaya, walked to the little town on the high plateau and told the authorities that some traveling companions would arrive momentarily. This man, who had gone to Sabaya a few days before to arrange the last details of this final stage of "Operation Escape," calmed his fellow townsmen by telling them that his new friends were Chilean businessmen who were anxious to cross the border. These "businessmen" arrived at 2 A.M.

on the fourteenth, got rooms at the same inn where Villca was staying, and were not bothered for the rest of the night.

The following morning—February 14—they visited the telegraph office in order to keep a watch on it. After a while the most eminent citizens in town appeared with the magistrate to request that the strange visitors show their identification papers. Only Villca was able to show his, while Aguilar gave the following explanation on behalf of himself and the others: "Some time ago we were arrested in Chile. They took us for smugglers and the authorities kept all our papers at that time. Right now we are on our way back to get them."

His explanation did not seem to convince the magistrate or the other citizens, and they began to argue with the fugitives. The villagers insisted on examining the contents of the knapsacks and the rest of their gear, but the guerrillas refused. When one of the local citizenry approached Urbano to search him, he waved a pistol in the air, took a step back, and fired a shot at the ceiling of the room, warning them: "I'll kill the first person who comes close to me."

His comrades calmed him down and his action dampened the curiosity of those who accompanied the magistrate. Both groups now sat down around a table in the inn's dining room and reached an agreement for a peaceful departure from the locality. The guerrillas naturally had to pay a price for this concession.

The guerrillas and their guides, in order to convince the townspeople that they were really peaceful businessmen, offered to leave a sum of money that they would pick up "when they returned to Bolivia, within fifteen days" with their identification papers. The practical townspeople could do no less than agree to such a reasonable proposition. The incident at the telegraph office had given them a clue as to the identity of their strange visitors, but although they were beginning to suspect that they were the last of the guerrillas, this did not keep them from their transaction. However, at about ten o'clock, taking advantage of a pause in this improvised "round-table discussion," the magistrate slipped away and sent a messenger to telegraph Oruro.

When the identity of the strangers was finally evident, a real commotion shook the little village. And for good reason: a sizable reward awaited whomever captured the unexpected visitors. Sabaya's most prominent citizens, led by Juan Gonzáles García, a La Paz businessman who made frequent trips to the Chilean border, tried to delay the departure of the fugitives. But they were becoming impatient, and at 2 P.M. they practically forced their would-be captors to accept the $400 bond after a receipt had been signed. Only then were they able to renew their march through the mud and snow as the unrelenting wind of the Andes pierced them to the bone. They left on foot, as they had arrived, with no possibility of getting help from the inhabitants of the unfriendly mountain town. Wrapped in heavy outer garments, their caps pulled down over their ears and heavy knapsacks on their backs, they walked toward Todos Santos, the town nearest to the Chilean border, followed by some curious townspeople.

As the fugitives crossed the last stretch that separated them from final safety, Bolivian land and air forces were keeping a close watch on the border area. On Friday, February 16, the command of the armed forces reported that the guerrillas had succeeded in reaching Chilean soil, explaining that the "delay in the message from Sabaya, caused by the lack of means of transmission, as well as the bad weather prevailing in the zone, were factors that kept paratroopers from arriving, as was necessary to cut off the guerrillas' retreat." On the seventeenth, President Barrientos personally flew over the Sabaya region, while the government of Chile announced that units of the Chilean air force, army troops, and border guards were watching the possible entry routes into the country.

In spite of the Bolivian command's communiqué, it was announced on the eighteenth that the fugitives were passing through the Chilean villages of Caranguiri and Negrillo, near the towns of Chilcayo and Canco in the province of Tarapacá. On that same day Peruvian police and immigration officials received instructions to cooperate closely with the Bolivian and Chilean authorities.

On the nineteenth it was learned that the guerrillas had been seen in the region of La Soga on the way to Camina, on Chilean soil. A rumor began to circulate to the effect that they were trying to escape the army troops and border guards for fear that they would be returned to Bolivia, preferring to surrender to the Chilean police. All trace of them was lost on the twentieth and the twenty-first, but rumors abounded: the guerrillas, now supposedly numbering twenty, were seen in various places, including the village of Chinchillani at the foot of the Isluga volcano.

Finally, on Thursday, February 22, patrols of Chilean border guards stopped the guerrillas at Alto Camina, 360 miles from Oruro, as they were going toward Iquique. They were unarmed and in a state of complete exhaustion and put up no resistance.

In spite of strict warnings from the Chilean government, the guerrillas were warmly received by the inhabitants of the north of Chile, where there is a strong Marxist electorate—the mayor of Arica is a member of the Communist Party and his colleague in Iquique belongs to the Popular Socialist Party. Along the whole route from Alto Camina to Iquique the escapees were constantly cheered by the population.

While they were being treated as heroes in the northern provinces, the government in Santiago was denying them political asylum and giving them forty-eight hours to leave the country. On the other hand, members of the Organization of Latin American Solidarity (OLAS), political leaders, and Communist and Socialist members of parliament mobilized to aid the guerrillas. The President of the Senate, Salvador Allende, assisted them personally in order to guarantee that they would receive treatment in accordance with international law.

Since there was no request for extradition and because the guerrillas were accused only of having entered the country illegally, on February 24 the government ordered that all five be taken to Pascua Island in the Pacific Ocean, 2481 miles off the coast, in the custody of Eduardo Zuñiga, Sub-director of Investigation of Chile, and five other police agents. On the following day—still in the company of Salvador Allende—they were taken to Papeete, the capital of Tahiti, an island territory of French Polynesia, where they were received by Baudillo Castellanos, Ambassador of Cuba in France. On Friday, March 1, they went on to Paris and from there safely to Cuba.

It should be added that this last adventure in search of freedom was the second one that the fugitives had undertaken; the first, which they attempted toward the end of January, 1968, was unsuccessful when their contacts failed.

Everything leads to the conclusion that the authorities have lost the trail of Inti and Darío; although they have repeatedly announced that they were keeping strict watch to see that these two did not resume their political activities, and it is logical to suppose that they are taking extreme security measures. Their attention is centered on Inti—Guido Peredo Leigue—who would now be head of the Army of National Liberation. What is known with some certainty is that while he was still in Cochabamba, Inti received concrete invitations to travel as a political exile to any country behind the Iron Curtain, along with his family and his last remaining guerrilla comrade.

Some people assert that Inti is somewhere in the vast tropic reaches of the region where he was born, the *departamento* of Beni, bordering on Brazil, and that personal friends and politicians are looking after him there. According to some sources, he is supposedly waiting for the storm that the guerrillas unleashed in the country to blow over; according to other sources, he has resumed all his former revolutionary activities in important cities and in centers where there is social unrest, including the capital, La Paz. At one time it was said that he had escaped from the country by way of the labyrinthine tangles of the Amazon jungle. But the most likely version insists that he left the country and crossed into Chile in the second week in May, 1968, passing himself off as a saltpeter engineer with an American company that did business in Bolivia and wearing the cap and jacket of a workman.

Che Guevara trusted Inti and his brother Coco Peredo implicitly, and was an admirer of their revolutionary conviction and their decisiveness in combat. On several occasions Che emphasized Inti's moral integrity, but he also regretted in passing that Inti had too little physical stamina for enduring the hardships of guerrilla fighting. Ironically, it was under the command of this man that the only survivors managed to get out of Ñancahuazú alive and head for home. This made Inti an undisputed political personality in the eyes of those comrades who share his ideals.

18

A Memory and
a Hope

Popular insurrection comes into being as a spontaneous response of peoples who have suffered foreign oppression. As an instrument of national liberation the phenomenon is not new, but today it is proving to be a historical constant in the four corners of the world because exploitation by imperialist powers has created an intolerable climate. Peoples in all five continents are taking up arms because they can no longer exist within the infrahuman scheme of life that has been imposed on them.

Guerrilla warfare is not foreign to Latin American history. In the colonial period the precursors of guerrilla insurrection were first the native chiefs; later, the mestizos and criollos were most active in rural areas. The leaders led agrarian communities to the mountains, where rebels with inferior materiel could have a chance to counterbalance the regular forces of the Spanish metropolis. The Indian rebels created what we would call today "free territories." The Royalist armies often put down these patriotic uprisings, crowning their campaigns with cruel and bloody reprisals. But they did not succeed in putting down the indomitable forces of rebellion, and they managed only to secure armistice until the next uprising.

At certain times during this period, the guerrilla factions grew stronger, created liberated zones, and tried to function as regular groups. Repression, failure of their efforts, and transitory pacification of the country were the immediate results. But it was the peace of the tomb, and lasted only as long as it took the guerrillas to get back up into the mountains and reorganize their cadres. Months or years later, after constant announcements by the Spanish generals that "the country is pacified," the country rose up in arms again. Thus, after a succession of bright days and dark and bitter days, the political emancipation long hoped for finally came about.

Alto Perú—today Bolivia—had to go through fifteen years of guerrilla struggle and civil uprising to consolidate the Republic in 1825, but it did not attain complete independence until our time. The Argentine historian and statesman, General Bartolomé Mitre, in his book on *The War of the Small Republics*, describes the struggle in Alto Perú succinctly and accurately:

> This was one of the most extraordinary wars because of the genius with which it was waged, one of the most tragic because of its bloody reprisals, and one of the most heroic because of its hidden, deliberate sacrifices. The lonely and isolated theater in which it took place, the multiplicity of interests and situations outside of the horizon of history, the humility of its leaders, its combatants, and its martyrs, has long hidden its true grandeur and prevented a real knowledge of its political scope.

And he adds farther on: "Each valley, each mountain, each town, is a little republic, a local center of insurrection, which has its independent leader, its flag, and its neighborhood Thermopylaes; their isolated efforts nonetheless converge toward a general result, which is produced without previous agreement of the parties."

The first guerrilla *focos* in Alto Perú were born in the native communities around Lake Titicaca, but the ideals they upheld were capable of being expanded, with blood and the death of their martyrs, to every corner of the country. The Universidad Mayor Real y Pontificia de San Francisco Xavier de Chuquisaca provided the ideology, the cities molded the political leaders, and guerrillas sprang up in the mountains, fields, and valleys. Chuquisaca, La Paz, Cochabamba, Oruro, Santa Cruz, and Tarija contributed the political principles and set the revolutionary keynote, while López, Ayopaya, Aroma, Tarata, Pocona, Chayanta, Porco, Cinti, Valle Grande, Florida, and La Tablada are like so many flags representing the conquests of the stubborn ideal of emancipation. Its names are engraved on the history of the country like paradigms for eternity. Its ideologies, its proto-martyrs, and its leaders mingle to form the common base of nationality. The list is long, and without special favoritism we may cite as examples Tupac Amaru, Tupac Katari, Julian Apaza, Murillo, Arze, Camargo, Muñecas, Zudañez, Lemoine, Monteagudo, Padilla, Warnes, Lanza, Méndez, Uriondo. Yesterday, as today, the enemy was the enemy of the social community and there was no discrimination of race, nationality, or creed in the defense of freedom. Mestizos from other regions of the continent and men from far-off places fought for this freedom: Frenchmen, Irishmen, Russians, Poles. And at their sides were the brave heroines, among them the outstanding trio Juana Azurduy de Padilla, Bartolina Siza, and Manuela Gandarillas.

Along with the inalienable patrimony of a free land, the guerrillas of the nineteenth century bequeathed to us a sentimental and romantic legend, accessible only to the sensibility of our Indo-mestizo people. Perhaps for that reason, even though they do not approve of any form of violence, a large part of the intellectual sectors of the nation did not condemn the guerrillas of Ñancahuazú with sectarian vehemence. If they did not sympathize openly with them, they at least tried to understand the reasons for their sacrifice, which from the beginning gave promise of being sterile, insofar as an immediate victory was concerned. Outwardly, at least, there was an attitude of general indifference, for people could not understand how a handful of men could disturb the stability of the nation and its historic continuity. It is possible that this attitude was due to the fact that the most vigorous nuclei opposing the government were in the mining centers and in the cities, among intellectuals, workers, and middle-class people, who have a definable influence on public opinion. It is also possible that this indifference, which resulted in only limited support for the guerrillas, was primarily rooted in disaffection toward the government in power rather than in genuine sympathy with the insurgents. The truth is that the majority of national opinion was convinced that the government was wrong in its policy toward the guerrilla problem, wrong to limit itself to liquidating it by force of arms without attacking its real cause: social injustice. This at least was the opinion expressed in the parliament by punctilious representatives of the nationalist parties (the FSB and the MNR). These legislators wanted it shown on the record that they recognized the existence of two different situations in the war against the guerrillas—that of the government and that of the armed forces—and emphasized that "they were with neither the guerrillas nor with the government, because both are negative factors contrary to [the interests of] the great national majorities." Only the conservative political parties and economic and social sectors, whose interests coincided with those of the government, mobilized votes in its favor and held lukewarm and indecisive demonstrations in the capitals of *departamentos* and some of the cities of the provinces, but the forced chauvinist speeches during these demonstrations did not impress the indifferent audiences. The women's committees and the committees for defense did not succeed in convincing people that the guerrilla movement might destroy the foundations of the nation.

The armed forces indirectly marshaled opinion against the guerrillas. Commanders of divisions and groups from the Acción Cívica Militar working in rural areas were generally represented in the committees for national defense.

Peasants, who have been a significant factor in elections since 1952, were easily manipulated by the authorities so that the shifts of opinion in this group were always led from higher up.

As one of the most important pressure groups, the Catholic Church maintained a cautious attitude. In accordance with its traditional position, it officially came out against Communism, but it abstained from marshaling support for the government in its fight against the guerrillas. Young laymen and post-Vatican II priests in some cases fully approved of the appearance of guerrillas, though this is not to say that they supported them fully.

The one who best summed up this state of collective consciousness in these days was the Bishop of Cochabamba, Monsignor Armando Gutiérrez Granier, who in part of his Pastoral Letter on the Guerrillas of August 1, 1967, stated:

> Although in the present historical circumstance the legally constituted government has the right and the duty to answer force with force, and in an emergency to defend itself, let it be remembered that lasting peace is not conquered by force of arms alone but the restoration of justice, for as Pius XII said, following Isaiah: "Peace is the work of justice."
>
> It is only right that we reflect that as long as our people live in misery with wages too low to provide for their human and family

necessities; as long as their jobs are not secure, and therefore they are in a state of permanent anxiety, not knowing whether tomorrow they will have bread for themselves and their family, there will always be people who will listen to agitators and even commit themselves to the tragic adventure of the guerrillas.

To attain the lasting peace to which our people aspire, it is indispensable to propose to them an immediate economic and social political program that will open perspectives allowing Bolivians to possess the necessary material goods and the minimum comfort compatible with the dignity of the human person; guarantee them job security through the creation of sources of work that will avoid unemployment and support union rights; a more equitable distribution of national income, avoiding the glaringly obvious inequality of wages and salaries between those most favored and those who are poorest; a politics of austerity in the daily lives of the ruling classes that will help the poorest to bear their previous sacrifices and those consequent upon the launching of a development program—all this within an Integral Development of "the whole of man and the whole of men," as Paul VI proposes in the encyclical *Populorum Progressio.*

And the distinguished prelate, one of the most brilliant minds of the Catholic hierarchy in Bolivia, concluded his document with this exhortation: "We will celebrate the mass of August 6, the anniversary of the Independence of Bolivia, in the cathedral church, in this intention, and I ask all priests to join with me in this intention by celebrating the 'sacrifice for the Peace of the Fatherland, the reconciliation of all Bolivians, and the eternal rest of the fallen guerrillas.' "

Ernesto Guevara was neither the standard-bearer of a Utopian messianism nor a borrower of concepts for confronting what happened to be the historical problems of his time. Nor were his actions during his life the consequence of resentment or unjust personal or family pretensions. He understood that the revolution is not a collection of schematic principles or an interpretive formula, but a historico-social phenomenon. For this reason he refused to cling to any theoretical dogmatism outlining revolutionary orthodoxy. Though he did not completely reject Lenin's postulate that "there is no revolutionary movement without a revolutionary theory," he understood that theory "as an expression of social truth, is above any enunciation of that theory; that is to say, that there can be a revolution if the historical reality is interpreted correctly and the forces intervening in it are used correctly, even without an acquaintance with theory."

It may be that he was wrong in his choice of means to transform the stiff mechanism of present-day society, but no one ever denied the noble sincerity of his ultimate aims since he always placed himself on the firing line, ready to give his life in the service of his ideals. He was not an imperturbable noisemaker but the revolutionary combatant par excellence. For this reason, his most recalcitrant enemies and even those who fought against him in the last campaigns respected his person and his sacrifice at the hour of his death, with rare exceptions that are lost in the thick shadows of hatred.

His death had world-wide repercussions and deeply touched collective sensibilities. Statesmen, politicians, thinkers, and men of eminence, without regard for ideology or personal creeds, emerged from the silence they maintained during his lifetime to express their grief. But it was among the most humble all over the world that the impact of his death was most painfully felt. We were the witnesses of the anguish experienced by the people of Cochabamba the night of Wednesday, October 11, 1967. The local newspapermen had been in Valle Grande that morning. Anxious knots of people crowded around the journalists and radio broadcasters, impatient to find out the latest details on the battle that was drawing to its close. And when the daily *Los Tiempos* scooped the world by putting out an edition around midnight with the latest news and the first photographs of Guevara's death, an invisible cloud slowly descended on the city.

Guevara was a combination of warrior and apostle, adventurer and prophet. He was a lay missionary for social justice. His personality was not shaped in gambling dens or aristocratic clubs, as he himself once said. He was a down-to-earth creature with deep human sensibilities, in spite of having imposed a severe Jansenist discipline upon himself. He demanded things from himself so as to demand them from others. He spontaneously gave up all comforts that life might offer him and only accepted and adapted himself to his ruling standards. When he decided to burn his bridges behind him, he drew a line between his past and his future destiny and flung himself into the fight. He has illustrious predecessors along the path of American freedom that he chose to take: Tupac Amaru, Bolívar,

Esteban Arze, César Augusto Sandino, Emiliano Zapata, and Gualberto Villarroel showed him the way. And like Camile Torres, he made himself worthy of following in their footsteps. He sowed and we shall reap. The seed will germinate and other generations will taste the new vintage in the wine-press of time.

His life and his death do not represent a truncated parabola, but a circle that connects the beginning and the end with mathematical precision. A life and a death that will have permanent continuity that no force will be able to trick us out of. His physical body may have been converted into rotting flesh or scattered ashes, but his spirit will endure throughout eternity because he entered the hearts of the humble.

So be it, leader of this continent!

In Bolivia it is traditional for markets of regional fairs to be held on certain days of the week in provincial towns and, on occasion, in the capitals of the departments. Aside from being an occasion to buy and sell goods, they are also rite and festival, and draw people from all over the region who have faith in magical cures. The fair is similar to the Moroccan marketplace, where contraband goods are sold as though they were legal, where people eat, drink, buy and sell everything, from pigs to nylons, from aspirins to the latest-model sewing machines, from rusty nails and tin cans to short-wave radios.

In Valle Grande the fair falls on Sunday. Since Guevara's death, peasants have come from the most remote corners of the province and formed lines to buy Che's photograph, which they take to the church to have blessed. This is in accord with their simple and innocent ancestral belief that those who have died a tragic death have the power to answer requests for miracles. A kind of legend has already grown up around the miracles of "Saint Che," whose portrait can frequently be found in peasant huts in the midst of Catholic images. Many people have even had masses said in his memory.

A rapid "Gallup poll" in the locality revealed the following statistical information: up to October 22, 1967—twelve days after his death—some 6700 photographs of Che had been sold.

Appendix I

ABBREVIATIONS

APRA   Acción Popular para la Revolución Americana [American Revolutionary Popular Front]

BID   Banco Interamericano de Desarrollo [Interamerican Development Bank]

CITE   Centro de Instrucción de Tropas Especiales [Center for the Instruction of Special Forces]

COB   Central Obrera Boliviana [Bolivian Labor Central]

CODEP   Consejo Democrático del Pueblo [Democratic Council of Peasants]

DIC   Departamento de Investigación Criminal [Department of Criminal Investigation]

FRB   Frente de Revolución Boliviana [Bolivian Revolutionary Front]

FLIN   Frente de Liberación Nacional [National Liberation Front]

FSB   Falange Socialista Boliviana [Bolivian Socialist Falange]

MNR   Movimiento Nacionalista Revolucionario [Nationalist Revolutionary Movement]

PCB   Partida Comunista Boliviana [Bolivian Communist Party]

PDC   Partido Democrática Cristiano [Christian Democratic Party]

POR   Partido Obrero Revolucionario [Workers' Revolutionary Party]

PRIN   Partido Revolucionario de Izquierda Nacionalista [Revolutionary Party of the Nationalist Left]

YPFB   Yacimentos Petrolíferos Fiscales Boliviana [Bolivian Fiscal Petroleum Deposits]

233

Appendix II

MEMBERS OF THE GUERRILLA MOVEMENT

Cubans

Alejandro. Major Ricardo Gustavo Machin Hoed de Bache, born 1936 in Havana. Married, two children. Chief of Operations of guerrilla command. Died August 31, 1967, at Vado del Yeso. Founder of the Revolutionary Student Directorate of Cuba. Fought in the Sierra del Escambray under the command of Rolando Cubela. Later was Under-secretary of the Treasury. Joined the Revolutionary Armed Forces as a member of the General Staff of the Western Army and military chief of Matanzas city. Completed technical-military studies in Russia. Entered Bolivia on December 9, 1966, via Chile, on an Ecuadorian passport, Number 49836, under the name of Alejandro Estrada Puig.

Antonio. Captain Orlando Pantoja Tamayo. Born in Contra Maestra, Oriente Province. Divorced, one daughter. Died October 8, 1967, in Churo ravine. After the revolution was chief of the Coast-and-Port Guard, of the Frontiers Guard, and of the Camarioca Operation. Lieutenant to Che Guevara in the Sierra Maestra and afterward confidant of Raúl Castro. Entered Bolivia via Brazil on December 12, 1966, with Ecuadorian passport, Number 49840, made out in the name of Antonio León Velasco. Was assistant to Ramiro Valdéz, Minister of the Interior in Cuba. Carried out intelligence operations abroad. Was in Bolivia in 1963 with the Peruvian guerrilla Hugo Blanco directing a group of Peruvian Trotskyites.

Arturo. Not identified. Died in Churo ravine, October 8, 1967.

Benigno. Daniel Alarcón Ramírez, thirty years old, born in Manzanillo, machine gunner of the Camilo Cienfuegos column during the revolutionary war; served in the same capacity in the Bolivian guerrilla war. Survivor.

Braulio. Major Rolando Quindela Blez. Born 1936 in Oriente Province. Entered Bolivia in November, 1966, through Chile on Panamanian passport, Number 62538. Second-in-command of the group commanded by Joaquín. Died at Vado del Yeso, August 31, 1967.

Félix. Wálter Pelaez Ríos. Died in the Los Monos region, Ñancahuazú. (*El Diario*, January 1, 1968.)

Joaquín. Major Juan Vitalio Acuña Núñez, born 1920 at Niquero, Oriente Province. Rear-guard commandant. Died August 31, 1967, at Vado del Yeso. Entered Bolivia November 24, 1966, via Brazil on a Panamanian passport, Number 65736, under the name of Joaquín Rivera Núñez. Was a guide for Fidel Castro's troops in the Sierra Maestra, one of the first peasants to join the cause; commanded a guerrilla school in Matanzas Province. Member of Cuban Communist Party. Fought in Vietnam and in the Congo. In September, 1966, he was chief of the Mixed Division of the Western Army in Guanabacoa, La Habana Province.

Marcos. Major Antonio Sánchez Díaz, doctor, born 1927 at Guane, Pinar del Río Province. Died June 2, 1967, at Iquira. Married, one son. Member of the Central Committee of the Cuban Communist Party. Entered Bolivia November 17, 1966, via Brazil, on Panamanian passport, Number 65896, under the name of Marcos Quintero Díaz. He joined Fidel Castro in the Sierra Maestra. Was chief of the Military Region of Isla de Pinos after the revolutionary victory.

Miguel. Not identified. Died in Abra de Picacho September 27, 1967.

Moro. Lieutenant and doctor, Carlos Luna Martínez Octavio de la Concepción Pedraja. Born 1933 in Havana. Married, one son. Fought under the command of Raúl Castro in the Sierra Maestra. After the revolution, was graduated as a doctor. Was Chief Surgeon at the Calixto García Hospital of Havana. Entered Bolivia under Ecuadorian passport, Number 49833, on December 7, 1966. Killed October 14, 1967.

El Negro. Gustavo Rodríguez Murillo, cardiologist, Cuban. Entered on passport Number 6078397, thirty years old. Died at Río Grande September 3, 1967.

Pacho. Captain Alberto Fernández Montes de Oca. Born 1936 in San Luís, Oriente Province. Divorced, no children. Member of the 26th of July Organization. Served under the command of Che Guevara in the

Sierra Maestra. Named Supervisor-Administrator of the Washington sugar complex in Las Villas Province in January, 1959, later became Director of Mines in the Ministry of Industry. Entered and left Bolivia repeatedly; entered for the last time in December, 1966, on Uruguayan passport, Number 12918, under the name of Raúl Bórguez; or Uruguayan passport, Number 12394, under the name of Antonio Garrido. Died at Churo ravine, October 8, 1967.

Pombo. Harry Villegas Tamayo, twenty-eight years old, born in Vieira, Oriente Province. Survivor.

Ricardo. Not identified. Died July 30 in Moroco. (Zenteno, *El Diario*, October 11, 1967.)

Rolando. Captain Eliseo Reyes Rodríguez. Born 1940 at San Luís, Oriente Province. Married, two children. Died April 24, 1967, in El Mesón. Member of the Central Committee of the Cuban Communist Party and the 26th of July Organization. Joined at the age of sixteen. Served under Che Guevara as Chief of Battalion at the fort of La Cabaña; was chief of Intelligence and Security in Pinar del Río Province. Entered Bolivia on November 17, 1966, via Brazil on Panamanian passport, Number 66019, under the name Rolando Rodríguez Suárez; intimate collaborator of Che's.

Rubio. Captain Jesús Suárez Gayol. Born 1928 at Manatí, Oriente Province. Died at Iripití, April 11, 1967. Was Vice-minister of the Sugar Industry and Director of Mineral Resources. Fought on the second front Frank País in the Sierra Maestra under Raúl Castro's command. Entered Bolivia under the name of Jesús Cuevas Ulloa with passport, Number 449839. High official in the INRA.

Tuma. Not identified. Died June 26, 1967, in Piraí near La Florida. (Zenteno, statement in *El Diario*, La Paz, October 11, 1967.)

Urbano. Captain Leonardo Tamayo Nuñez. Born in Boyano. Married, two children. Was secretary to the Cuban Delegation at the conference of the Inter-American Social and Economic Council that met at Punta del Este in August, 1961. One of the five survivors who escaped through Sabaya.

Bolivians

Aniceto. Elia Cabrera, from the San José-Oruro mine. Died in Churo ravine October 8, 1967.

Antonio. Rodríguez Flores. Turned himself in to the army in the Peñones zone on September 30, 1967.

Pastor Barrera Quintana. Born in Oruro. Deserter, tried at Camiri. Was released.

Benjamín. Benjamín Coronado, died by drowning in Río Rositas during Guevara's march. (February 25, 1967, according to statement by General Alfredo Ovando Candia.)

Camba. Orlando Jiménez Bazán. Born in Riberalta, thirty-three years old. Was taken prisoner on September 30, 1967.

Carlos. Not identified. Drowned in Ñancahuazú River, March 10, 1967. (Diary of Che.)

Chapaco (Luís). Jaime Arana Campero, hydraulic engineer, killed in Los Cajones at the junction of the Río Grande and Mizque on October 14, 1967.

Chingolo. Hugo Choque Silva, captured at Monteagudo July 23, 1967. Exposed the Ñancahuazú arms caches. Recruited into the Center for the Instruction of Special Forces (CITE) where he is now.

Salustio Choque Choque. Miner. Born in La Paz. Deserter, tried at Camiri. Was released.

Coco. Roberto Peredo Leigue. Born May 23, 1939, in Trinidad. Studied in Trinidad at the "Sixth of August" school and later at the Hugo Dávila and Bolívar schools in La Paz. Was active in the Bolivian Communist Party from the age of eleven. Later he became Director of Youth and after that Intermediate Director of the Regional Committee of La Paz. He traveled to Cuba in 1962, to the U.S.S.R. in 1964, and again to the U.S.S.R. and Cuba in 1965 and 1966 respectively. He was the son of Rómulo Arano Peredo and Selina Leigue de Arano Peredo. In 1960, he married Mireya Echazú, who gave him three children, Roberto, Katia, and Yury, six, four, and three years old. Trained as a guerrilla in Cuba and in Vietnam. Later he became part of the Bolivian guerrilla army. He was killed at Higuera by the company under Lieutenant Galindo on September 27, 1967.

Curu. Not identified. Died in Ayango near Muyupampa. The commission's doctor saw him.

Darío. David Adriázola, another of the five survivors who broke through the military encirclement at Higuera. His whereabouts are unknown.

Ernesto or **Chino.** Fredy Maimura Hurtado, doctor, born in Beni. Killed in the Vado del Yeso ambush on August 31, 1967.

Eusebio. Eusebio Tapia Aruñe, born in La Paz. Twenty years old, deserter. Turned himself in July 23, 1967, at Monteagudo.

Gabriel. Rodolfo Saldaña, chief of urban liaisons. (*El Diario*, January 16, 1968.)

Inti. Guido Peredo Leigue. Born April 30, 1938, in Trinidad. Coco's brother and son of Rómulo Arano Peredo and Selina Leigue de Arano Peredo. Studied at the Juan Francisco Velarde school and in the "Sixth of August" school in Trinidad and at the Bolívar and the Hugo Dávila schools in La Paz. Active in the Bolivian Communist Party since he was twelve. Was chief of the Pioneers; later, Director of Youth and finally First Regional Secretary of La Paz. Married Matilde Lara in 1963; two children, three and two years old. He is at present commandant of the Army of National Liberation and one of the five survivors of the war.

Julio. Mario Gutiérrez Ardaya, doctor, born in Cochabamba, thirty-two years old. Killed in Higuera by Lieutenant Galindo's company, September 27, 1967.

León. Antonio Domínguez Flores, born in Trinidad. Turned himself in to the army on September 27, 1967.

Lorgio Vaca. Died at Río Grande on October 13, 1967.

Loro. Jorge Vásquez Viaña, geology student, born in La Paz, captured in Monteagudo on April 27, by the farmer Nicolas Montaño and the prefect of that province. He was killed in the military hospital at Choreti on May 27, 1967.

Moisés. Moisés Guevara Rodríguez, miner, killed at Vado del Yeso, August 31, 1967.

Ñato. Julio Méndez Cano, MNR militant. Managed to escape the encirclement along with the five survivors of Churo. Died in Mataral in 1967.

Pablo. Francisco Huanca Flores, university student from Oruro, twenty-one years old, killed in Los Cajones at the junction of the Río Grande and Mizque on October 14, 1967.

Paco. José Castillo. Recruited by Raúl Quispaya in La Paz. Sole survivor of the Vado del Yeso ambush. Captured by Captain Mario Vargas and transferred to Valle Grande. Is being detained by the armed forces; no trial date has been set.

Pedro. Antonio Jiménez Tardío. Born in Tarata, capital of Estevan Arze Province. Died at Iñau, Taperillas region, August 9, 1967. (Ovando's statement.)

Pepe. Julio Velasco Montaño. Turned himself in to the army on May 25 at Ipitá. Was executed two days later by troops of the company under the command of the Second Lieutenants Javier Hinojosa Valdéz and Carlos Monje. Velasco's body was transferred to Choreti for identification. General Ovando and Colonel Joaquín Zenteno Anaya confirmed his death in declarations of September 23, 1967.

Polo. Apolinar Aguirre Quispe, died September 31, 1967, according to Ovando. (Died August 31, 1967, at Río Grande, according to Zenteno, *El Diario*, October 11, 1967.)

Epifanio Quiñonez Aguilar. Born in Oruro, twenty-five years old. Guerrilla guide. Escaped through Sabaya. Lightly wounded in the foot.

Raúl. Raúl Quispaya, died at Moroco on July 30, 1967, according to Ovando. (Zenteno, *El Diario*, October 11, 1967.)

Vicente Rocabado Terrazas. Born in Oruro. Deserter, tried at Camiri. Was released.

Serapio. Not identified. Died at Iquira on July 10, 1967.

Tomás. Tomás Rosales Vargas, taken prisoner at Santa Cruz de la Sierra, hanged himself in the cells of the Department of Criminal Investigation of that city on April 12, 1967.

Víctor. Víctor Casildo Vargas Condori, died June 2, 1967, at Iquira, along with Marcos.

Estanislao Villca Cohue. Born in Sabaya. Law student from Oruro, twenty-nine years old. Guerrilla guide.

Wálter Arancibia. Killed August 31, 1967, at Vado del Yeso.

Willy. Simón Cuba, mining director from Huanuni, taken prisoner at the same time as Che Guevara in Churo, October 8, 1967. Killed the next day by Sergeant Francisco Huanca in La Higuera.

Argentinians

Pancho. Not identified. Argentinian, according to Zenteno. Killed at Higuera by Rangers Regiment Number 2, on October 8, 1967.

Tania. Tamara Bunke. [Laura Gutiérrez Bauer.] About twenty-nine years old. Killed at Vado del Yeso by Captain Vargas on August 31, 1967.

Peruvians

Chino. Juan Carlos Chang, law student, member of the Peruvian Communist Party. Fought in the Army of National Liberation of Peru. Thirty-seven years old. Began his political activities in the APRA. Died in Higuera on October 8, 1967.

Eustaquio. Edilberto Galbán Hidalgo. Radio operator. Twenty-five years old. Died in Los Cajones at the junction of the Río Grande and the Mizque, October 14, 1967.

Guerrillas of Unknown Nationality

Loco. Unidentified.

Marco. Not identified. Fell at Caripatí on April 27, 1967. (Braulio's diary and Ovando's statement.)

Appendix III

PHYSICAL DESCRIPTIONS OF THE GUERRILLAS
MADE BY CIRO ROBERTO BUSTOS FOR THE
MILITARY AUTHORITIES

POMBO: Negro; tall (approximately 5′ 10″), thin, very fine features; fine, straight nose; dark, large eyes; smooth skin; clearly defined lips, not very large; a classical face, but dark; salt-and-pepper beard, full and thick; thick, black hair; long arms and legs; 28 to 30 years old; does not smoke.

URBANO: Also Negro; approximately 5′ 7″; robust; he was the best walker and strongest of all, never sick; face more typically Negroid; wide nose with full base; medium-sized eyes, light (brown, perhaps); thick lips, the lower protruding; heavy, curly beard; thick, long hair; skin more chocolatey; used a dental bridge (two upper teeth, I think); 26 to 28 years old.

TUMA: Mestizo, olive-colored; angular cheekbones; medium nose; medium forehead; a lot of hair with somewhat Negroid kinks; long beard, but only along the jowls and under the chin; medium height, about 5′ 5″; legs bowed like a horseman; quiet type; 26 to 30; a strong man even when exhausted; like the first two, he always hung around Ramón and carried part of his numerous things (books, cases, flashlights, etc.).

RICARDO: Mestizo; he was the most robust of them all; 5′ 10″; he looked like a wardrobe; tremendous black beard that covered nearly his whole face; straight nose; thick eyelashes; eyes medium-sized, brown;

240

straight forehead; lots of loose, wavy, long black hair; light olive skin; strong arms and legs; large hands; over 30; does not smoke.

ALEJANDRO: White; long, thin nose, maybe slightly aquiline; more or less large, light eyes; very long beard, straight (vertical); straight, long, brown hair; small light freckles; about 5′ 9″; thin; over 30; clear brow.

MIGUEL: White; long face; straight, long nose; thin beard, more thin at the sides; full mouth with a wrinkle in the left side, like somebody who laughs sideways; firm, angular chin; approximately 5′ 10″; thin; long hands; very quiet and disciplined; appeared to be the preferred scout; brown hair, long and loose; horizontal wrinkles on his forehead; medium-sized eyes; 28 to 30 years old; eternally smokes a pipe.

ROLANDO: White; ovoid head; bulging eyes, very large; medium nose, rather prominent; nearly beardless with something of a sparse goatee; sensuous fleshy mouth; almost a baby face; very prominent Adam's apple; very long tangled hair, cowlicks in all directions, falls on his medium forehead; gives the impression of having a very big head or a very small face; smallish body; height about 5′ 5″; very thin; yellowish skin; about 26.

MARCOS: White; middle-aged, over 40; not very tall, about 5′ 6″; face furrowed with wrinkles; beard more or less sparse, graying; curly hair, also graying; nose a bit prominent; eyes very lively, dark; very slangy and nervous, like a Spaniard; a talker; thin; had been very heavy before; always smoking a pipe, even when walking.

BRAULIO: Negro; tall, about 5′ 10″; a shouter, typical Negro voice; squarish head; flat chin; wide forehead of medium height; hair with tight curls; flat, medium nose; black; sunken eyes, medium-sized; ordinary beard under the chin; 30 years old.

PACHO: White, beard and hair very curly and black; medium, straight nose; large eyes with long lashes and heavy eyebrows; height about 5′ 6″; thin but strong; about 28 years old.

BENIGNO: White; about 6′ tall; large, straight nose; middle-sized mouth; prominent chin; goatee and lots of straight black hair; long arms and large peasant hands; about 28; long strides; smokes a pipe.

JOAQUÍN: Older man, over 40; tall, around 5′ 10″; a bit stooped; thin arms; medium-sized eyes, half-closed; thin wide mouth; large nose, a bit hooked; sparse beard; medium chin; air of a simple man; they said he was one of the peasants that enlisted in the Sierra Maestra and was a major.

MORO: White, perhaps mestizo; round head; very prominent cheekbones; lively eyebrows; large, wide-open eyes; long lashes; medium nose; beard and hair very tangled; lots of black hair falling in his face; very short, not more than 5' 2"; chubby; short arms; small hands; small feet— he took the same size shoe as Tania (7); about 30 years old; surgeon; does not smoke.

ARTURO: Mestizo; Ricardo's brother; strong; about 5' 6"; medium complexion; large head; abundant black hair, long and wavy; big black beard; medium nose, fleshy; mouth the same; dense eyebrows; large, very black eyes; wide cheekbones; light olive skin; about 25 years old.

ANTONIO: White; yellowish skin; curly, thick, black beard; hooked nose, medium-sized; medium eyes, flashing black; arched black eyebrows; upper lip somewhat prominent; gets all tangled up talking; smooth forehead; short hair; very nervous; well-proportioned body; medium height, about 5' 4"; about 35 years old.

EUSTAQUIO: Mestizo (Peruvian); short, about 5' 2"; thin; narrow forehead; medium-sized aquiline nose; fairly large black eyes; medium mouth; nearly beardless, with a few hairs on his chin; lots of long hair; about 26 years old.

MÉDICO: Negro, but Caucasian features; fine nose with small base; medium mouth; large cranium; black, somewhat curly, long hair; short, sparse, speckled beard; thin mustache; large smiling eyes; very tall, about 6' 2"; medium complexion; long arms and hands; cardiologist; about 30.

CHINO: Looks more or less like a Chinese; wears glasses, without which he can see almost nothing; permanent smile; round face; wide forehead; neat beard on jowls and under chin; long black hair; fleshy face; slow and plodding; somewhat lethargic; about 5' 4"; 30 or over; he said he'd lost 25 or 30 pounds but he was still pretty fat.

PEDRO: Wide face marked by a round black beard; eyes that open wide; narrow, somewhat aquiline nose; long, curly black hair; about 5' 4"; medium build; 27 or younger.

ÑATO: Swarthy; tall; thin but strong; large, very black eyes, somewhat sunken; nose has flat, fairly wide base; enormous black mustache growing down to a long, thick, black chin beard; straight, black, profuse hair; Easterner; alligator hunter; a strong man about 30 years old; about 5' 10".

CAMBA: Also a swarthy Easterner; about 5' 10"; long neck; medium-sized head; prominent cheekbones; large eyes; heavy eyelids; sparse mustache; goatee; pointed chin; narrow forehead; lots of black hair; thin but wiry; from 30 to 35 years old.

MÉDICO CHINO: Round face; very black beard, flaring out a bit like a lamp-shade; small eyes and mouth; medium-sized nose; medium build; about 5′ 4″; about 26 years old.

WILLY: Short, stocky; short neck; eyes with hooded lids and a kind of blemish in the white of the left eye (I think); stubby nose, it seems to me, like a boxer's; thick mouth; sparse beard and mustache; low forehead; about 5′ 2″; long-suffering expression; miner; 36 or older.

PABLO: Young highlands type; round face; swarthy; beardless; strong, not particularly thin; about 5′ 6″ (perhaps less); about 20.

ANICETO: Swarthy; oval face; widespread cheekbones; beard on jowls, chin; has a goatee; medium-sized aquiline nose; wide-open small eyes; about 5′ 6″; 27 years old, more or less.

RAÚL: Somber expression; narrow forehead, sparse black beard; about 5′ 4″; about 26 to 30.

ANDRÉS: I remember little about him, since I only saw him for about 30 minutes; he's a man of about 30, Bolivian type, swarthy; black hair, more or less straight and abundant; thin black mustache; thin, aqui-line nose; fine chin; high, prominent cheekbones; thin frame; 5′ 4″; worn, dark suit; general look of middle-class worker; head a bit stooped; eyes with heavy upper lid, fairly large and very black; very quiet, talks softly with a typically unemphatic Bolivian accent; doesn't give one the impression of being very sure of himself, but rather timid, although maybe I couldn't tell about this in so little time.

ISAAC RUTMAN: He's about 35 or 40; Jewish; merchant or mercantile family; straw-colored hair, freckles; rather thick glasses, probably myopic; bland face or gives the impression of being bland, soft; fleshy lips and ears; nose a bit hooked, very Jewish; large eyes that don't pop out but seem very big, very thick lids, I don't remember what color they were, I think light; clear forehead, hairline beginning to recede; carefully combed hair, whether with brilliantine, I don't know, but it gives that impression; hair well cut, longer on top; generally elegant appearance, but not distinguished, just ordinary; medium height, low-slung, about 5′ 2″; not fat but plump, fleshy, probably weighs about 165 pounds; very cultured speaker, talks with a clear voice with round tones, neither high nor low; highly developed intellectually and I'd say very intelligent; not a spectacular type nor one that attracts atten-tion at meetings.

Appendix IV

DECREE OF THE COUNCIL OF MINISTERS PROSCRIBING THE COMMUNIST PARTIES AND THE WORKERS' REVOLUTIONARY PARTY, APRIL 11, 1967

Considering:

That, after a long process involving many sacrifices, Bolivia has entered an active period of social, political and economic development, so that any interference constitutes the crime of high treason,

That armed groups of irregulars made up of elements of various nationalities, obeying orders from International Communism, have organized a base of operations that affects the provinces of Hernando Siles and Luís Calvo of the *departamento* of Chuquisaca, and Cordillera and Vallegrande of the *departamento* of Santa Cruz,

That the presence of these forces constitutes an attack on the national sovereignty and affects internal security because it is associated with extremist national groups,

That the above-mentioned foreign forces have been publicly supported by the International Communist movement, by the Communist Party of Bolivia, by the Workers' Revolutionary Party, and by other extremist groups,

That these armed groups have caused serious damage to the peasants of the affected zones, violating their property rights, carrying off their cattle, their means of subsistence, and other possessions,

That such acts of vandalism constitute a threat against the life and tranquillity of the inhabitants of the region,

That the foreign mercenary groups have confronted the armed forces

244

of the Nation using armament and subversive techniques typical of the Communist guerrilla movements,

The Council of Ministers DECREES:

Article 1. While the conditions previously mentioned in the preamble of this decree obtain, the area comprised of the provinces of Luis Calvo and Hernando Siles of the *departamento* of Chuquisaca, and the provinces of Cordillera and Vallegrande of the *departamento* of Santa Cruz is declared a military zone and the armed forces are charged with the defense of the national sovereignty and the maintenance of public order in the above-mentioned provinces, and the political and military authorities are to submit to the respective military jurisdiction.

Article 2. The appearance of irregular armed groups in other zones will *ipso facto* cause the affected area to be submitted to military jurisdiction.

Article 3. The activities of the Communist Party and the Workers' Revolutionary Party are proscribed.

Article 4. Those persons who aid the formation of irregular armed groups either directly or indirectly will be liable to the maximum sanctions established in the Military Penal Code and the Law of Security of the State.

The Ministers of State for National Defense and the Interior are charged with the execution and fulfillment of the present decree.

Appendix V

MANIFESTO OF THE ARMY OF NATIONAL LIBERATION OF BOLIVIA

The Army of National Liberation to the Bolivian People:
The history of the misery and suffering that our people have had to bear and are still bearing is a long one. Torrents of blood have run in a steady stream for hundreds of years. Thousands of mothers, wives, sons, and brothers have shed rivers of tears. Thousands of patriots have been cut down.

We men of this earth have lived as strangers on it; any Yankee imperialist has more rights than we to the national territory that he calls his "concessions." He can destroy, demolish, and burn the homes, the crops, and the possessions of Bolivians. Our lands do not belong to us; our natural resources have served and continue to serve to enrich foreigners and leave only empty mine shafts and deep hollows in the lungs of us Bolivians; there is no school for our children; there are no hospitals; our living conditions are miserable; our pay is starvation wages; thousands of men, women, and children die of starvation every year; the misery in which the peasant lives and works is frightful. In other words, we live in conditions of slavery with our rights and conquests denied and trampled upon.

Before the horrified eyes of the whole world, in May, 1965, wages were lowered, workers thrown out of work, jailed, exiled, massacred, and their camps with defenseless women and children bombarded and sacked.

Even if this is the background against which we live, ours was and is a people who fight, a people who have never given in.

How many heroes at the side of the miners, the peasants, the factory workers, the teachers, those of the liberal professions, and this glorious youth of ours have written the most glorious pages in our history in blood! Before our eyes and the eyes of the world we have placed the legendary figures of Padilla, Lanza, Méndez, Zudañez, Rabelo, Murillo, Tupac Amaru, Warnes, Arze, and also the peerless heroines of La Coronilla, Juana Azurduy de Padilla, and Bartolina Sisa, whose glorious example preserves our heroic people who remember and are ready to follow it.

Even if the generations before us fought a bloody fifteen-year battle to build a free and sovereign country, driving the foreign master from our soil, it was not many years later that new capitalist powers sank their claws into the land that Bolívar and Sucre built. The peasants that have been brutally murdered since the founding of the Republic number in the thousands; the miners and factory workers that have had their demands answered with machine-gun fire number in the thousands. The "valiant" colonels who have earned their promotions and their rise in ranks in this unequal battle, machine-gunning and bombarding the defenseless people who at times rise up, armed only by this wall of courage that will not yield, will not be degraded, also number in the thousands.

The memories of the massacres, the crimes, and the insults to which the Bolivian people have been submitted remain fresh in our minds. Cops, generals, and Yankee imperialists, you have your claws and your gullets stained with the blood of the Bolivian people, and your final hour—the end of the pools of blood that you have caused to be shed, of the ashes of the thousands of patriots that you have murdered, persecuted, jailed, and sent into exile—has sounded today. Today the Army of National Liberation has risen. Valiant men of the fields, men of the cities, of the mines and the factories, of the schools and universities, take up a gun.

It also announces, murderers, that your end has come, and the voice of justice, well-being, and freedom resounds, deep and uncontainable, in the Bolivian people, in the mountains and the valleys, in the forests, and the *altiplano*.

Generals: When today you have received the first blows, cry out for your mothers and your sons; we too feel for them, but do you perhaps believe that those thousands of peasants, workers, teachers, and students did not have sons, mothers, and wives? Those whom you have mercilessly murdered in the streets of the cities, in Catavi, Cerdas, Villa Victoria, El Alto, La Paz, Milluni, Siglo Veinte?

Faced with the powerful beginning we have made, the inner clique of the government and its master, Yankee imperialism, tremble with fear; they lash out like cornered beasts, they persecute all the more, they see themselves forced to commit even more crimes, to violate their pseudo-democratic constitution that they have sworn to uphold. Their hysteria where the guerrillas are concerned brings them to force political parties of the left aside, as if ideas could be killed by decree. They persecute, they jail, they cause free citizens to "commit suicide," accusing them of being guerrillas. They imprison and torture foreign journalists, saying that they are guerrillas; they invent calumnies and write propaganda based on such ridiculous lies that the people scorn them. This attempt, or any other, to stifle the guerrilla movement will be in vain, like everything these men do to maintain themselves in power. Their end as the government clique has come.

We regret that this struggle is necessary to put an end to the systematic robbery, the abuse, the injustice, the crime, the benefits that a few enjoy, to secure a new classless society where social justice, with equal duties and rights for all, holds sway; where the natural resources are enjoyed by the people; many lives are going to be lost that are useful to the country, both the lives of military officers and of soldiers in the ranks, because it is certain that not all of those who are sent onto the battlefield think like the pro-Yankee inner clique that has power.

We call upon all patriots, officers, and soldiers in the ranks, to lay down their arms; on the glorious youth of the country not to join the army; on mothers to prevent their children from being sacrificed to defend an insiders' clique that has sold out to the foreign dollar and hands over the better part of our resources to voracious Yankee imperialism.

The Army of National Liberation calls upon the Bolivian people to close ranks, to forge the strongest possible unity without regard for the various political colorations, and calls on patriots who are able to fight to join the ranks of the Army of National Liberation. It is also possible to help from outside. There are a thousand ways to do so, and the creative ingenuity of the people will find a great many methods for doing so, from groups of friends to more daring forms. The problem is to get started and make the governing clique and its master, Yankee imperialism, feel the Bolivian earth tremble beneath their feet. We warn the people that in order to keep our country under its sway, Yankee imperialism will have recourse to new generals and civilians, including pseudo-revolutionaries, and in turn will get rid of these. Do not let yourselves be surprised and fooled as has happened throughout our history. This time the fight, once begun, will not end until the day that the people govern themselves and foreign domination has been eradicated.

Notice is hereby given that the Army of National Liberation will watch over the faithful fulfilling of popular ideals, that at the proper time it will mete out punishment to today's oppressor, informer, or traitor, to those who are committing injustices against the poor with impunity. Organizations for civil defense are being formed. Popular revolutionary tribunals will begin to hold trials and pass sentences.

The Army of National Liberation, finally, expresses its faith, its confidence, and its certainty that it will triumph over the Yankees and all invaders in the guise of advisers, Yankee or not. We will not allow ourselves rest or repose until the last redoubt of imperialist domination has been freed, until the happiness, the progress, and the good fortune of the glorious Bolivian people shines forth.

Die rather than live as slaves.

Long live the guerrillas.

Death to Yankee imperialism and its military clique.

Freedom for all patriots arrested and jailed.

Ñancahuazú, April, 1967,
The Army of National Liberation

Appendix VI

ATTACHMENT 1: Following are the death certificate and the report of the autopsy conducted on the body of Ernesto Guevara.

Death certificate—the undersigned doctors, the directors of the Señor de Malta hospital, and the resident physician, certify that on Monday, the ninth of this month at 5:30, the corpse arrived of an individual whom the military authorities said was Ernesto Guevara Linch,[1] of approximately forty years of age, it having been noted that his death was caused by multiple bullet wounds in the thorax and extremities.—The corpse was then embalmed—Vallegrande, Oct. 10, 1967.—Signed: Dr. Moisés Abraham Baptista.—Signed: Dr. José Martínez Casso. There appears a seal with the following inscription: Señor de Malta hospital. Address—Vallegrande, Bolivia.

This is an exact copy of the original that I submit in your case.

Hugo Pelaez Martínez, Secretary of the Department and Organization of the General Staff.

La Paz, Oct. 16, 1967.

ATTACHMENT 2: Report of the autopsy of October 10 of this year that was carried out, by military order, on the corpse that was identified as that of Ernesto Guevara.

---

[1] The proper spelling is Lynch.—*Trans.*

250

Age: approximately forty years.

Race: white.

Height: approximately 5′ 9″.

Curly chestnut hair; long mustache and beard, also curly; thick eye-brows, straight nose, thin lips, open mouth, teeth in good condition with nicotine stains, with a floating lower left premolar; light-blue eyes. Normal build.

Extremities: Well-preserved feet and hands; a scar that covers almost the whole back of the left hand.

The following injuries were noted in the general examination:

1. Bullet wound in the left clavicular region, with the exit in the scapular region on the same side.

2. Bullet wound in the right clavicular region, with a fracture of the same and no exit.

3. Bullet wound in the right costal region without exit.

4. Two bullet wounds in the left lateral costal region, with the exit in the dorsal region.

5. Bullet wound in the left pectoral region, between the ninth and tenth ribs, with the exit in the lateral region of the same side.

6. Bullet wound in the middle third of the right leg.

7. Bullet wound in the middle third of the left thigh in seton.

8. Bullet wound in the lower third of the right forearm, with a fracture of the ulna.

When the chest cavity was opened, it was seen that the first wound injured the vertex of the left lung.

The second injured the subclavian vessels, incrusting itself in the body of the second dorsal vertebra.

The third pierced the right lung, incrusting itself in the costal-vertebral articulation of the ninth rib.

The wounds mentioned in Point 4 slightly injured the left lung.

The wound mentioned in Point 5 pierced the left lung in a tangential trajectory.

The chest cavities, above all the right one, showed an abundant pool of blood.

When the abdomen was opened, no traumatic injury was found, there being only distention produced by gases and a citrine liquid.

Death was caused by the wounds in the thorax and the resulting hemorrhage.

Vallegrande, Oct. 10, 1967.

This is an exact copy of the original.

[Signed] Dr. Abraham Baptista; [Signed] Dr. Martínez Casso.

ATTACHMENT 3: Identification by the Argentinian police. Certificate.

In the city of La Paz, Republic of Bolivia, on this day, Saturday, the fourteenth day of the month of October of the year 1967, at 4 P.M., the undersigned officials, Inspector Esteban Relzhauzer, in his capacity as a handwriting expert, and Sub-inspectors Nicolás Pellicari and Juan Carlos Delgado, fingerprint experts, of the Bureau of Investigation of the Argentinian Federal Police, do hereby testify for whatever purpose that may be needed: that complying with the express orders of the Chief of the Argentinian Federal Police, Divisionary General Mario A. Fonseca, prompted by a request for aid submitted by the Ministry of Religious and Foreign Affairs, came to this city and put themselves at the disposal of the Argentinian Embassy here, which provided the instructions they were to follow. For this purpose they were told that they should proceed to make an examination of fingerprints and documents of elements that they would receive. In the company of Naval Captain Carlos Mayer, Naval Attaché to the Argentinian Embassy, Embassy Secretary Jorge Cremona and the Consul in charge of the Consulate General in La Paz, Miguel A. Storppello, they went to the offices of the Bolivian General Headquarters in Miraflores, where they were received by Naval Lieutenant Oscar Pano Rodríguez, the Adjutant of General Alfredo Ovando Candia, Commander in Chief of the armed forces, and Major Roberto Quintanilla of the Ministry of Government. The latter presented the experts and the above-mentioned officials with a closed cylindrical receptacle of metal, which was opened and contained two hands submersed in a colorless liquid that smells like formaldehyde, a strong disinfectant used to preserve such elements. At this point the fingerprint experts mentioned above, Sub-inspectors Nicholás Pellicari and Juan Carlos Delgado, proceeded to carry out the corresponding technical operations in order to identify, using the "Juan Vucetich" fingerprinting system which is employed by the Federal Police, the papillary designs on the fingers of the amputated hands that had been presented to them. They followed the technique which is given below in order to provide correct information as to the process and the result at which they arrived:

The papillary tissue, due to the long action of the formaldehyde in which the hands had been submerged in order to preserve them, had deep wrinkles in the area corresponding to the balls of the fingers, which made it difficult to ink them and thus obtain impressions. When the technical procedures which are advisable in these cases did not produce the desired results, they proceeded to obtain fingerprints on sheets of polyethylene and in some cases on pieces of latex, which were classified and will be sent to the Office of the Identification Section of the Argentinian Federal

Police in order to be tested. When the prints from the above-mentioned hands had been obtained in this manner, they proceeded to compare them with the individual prints shown on the photostatic copy of the record (of all ten fingers) corresponding to the original recorded in the files of the Identity Section by the Argentinian Federal Police under the numbers 3.524.272 in the name of Ernesto Guevara, establishing irrefutably and in a manner consonant with the Argentinian Dactyloscopic System, his perfect identity, that is to say, corresponding to one and only one person. It is hereby recorded that the document given Major Roberto Quintanilla, Adjutant-General of the Ministry of Government, Justice and Immigration, was a photostatic copy of the ten-finger dactyloscopic record corresponding to the original in Ernesto Guevara's file. There was likewise received from this official a fingerprint record obtained on the ninth day of this month in the town of Vallegrande in the Department of Santa Cruz from a corpse of masculine sex. M/N. That establishes that these prints are those of the above-mentioned Ernesto Guevara. In a second instance, the handwriting expert, Inspector Esteban Rolzhauzer, of the office of the handwriting section of the Argentinian Federal Police, received for his examination two notebooks: one of them of manuscript notes of standard size, 20 centimeters by 14.5 centimeters, with a brown plastic cover, with an inscription on the title page that says: "1967," in low relief; and on the lower border and at five centimeters to the right of the back of the book of the above-mentioned object of analysis there is a sign of a mark probably produced by heat. The above-mentioned notebook is in a good state of preservation without stains or evident rips in the pages. Inside, on the reverse side of the title page, a small red seal is stuck on the lower left corner that says: "Carl Klippel - Kaiserstrasca 75 - Frankfurt a. M." The imprint reads: "Harstellung Baier Schosider" (Neilbreum A.N.)," all of which confirms the German origin of said element. The pages are of smooth, white paper, printed with the dates of the year 1967, and each page has the hours of the day indicated twice.

On each one of the pages observed are manuscript texts that correspond to notes written describing operations and movements of the persons who are mentioned. Said cycle begins on January 1 of this year and ends on October 7, after which date the pages are blank. Applying the technique of the identification of manuscripts that is called the "scopometric study of documents" and having authentic elements for comparison belonging to Identity Card No. 3.524.272 of the Argentinian Federal Police, issued to Ernesto Guevara, in the form of signatures and writing produced when Guevara requested documents from the Argentinian authorities, and these latter elements having been brought here as photostatic copies of the originals, they were compared with the new documents.

In a study of this nature one takes into account the date when the above-mentioned authentic writings were produced, the fact that they only contained signatures on the one hand, and writing (only just the words "Guatemala—Panama—Chile and Colombia) on the other, while they were being compared to writing alone, not signatures, and the fact that the authentic signatures presented the typical characteristics and structure of pure literal forms with some tendency toward simplification that did not affect the general examination, and that therefore they were adequate for the extrinsic and intrinsic formal comparison which is the basis of scopometric identification, at the same time that an adequate optical instrument is employed. Under the above-mentioned conditions, the authentic elements constitute only a very small part of the material which the expert has available for his examination, which demands a statistical examination of the characteristics of the writing in the first notebook, and the notebook with a brown plastic cover with the inscription "Elba 66509" that contains forty-four pages of writing. By means of the technique we have described and through its principles there are established in common a significant regularity in the writing, structure, graphic culture and existence of characteristic formations that permits us to establish a relationship between them and the notebooks that were presented to us and that show the same graphic characteristics of those samples found in Ernesto Guevara's file. We also wish to state here that no copies of the writing analyzed at this time were received by us, but that they will be sent subsequently to the Federal Police so that there may be better documentation of the examination. With which this certificate is concluded. It is read to those present, who sign at the end and in the order in which they were mentioned above, to indicate their approval. I so certify. [Signed] Esteban Belzhauser. [Signed] Juan Carlos Delgado.